William E. Caldwell,
Union Theol. Seminary
New York 1854

THE

EVIDENCES OF CHRISTIANITY,

AS EXHIBITED IN

THE WRITINGS OF ITS APOLOGISTS DOWN TO AUGUSTINE.

HULSEAN PRIZE ESSAY.

BY

W. J. BOLTON,

PROFESSOR IN GONVILLE AND CAIUS COLLEGE, CAMBRIDGE.

"Πείθομαι σοφῶν λόγοις."—GREGORIUS NAZIANZENUS.

"Discussi, fateor, sectas Antonius omnes,
Plurima quæsivi, per singula quæque cucurri,
Sed nihil inveni melius, quam credere Christo."
PAULINUS.

BOSTON:
GOULD AND LINCOLN,
59 WASHINGTON STREET.
1854.

PREFACE

TO THE

AMERICAN EDITION.

THE work which is introduced to American readers, in this volume, received the Hulsean prize in England in 1852. This prize has been conferred annually for many years, and was originally established by a legacy from the Rev. John Hulse, of Elworth, England, his will bearing date of July 21, 1777. The will directs that certain rents and profits (amounting now to about five hundred dollars yearly) shall be paid to such learned and ingenious person, in the University of Cambridge, under the degree of Master of Arts, as shall compose the best Dissertation on the Evidences in general, or on the Prophecies or Miracles in particular, or any other particular Argument, whether the same be direct or collateral proof of the Christian Religion, in order to evince its truth and excellence. The subject of the Dissertation is required to be assigned by certain authorities in the University, on the first day of each year, and the award in favor of the successful candidate is to be made annually on Christmas day, after which the Dissertation must be published for general circulation.

The subject proposed by the Trustees in Jan. 1852, was "THE EVIDENCES OF CHRISTIANITY, AS EXHIBITED IN THE WRITINGS OF ITS APOLOGISTS DOWN TO AUGUSTINE INCLUSIVE." The Dissertation by Mr Bolton, which gained the prize, will be found worthy of attention from American readers, for two particular reasons, in addition to those more cogent claims submitted by the author.

Elegant scholars in this country have discredited the grossness of Pagan idolatry. They have revived the new Platonic theories of the symbolic nature of Classic Mythology, and have denied that material images were objects of worship, or that the gods of Greece and Rome were adored as living and personal existences. The writings of the early Apologists give conclusive testimony on this point, and demonstrate that poets and philosophers, no less than the people, believed in the essential deity of the gods of the classic Pantheon, and paid devout adoration to their sculptured images. The apostle Paul's picture of ancient Paganism, in the first chapter of Romans, is a sketch taken from actual life.

The intellectual ability exhibited in these extracts from the Fathers, will restore also, in some degree, the confidence and respect of the Christian world, which have been rudely shaken by the publications of the Oxford Divines, and of the Mercersberg Professors. The Fathers were but men, of like passions with others, and the false philosophy in which many of them had been trained, and the wild speculations in which they indulged unchecked, led them often astray from the truth, and corrupted the simplicity of the gospel faith and ordinances. But this volume indicates their strength, when leaning only on the Divine Word, and reveals the noblest elements of Christian character. It will confirm the confidence of the American churches in the divine origin of Christianity, and in the substantial piety of its early Apologists.

CONTENTS.

INTRODUCTION.

CHAPTER I.

THE ARGUMENT FROM ANTECEDENT PROBABILITY.

SECTION 1.

SECTION 2.

SECTION 3.

SECTION 4.

CHAPTER II.

THE ARGUMENT FROM ANTIQUITY.

CHAPTER III.

THE ARGUMENT FROM PROPHECY.

CHAPTER IV.

THE ARGUMENT FROM MIRACLES.

CHAPTER V.

THE ARGUMENT FROM THE REASONABLENESS OF DOCTRINE.

CHAPTER VI.

THE ARGUMENT FROM SUPERIOR MORALITY.

CHAPTER VII.

THE ARGUMENT FROM THE SUCCESS OF THE GOSPEL.

INTRODUCTION.

The general subject of these essays, — the setting forth of the claims which Christianity has in the way of evidence upon our faith and affection, — commends itself to every man's conscience. If religion is important, whatever calls our attention to it must be important also. But "the Evidences" do more than recommend Christianity: they are the groundwork of the sacred building. Every appeal to the believer or unbeliever stands upon their truth; and whether viewed as external or internal, historical or moral, objective or experimental, argumentative or testimonial, direct or auxiliary; they constitute the substance on which all true spirituality of mind rests and operates. In this respect our religion differs from others, and enables us to invite and welcome that rigid examination from which they all instinctively shrink. But without entering upon such a boundless subject, we may take for granted that its nature is understood, and its value appreciated, and proceed at once to the more specific matter in hand; the part of this grand whole selected for our present consideration.

It consists of a *particular* view of the Evidences for the truth of Christianity; a view that may fairly be called the original view; taken not by ourselves, but by others; from a point in past ages, and in foreign lands. I may therefore be allowed to say here, once for all, that in transporting our thoughts, as we must needs do, to times, places, and situations, so distant and different from our own, we shall require both patience and candor; patience in surveying exotic and rather extensive materials, and candor in judging of them, with modern, perhaps preoccupied minds.

There is much, however, to make this an *interesting*, and still more, an *instructive* matter of research. Its interest arises from its connection with history, — not with civil history so much, though any experimental reference to this increasingly important study (much more the entire bearing) must be welcome in an age of inquiry and eclecticism like the present, — but rather from its connection with the history of the *Christian religion*. Our subject is ecclesiastical in its very nature; an essential page of Church history. It involves a review of the first four, possibly the most important centuries the world ever saw; and an exhibition of the earliest combined intellectual defence of Christianity, in which and by which the primitive converts were enabled to give "a reason of the hope that was in them." Surely to those of us who indulge the same hope, this period of the Church's great and *predicted** conflict; these Apologists, our own elder brethren and fellow Gentiles, who fought and in some measure bled for us; and these arguments, the weapons they wielded with considerable energy and success, present altogether a most inviting field of thought.

Nor is there wanting another claim to our regard of quite a *personal* kind. When the heavenly command was issued to enlarge the borders and strengthen the stakes of the Gospel tent, it pleased God that one of the cords should be fastened in our isle. Our rude and painted forefathers were

* I believe all the schools of prophetical interpretation, however they may differ on other points, coincide in finding intimations of the sufferings of the early Church in the Revelation of St. John.

early made the recipients of the "good tidings of great joy." For the preservation of this pleasing tradition we are mainly indebted to the writings of the Apologists. Whilst Tacitus was meditating his terse and cold speculations upon our climate and our pearls,* these men were delighting to tell each other and the whole world of the mercy of God towards a little island set amid the mists and waves of "the Western ocean." They felt for us as we feel for the natives of a Madagascar or a Tahiti now. Their hearts throbbed with sympathy at each assurance, brought perchance by a returning legion or home-bound vessel, of the progress of our happiness. At length our name became quite familiar to their pen: we seemed to furnish a standing proof of the power and extent of the Redeemer's kingdom. It was just because we were so remote, so barbarous, and as it were so unlikely, that our country became a sacred land-mark: what *ultima Thule* had been to the poets of antiquity, such *ultima Britannia* was to the Christian Apologists. Here then is a theme of grateful reflection for us, and for Britons at all times: "a psalm to bring to remembrance." Let others attribute the prosperity of our country to geographical position, to the physical determination of a race, or to a happy adjustment of laws; the Christian mind can only count upon those blessings, as they were sheltered under "that righteousness which exalteth a nation," first taught us ages ago, and marvellously preserved with us to this hour.

The *usefulness* of our task may be presumed from the following suggestions among others. First, such a review is calculated to disarm and dissipate *prejudice.* However much there is of the erroneous, absurd, or obscure in the esoteric systems of the Fathers, and whatever misuse has been made of such imperfections by a patronizing heresy, or a sneering scepticism, (rendering caution doubly necessary,) nothing of

* Vid. Tac. *Agric.* c. 12.

the sort obtrudes on us here. From vexed questions, the sad details of civil strife among Christians, and all the disturbing associations that cling to internal and long-continued controversies, the present inquiry is free. We are invited to a nobler, fairer view of the Fathers unanimously contending in all simplicity and earnestness, and against each external foe, "for the faith once delivered to the saints." We have to consider them not as preachers or catechists, but as Apologists; not as disputants in a council, but as defendants in a court: and though considerable blemishes undoubtedly attach to many of them under these as well as under any other characters, yet they will be found of such comparatively rare occurrence, and bearing so little upon the main topics and design of the present investigation, as scarcely to require a place in our thoughts.

Moreover, it would seem that a resort *of this kind* to antiquity, is peculiarly agreeable to the temper of our Church. Neither exalting the ancient Fathers on the one hand, as authorities coequal with the word of God, or as divine authorities at all, — a position which reason, the sacred Scriptures, and their own works, cannot endure for a moment; — nor, on the other hand, disparaging and rejecting them altogether as worthless or worse, — another extreme condemned alike by common justice and common prudence, — the Church of England takes a more moderate and judicious course: and having established as a fundamental article of religion, "that Holy Scripture containeth all things necessary to salvation; so that whatsoever is not read therein, nor may be proved thereby, is not to be required of any man, that it should be believed as an article of the faith, or be thought requisite or necessary to salvation;" she can afford both to permit and encourage the study of the patristic writings and the whole circle of history, for evidence of facts and confirmation of doctrines; thereby indicating to her friends that they need fear no thorough examination of any sort, but rather boast with Tertullian, that "truth dreads nothing but concealment."

Under such a guidance and with all those sentiments which become the investigation of venerable and Christian records, I shall proceed presently to extract and furnish the arguments of the Apologists for the truth of Christianity, not doubting that the honest, the courageous, the pious disposition they discover will speak for itself, and raise our authors in the estimation of all impartial minds.

A further result of the discussion before us must be to deprive the modern sceptic of his claim to *originality*. I think it will appear in the sequel that most of our present popular objections to Christianity have been anticipated centuries since. With the exception of a few sophistries and transcendentalisms, which destroy themselves, I scarcely know of an infidel position that we do not find taken up and exploded by such writers as Origen, Arnobius, Eusebius. Perhaps the exposure of such a circumstance, considering what a sharp spur notoriety is, may serve to lower the value of rash opinions, even in the eyes of the inventor himself; or, the bloom of freshness being lost, more certainly in the eyes of others also.

And this idea leads us on to another somewhat akin to it. Our subject is of value as proving collaterally the intellectual *capacity* of the early Christians. For not only are adverse and infidel objections quoted or presumed in these documents, but they are also shrewdly and substantially answered: and thus we find modern defenders of the faith as well as modern objectors, have been superseded. Much that Grotius, Pascal, Fenelon, Paley, have produced on the Evidences of Christianity will find its precedent, if not its original, in these Christian Classics. What has been said of Arnobius may be said with more or less truth of the rest of the Apologists; "the reader will recognize many a familiar thought, and remark how many arguments of modern Apologists have been anticipated here." An investigation of this sort, therefore, cannot but do some justice to memories of the past. But it will do something more. This is not a mere compliment to the pious dead: it is material to our own confidence in the common cause. The importance of establishing the right of early Christian converts to be reckoned intelligent as well as sincere men, is pointed out by Dr. Woodham in his preface to *Tertullian's Apology.** He shows that the learned Grotius† in making miracles decisive evidence for the truth of Christianity, draws his inference, not as Paley does, from the *sufferings*, but rests it upon the *circumstances* of the early converts; especially upon the fact that such professed philosophers, "men of good judgment and no small learning" as most of the Apologists were, became disciples after due examination.‡

The last point I need notice in order to claim the most serious attention of the reader, is the general *applicability* of the apologetic arguments to the times in which we live. This, the most important quality, involving as it does great practical utility, will require a little thought. There are many things that as they become old become obsolete, or which when transferred from one country to another are as useless in their new relations, as they were valuable before. The era or the climate whose peculiarity gave them birth being changed, their use is gone. Among these transitory existences, the evidences of the Christian Religion are certainly not to be classed. Like the cause they support, they belong to every age and every zone. This universality of application arises from two things. First, from the ethical nature of Religion itself, which being unaffected by temporal changes and admitting neither of discovery nor development, lends a glow of immortality, a perpetual youth to any prin-

* Tertul. Lib. *Apol.* Ed. Woodham.

† Grotius, *On the Truth of Christianity*, Lib. II. § 4.

‡ That this careful examination was made may be gathered from the scraps of autobiography, as well as from the substance of these apologies.

ciples of reasoning that have ever been of considerable service to its interests. And secondly, from the unalterable character of the errors such arguments are invented to counteract. Error is as immutable as truth. Its outward couching of language or logic may vary; but its direction and force are the same: its masks may be many, it has but one face.*

The Chevalier Ramsay, in his Essays on *Pagan Theology*,† has taken the trouble to trace an identity between the ancient and modern systems of philosophy. But without quoting his details, we may at once adopt his conclusion: "Modern free-thinkers have only revived the ancient errors, disguising them under new terms. The history of former times is like our own. The human understanding takes almost the same forms in different ages, and loses its way in the same labyrinths." Especially is this true of the opposition the human heart feels to the system of Divine *grace*. Herein the world for once maintains a uniform consistency. It thinks and acts much alike everywhere, and at all times. Indeed on no other hypothesis could we explain the fact already advanced, that most of the old objections to Religion have their representatives still: that, for example, the difficulties noted by Athenagoras concerning the resurrection, and by Origen concerning the evangelistic history, are just what are now going the rounds of our workshops and lecture-rooms with all the credit of a patent invention. But I would ask who needs any other witness to the truth of this proposition than his own daily observation? Surely no one can have reflected upon the state of society (whatever its range) in which he moves, without perceiving that our own country and day furnish living specimens of all those classes of mind with which St. Paul, and his successors in the *Apologetic* work,

* "Manabat saxo vena perennis aquæ."

† Annexed to this author's *Cyrus*. Tenth Edition, p. 341.

had to contend; that the Sadducee and the Cabalist, the Epicurean and the Gnostic, have disappeared only in name. How many of our scientific professors are but materialists; of our theologians, but Neoplatonists; of our sentimental poets, but worshippers of nature, and that too in *this* land of light! "Little do they know," says Chalmers,* "of our men of general literature, who have not observed the utter listlessness, if not the strong and active contempt, wherewith many of them hear the doctrine of God's word." In fine, if we allow with Baxter, "he that maketh not God his chief good and ultimate end, is in heart a pagan and a vile idolater,"† who is not a party concerned? Would that this were a mere play upon words; but there is too serious a reality in it. It exhibits a parallelism of *principles*, if not of expression, underlying all periods of time.

Things being so with regard to *truth* and *error*, the adaptation and virtue of our subject follow almost as a matter of course. The only remaining question can be as to the actual capacity and appliances of the Fathers. This, like any similar question of fact, can be alone solved after a careful consideration of contemporaneous reputation — of position, — of writings, such as these now under discussion, formerly unanswered and since unsurpassed, — and finally of attendant success. Meanwhile, there is this to be said. We have no *à priori* reason to doubt that the Apologists were quite as capable of using their faculties and their materials as any later class of advocates. It is a very easy thing for gentlemen of leisure on the banks of the Thames or the Rhone, and at the distance of fifteen hundred years, to complain of the style and method of controversy adopted by the early Christians. But their criticism must needs fall short of its mark, unless they can show that the Apologists were more

* Sermons.

† *Saints' Rest.*

incompetent than ourselves from any necessity of the case. Until this is done the *probabilities* are against every partial quotation, every perverted view, every malicious innuendo that either ignorance or impiety can suggest. The presumption must remain, that in an intellectual exercise of this kind the Apologists were masters of their subject.

Nay, possibly, they had an advantage over us, the advantage of *practice.* They were in the heat of the battle. A multitude from every quarter of the globe, a variety from every class of enemies, surrounded them. There was the subtle and metaphysical Eastern, the strong-minded African, the imaginative Greek, the practical Roman, the elder Jew; there was Lucian classing Christianity with every kind of fanaticism and fraud; there was Celsus attacking it through the sides of Judaism with all the shafts profane wit could command; there was Porphyry, the pupil of Longinus, with as much sophistry as learning, denying everything save the operations of nature; and Hierocles bent, like some alchemist at his occult art, upon imitating the gold he could not but admire: * there was the superstitious multitude, the interested artisan, the responsible governor, the jealous emperor, each and all to be met in their own way.

It was likewise a *deadly* struggle: our Apologists endured this great fight of affliction, not in the shape of a mere paper war, or platform controversy, the end of which is often only to "gravel" an opponent; but for body and soul, religion and character. It is plain that every thing dear to the man or the Christian hung on the issue.

And once more, it was *protracted.* The controversy was of no temporary nature, nor belonged to one generation alone.

* Besides the life of Apollonius, Hierocles wrote a book to prove the Scriptures guilty of falsehood and contradiction; so punctiliously naming everything, that Lactantius considers him to have been an apostate Christian.

The clouds returned after the rain; and "neither sun nor stars in many days appeared." The whole term of persecution is reckoned not by years but by centuries, during which time, it may be fairly presumed, that every question was raised which was worth an answer.

Such practice, and such experience as this practice implies, must have necessitated the invention of sharp weapons, and skill in handling them. We cannot but think, then, inasmuch as there seems to be no reason why sound Christian evidence effective in a former age, should become worthless by lapse of time; and as neither Christianity on the one side, nor scepticism on the other, have much altered their ground of opposition since the first days of conflict; and, lastly, seeing that the Apologists may have been as clever (at the least) as ourselves; I say, we cannot but think that their arguments demand a careful examination at our hands, and bid fair, like the renowned sword of old that had long lain "wrapped in a cloth behind the ephod,"* to do good service still, as well by their own temper and weight, as by their hallowed and victorious associations.

The following remarks of Dr. Hundeshagen, of the University of Heidelberg, are based on the same principles, and tend to the same practical conclusion. Bewailing the spread of infidelity in Germany, he observes: "The first age of the Christian Church is rightly called the Apologetic, for the Christian religion had then to win its right to existence by its struggles. We of this age are in this respect carried back to the commencement of Christianity, for the forefront of the battle of parties relates to the very existence of the Christian Religion. So that without doubt we are called upon to apply our Christian attainments to that same Apologetic task which engaged the attention of the first centuries."†

* 1 Sam. xxi. 9.

† *Studien und Kritiken* for 1848. See Appendix to *Hulsean Essay* for 1849. Tomkins.

Still less hesitancy can be felt as to the appositeness of these arguments to the case of countries yet shrouded in heathen darkness. Take, for example, our largest dependency, India. *There* we have a land boasting at this hour of as many gods as swarming inhabitants; its idols under every spreading banyan-tree, by the side of every road, by the bank of every river: *there* a priesthood, crafty alike by nature and education, who when hard pressed by the technical difficulties surrounding the subject of Polytheism, fly to the metaphysical subtleties of their schools: *there* a confusion of religions, a moral Babel; superstition strangely shared between the Pundit, the Brahmin, the Parsee; each with dogmas diverse as their races, only united in their determination to resist whatever is holy and true, and all publicly encouraging licentiousness and cruelty. In a word, *there* we recognize the usual phases of Paganism, — literal idolatry, — a religion with its convenient senses, vulgar and mystic, — a philosophy as discordant, and vices as inveterate as ever.* For such symptoms, Apologetic practice might certainly be made available with a little address, and the modern missionary furnished with hints out of these stores of ancient and Christian learning. It is interesting to find that the gifted Henry Martyn† used with effect some of the natural arguments of the Fathers on Christian theism, in his public addresses at Cawnpore. And thus may others, by appeals to conscience, to nature, to universal tradition, catch the attention of hearers (dark in mind as in feature), and rouse them from their fascinating self-delusions, to some consciousness of the light that shines all unheeded around. On these as on common grounds, and with some appearance of equity, and the assurance of being understood,

* Palmer, in his *Development and Conscience*, says that some of the arguments of the Apologists are exactly applicable to the heathen systems of the present day. Observe his note, p. 8.

† See Life, p. 327. 8vo.

a hearing at least might be obtained, and a door opened for more important matters.

From these suggestions it would appear that our subject is one of considerable practical importance. It is surprising therefore that we have no direct treatise upon it. Yet such is the fact. Fabricius has given little more than a list of authors who have pleaded the cause of Christianity, from Apostolic times to his own, and a series of the Apologetic works of the Fathers is slowly issuing from the press; but I am not aware of any synopsis or review on the proposition that heads this essay. The notices of the Apologists in our Ecclesiastical Histories must necessarily prove unsatisfactory. By the compression of so wide a theme into a few paragraphs, more injustice than justice is commonly, though unintentionally, done.* Hence little is to be gleaned in that direction. I have, however, to acknowledge my obligations to the bishop of Lincoln's *illustrations* from the treatises of Justin, Tertullian, and Clemens, than which nothing can be more fair or complete; as also to Dr. Woodham's valuable Introduction to Tertullian's *Apologeticus*, already consulted; and to the first chapter of Palmer, *On the Doctrine of Development and Conscience;* as being the best, indeed the only, notices I have met with on the special point of the Apologetic arguments.

I now pass on to consider more definitely our *sources of information.* They consist of the Apologies and Apologetic works of the early Fathers. And, I think, we cannot do better for a thorough understanding of what lies before us, than devote a few minutes in glancing at the general history of these works, and the circumstances under which they were produced. It is scarcely possible to judge of the force and propriety of what an author advances, unless we know something of his *situation.*

* Neander's *Church History* is almost an exception.

In doing this, need I observe, that there will be no attempt to do justice to such an interesting topic as the History of the Apologies? My business is simply to extract the dates, the order, the language, the locality, the standing and the principal works of the Apologetic Fathers, together with the special occasions that called them forth; in short, just those details which serve to throw light upon *their arguments*, — the immediate subjects of our investigation.

The portion of time these writings embrace is about three hundred years, commencing with the second century.

THE APOLOGIES OF THE SECOND CENTURY.*

QUADRATUS (Greek), of the apostolic age, and ARISTEIDES (Greek, A. D. 126) originally an Athenian philosopher, address apologies to the Emperor Hadrian during a popular tumult raised in Greece, probably on the plea of Trajan's prohibition of the Heteriæ, which the Christian assemblies appeared to contravene. Of these, nothing but a fragment or notice remains; as is the case also with some other apologies presented to Marcus Aurelius by ABERCIUS (A. D. 150), MELITO (A. D. 169), and to M. Antoninus by APOLLINARIUS (A. D. 170), all Eastern bishops, a little later. These latter pleas were drawn forth by severe but partial persecutions in Asia Minor, instituted under cover of informations, rather than by express edicts.

THE EPISTLE TO DIOGNETUS (Greek) is addressed about this time to an inquiring heathen of rank. The style of this "valuable remain of antiquity" is classical, and the

* I chiefly follow Spanheim's Chronological Tables.

doctrine truly apostolical. Its object is to explain the nature of a religion, which induces its followers to love one another, and to despise at once the blandishments of the world, and the terrors of death; which honors neither the heathen gods, nor the Jewish ceremonies; and which yet is of so recent a date as only just to have made its appearance among men. The writer claims to be a disciple of the apostles, and alludes to persecutions by the Jews and Greeks.

JUSTIN MARTYR (Greek) was a Platonic philosopher, born in Palestine.* He traces his conversion to an aged Christian,† whom he met by the sea-shore, and at whose recommendation he began to study the prophets.‡ Afterwards, being at Rome during the persecution under Antoninus Pius, he dedicated his *First Apology* (A. D. 148) to the emperor and the young princes, Verissimus and Lucius. About this time the infamous charges against the Christians were set afloat, (Justin says,) by the Jews. He therefore applies himself to the defence of Religion, on the ground of the reasonableness and morality of its precepts, as contrasted with those of heathen systems; and also on the ground of corroborative prophecy. His *Second Apology* (A. D. 164) is addressed to the senate, and pleads for the superiority of the doctrines of Christ over those of devils; demanding protection

* Though he calls himself a Samaritan, he appears to mean no more than that he was born in the country of Samaria; not that he was a semi-Jew.

† This person is fancifully supposed to be an angel, by Reeves; which Brown likewise thinks not an unreasonable conjecture, "if the dialogue with Trypho be true; because the meeting with such a grave and wise old man looks altogether miraculous." Surely the difficulty vanishes when we consider the persecutions at that time pending, and the solitude and reserve they rendered necessary. Moreover, this venerable old gentleman, as Justin styles him, affirms that he is in search of some of his family—a strange expression, to say the least of it, in the mouth of an angel.

‡ By prophets the Fathers often meant the whole Scripture. Jortin gives instances of this.

for his brethren on account of the innocency of their lives. In his *Oratio ad Græcos* he attacks the flagitious immoralities ascribed by the heathen to their deities, and committed by themselves in their religious festivals;* founding thereon an exhortation in favor of Christianity. The treatise *De Monarchia* is an argument for Monotheism, supported by numerous quotations from the ancient classics. His fragment *On the Resurrection*, (thought by Otto to belong to a lost work *against Marcion*,) is an exhibition of the Christian's hope concerning the tenet in question upon abstract grounds, the only way of establishing what is future. In the *Dialogue with Trypho* the Jew, Justin's chief aim is to prove from the Old Testament that Jesus was the Logos and the true Messiah, by his having fulfilled in person the ancient prophecies therein contained; and to refute the common objections urged by the Jews against the new and rival sect. This disputation is supposed (by Eusebius) to have taken place at Ephesus, in one of the piazzas of the city, and in the presence of several other Jews. The *Cohortatio ad Græcos* sometimes passing under our author's name (whether genuinely or not, can be of no consequence here, since its date is unquestioned), consists of an examination of the doctrinal formulæ of heathenism and Christianity, by which the writer plainly shows the absurdities and disagreements of the one and the simplicity and harmony of the other; and also of an investigation into the rival claims of the two systems, to antiquity. It is probable that the fearless stand Justin took in these works had the effect of mitigating the persecutions of his day, though they seem to have accelerated his own martyrdom, which occurred, according to the Chronicon Paschale, A. D. 165.

TATIAN (Greek), a pupil of Justin Martyr, an Assyrian by birth from beyond the Tigris, and a Cynic or a Sophist by

* Smith's *Dictionary of Biog.*, &c.

profession, was the next defender of Christianity. He wrote the *Oratio adversus Græcos,* in which he remonstrates with the Greeks for their repugnance to the opinions of foreigners, and points out the purer morality; the higher and more elevated views respecting the universe, God, and the divine administration generally; and the greater antiquity of the Christian system. It is cited by Jerome as "a distinguished work." Tatian lapsed into heresy; this circumstance however does not affect us, as the work in question was written before his fall, and contains none of the erroneous sentiments of the Encratites, or the Gnostics, though some of its speculations are sufficiently fanciful and remote from the simplicity of Christian truth. Neither the date nor place of his death is known.

ATHENAGORAS (Greek, A. D. 178) follows. He was born at Athens, and had been a Grecian philosopher, but now undertook the defence of the Christians in an address dedicated to Marcus Aurelius and his son Commodus, and usually entitled, *Legatio pro Christianis.* This work discusses the respective merits of the heathen and Christian systems, laying the greatest stress on an exposure of the follies and idolatries of Paganism. It also touches by the way, upon prophecy and the antiquity of the Scriptures. We have likewise a treatise of this Father *On the Resurrection,* an excellent piece of reasoning, wherein he shows with no little ingenuity that the presumptive arguments against the doctrine of a Resurrection are inconclusive. Of his personal history we know but little. It is asserted by P. Sidetes that he owed his conversion to a perusal of the holy Scriptures, with a view to ridicule them as Celsus did subsequently.

THEOPHILUS (Greek, A. D. 180) of Antioch, about this time furnishes us with an apologetic work in three books, addressed to *Autolycus,* a learned heathen of his acquaintance.

He tells us that his design is to give a chronological view o epochs from the creation of the world down to the year in which he writes, by which he will prove that the divine oracles in our possession are more ancient and more true than the statements of Egyptian, Grecian, and all other historians. The first book is an answer to what the ingenious Pagan had maliciously and strenuously objected against the religion of Christ.* In the second, he proceeds to an examination of the profane histories, in the course of which he confutes the opinions that were maintained by the Pagans, concerning their gods, and shows the absurd contradictions of their poets and philosophers upon this subject. He then turns to the sacred writings, explains at large the creation of the world and the occurrences of succeeding ages, and demonstrates that the history of Moses is the most venerable, and that from which other writers have borrowed. In the third book he exposes yet more the notions of the heathen, as inconsistent and contrary to humanity, to reason and to morals. He also shows that the doctrines of the Christians are far from those horrid crimes imputed to them; and lastly, he appends to the whole a sort of historical chronology to confirm the truth of the Scriptures. Neander says these books display much erudition and proof of thought. Our author confesses to his having been originally a pagan in Lib. II. c. 78.

HERMIAS (Greek), a contemporary of Tatian, presents us with a satirical piece called *Irrisio Gentilium Philosophorum*, in which he has brought together a number of the absurd and contradictory opinions of the Greeks on nature, the world, God, the human soul, &c., proving by their discrepancies how useless and insufficient they are. He styles himself a Christian Philosopher.

CLEMENS ALEXANDRINUS (Greek, A. D. 190) next addresses the Gentiles in an *Exhortatio*. It forms the first

* Cave's *Lives*.

part of his celebrated work on divine Gnosticism. He himself describes it as a treatise on morals, which he says, like the keel of a ship, must first be laid for the edification of faith.* It trusts mainly to an exposure of the impurities of Polytheism as contrasted with the spiritual nature of Christianity, and demonstrates the value of the Gospel by showing that it effectually purifies the motives and dignifies the character. There is some reference also in his *Stromata* or Miscellanies, to the questions of antiquity and plagiarism. It is to be observed that he quotes from the address of Tatian to the Greeks. Clemens was probably an Athenian by birth, and had been a philosopher of the Platonic school. In the *Stromata* we are informed of his having been indebted for his education to two masters, the one a Cœlo-Syrian, the other an Egyptian. He does not seem to have felt the attractions of the Gospel until the age of manhood; for he classes himself among those who had left the sinful service of Paganism, for that of simple faith in the Redeemer. This fact may account in some measure for the philosophical views he took of profane learning as well as of Christianity, and which indeed so entirely tinctured his mental character. For whilst it cannot be questioned that he was pious, it must be allowed at the same time that he was unduly prone to theory, and by no means comprehensive or connected in his development of Christian doctrine. An Eclectic, sometimes leaning towards the Stoics, he was altogether more attached to philosophy than any of the Fathers, with the exception of Origen. Of course these reflections hardly bear upon any of his Apologetic writings. Jerome pronounces his works to be full of learning and eloquence. His conversion is attributed to free inquiry made under the direction of Pantænus, once a heathen philosopher like himself, but afterwards the president of the Catechetical school of Alexandria.

* *Pædag.* cap. I

TERTULLIAN (Latin) was a native of Carthage, the son of a proconsular centurion, and in early life a heathen advocate, or rhetorician. His cession to Montanism, happening as it did in his later years, does not interfere with the few polemical works now under review. In his *Apologeticus*, addressed to the chief magistrates of his province, in consequence of their unjust treatment of the Christians (under Severus), he adduces the argument drawn from antiquity, and the evidences of prophecy and miracles; but places the greatest reliance for his cause upon an exhibition of the folly and immorality of heathen worship, occasionally parrying and even hurling back upon his assailants the reproaches of lewdness and cruelty which they had cast at the Church. In the two books, *Ad Nationes*, he pursues a like train of thought; indeed there is frequently an identity both in words and substance. His treatises *De Resurrectione Carnis*, and *De Testimonio Animæ*, contain some fine abstract arguments from nature, in support of Christian doctrines. Of the former, Milner, (no usual admirer of this author,*) allows in his *Church History* that "he scarce remembers a finer observation made by any author in favor both of the natural voice of conscience and of the patriarchal tradition of true religion; for both may fairly be supposed to be concerned." The tract styled *Adversus Judæos Liber* appears to have sprung out of a public debate held between a Christian and a Jewish proselyte, at which our author was not able to deliver his opinions freely, on account of the party clamor that prevailed. Upon his return, therefore, from the meeting, he composed this short piece to show how the Jew might be confuted out of his own Scriptures.† Tertullian is certainly the most original and forcible of the Latin Fathers. Reeves says of him, that while it is admitted his style is iron, it cannot be denied that

* Bishop of Lincoln's *Eccles. Hist.*

† See Smith's *Biographical Dictionary*, Art. Tertullian.

he has forged out of it most noble weapons for the defence of our holy religion; and Dr. Woodham remarks upon *The Apology*, that its arguments are astonishingly clear, and, if contemplated *quoad homines* and *quoad causam*, can hardly fail to command our assent.

THE APOLOGIES OF THE THIRD CENTURY.

MINUTIUS FELIX (Lat. circ. A. D. 230). *The Octavius* of this author purports to have originated in the following circumstance. Minutius, an advocate of the Roman bar, and two of his legal associates (Octavius Januarius, a true believer, being one, Cæcilius Natalis, a pagan, the other) take advantage of the holidays to visit Ostia during the heat of the Italian summer. As they stroll along the coast, a statue of Serapis comes into sight. Cæcilius at once salutes it with his hand. This incident leads to a discussion of the entire subject of religion, between Octavius and his heathen friend; Minutius agreeing to act as umpire on the occasion. The result is the conviction of Cæcilius, who charmingly concludes the dialogue by acknowledging that there is no need for any judicial decision, since both parties have conquered; "Octavius has conquered me, and I have conquered error." After the death of Octavius, the disconsolate Minutius recalls this interesting and memorable conversation, and publishes it *in memoriam* of his friend. The body of the book consists of a contrast of the degradation and inconsistencies of idolatry, with the high tone of Christian morals. The author is careful likewise to show that even the heathen allowed some of the great truths of religion; and to defend Christians against the usual reproaches cast upon them. Dr. Woodham says of this dialogue: "it will be seen, on a careful perusal, that it is occupied in clearing away any antecedent objections to the consideration of Christianity; it shows the existence of a

God, and offers proof of his unity; it demonstrates the folly of the existing religion, and removes the superficial prejudice against the new one; and its effects upon its readers must have been to convince them there was a God, to whom their worship was due, that they had not known him yet, and that to say the least there was no *á priori* evidence that the teaching of the despised Christians would not supply the knowledge." Even Gibbon admires some parts of the *Octavius.* Minutius, or Octavius (it matters not which speaks), was by birth a Gentile, and a lawyer for some time before his conversion to Christianity. He seems to have been well versed in the classics, and drew largely from Cicero and Seneca, as well as from Tertullian.

HIPPOLYTUS (Greek) probably an Arabian Pastor,* is found about this period writing a *Demonstratio adversus Judæos.* Photius makes him a disciple of Irenæus, the bishop of Lyons, and, like his master, a martyr.

ORIGEN (Greek) follows in point of time. He says in his preface to the eight books *against Celsus,* (A. D. 244–249,) an Epicurean philosopher, that he writes "to vindicate Christians from foul aspersions, and because the common people may be in danger of listening to scepticism, and turning apostates from the faith." It is difficult to give any general description of this work, inasmuch as it consists of a string of scarcely connected chapters or criticisms, closely following upon the track of Celsus. Origen more than once complains of this disorder, and attributes it to the blindness of his opponent's malice, confessing that the frequent repetitions of which

* Bunsen's researches have refuted the conjecture of Le Moyne, that Hippolytus was bishop of Aden in Arabia. He was bishop of Portus, the new harbor of Rome, on the northern bank of the Tiber, and his most celebrated production, discovered in 1842, in a Greek library at Mount Athos, and published at Oxford in 1851 as a work of Origen, is entitled "*A Refutation of all Heresies.*" *Am. Ed.*

Celsus forces him to be guilty, make him appear almost as impertinent as himself. The first two books are levelled principally against Jewish objections, behind which Celsus at first conceals his own views. In the third, both the Mosaic and Christian institutions are defended against Epicurean assaults and ribaldry, (as in the very opening of the book, where the Christian and the Jew are charged with contending, according to the old proverb, about the shadow of an ass,) after which the author proceeds to resolve the confusion Celsus endeavors to throw around the religion and character of Jesus by comparing him with the Grecian heroes. The fourth enlarges upon the prophecies and antiquity of the Hebrews. The fifth answers a variety of charges brought against practical Christianity. In the sixth, the marked difference between the writings of the Christians and Greeks is treated of. In the seventh, their respective claims to the prophetic spirit, and in the eighth, their modes of worship, are contrasted. The value of this work could scarcely be told, were it less discursive. Origen's treatise, *De Principiis*, likewise contains some material for our purpose, though it stands doctrinally charged with Neo-Platonism, and even Arianism. What makes the peculiar tenets, especially the freedoms of Origen with the interpretations of Scrip ture, the more remarkable is, that he is one of the few Apologists who received a Christian education. He was brought up at Alexandria, where his father, Leonides, once a rhetorician, afterwards a devout Christian, was beheaded for Christ, in a persecution which befell the disciples in Egypt under Sept. Severus. Origen was then a youth, but had already distinguished himself by his piety, learning, and indomitable courage. He is said to have had Clement for a master, and to have been elected a catechist at the early age of eighteen. He died at Tyre A. D. 253; his health having been impaired by torture during the Decian trials.

CYPRIAN (Lat.) writes an apologetic letter, or rather a formal discourse, *De Gratia Dei*, (A. D. 246,) which he addresses *to Donatus*, a young fellow disciple. The two friends are supposed to be seated under the shade of vines, enjoying the mild airs of autumn and an agreeable prospect, whilst they converse on their favorite theme. Our author begins by taking an imaginary view from an eminence, of the ways of the world, which is found calculated to excite both pity and gratitude in the mind of a Christian man. He then points out particularly the vices of cities, and draws a striking parallel between the holy and happy condition of such as have turned from Paganism, and the grossness of their former state.

The tract *Ad Demetrianum* (A. D. 252) is of the same character. It defends Christians from the charges of the Proconsul and other persecutors, to whom it offers in return some home truths. Lactantius quotes from it.* *The Vanity of Idols* is dated the year after the letter to Donatus. The title speaks for its contents. This author borrows largely from the *Octavius* of Minutius Felix. Among his smaller works are two books, *Testimoniorum adversus Judæos*, consisting of Scripture proofs of the fulfillment of prophecy. They are noticed by Jerome and Augustine. Cyprian was an African, of heathen parentage, brought up to rhetoric, and induced to embrace Christianity by an aged presbyter of Carthage, A. D. 246. He suffered much in the Decian persecution, A. D. 250, but was not martyred until the reign of Valerian, A. D. 258. It was a custom with him to call Tertullian his "Master," from the veneration he had for his great countryman's works.

ARNOBIUS (Lat.), likewise an African, "of which there can be no doubt," says Cave, "for his speech agreeth thereto,"

* *Div. Instit.* v. 4.

has left us seven books of *disputations*. He was not a Father of the Church, but a neophyte or candidate for institution, to forward which, it is said, he wrote this work. Little is known of his personal history. That he had been a heathen and a professor of rhetoric at Sikka, in Africa, is certain, as also that he continued a heathen until the Diocletian persecution, when the constancy and meekness of the Christians under their severest trials awakened his mind to a more serious and impartial inquiry after truth. He writes now, he says, in consequence of the calumnious charges brought against the Christians, and the assertion that the gods have afflicted the human family with evil on their account. The latter point he determines principally to answer to the best of his ability. There is a great amount of original and bold reasoning in these books. They contain the usual vindication of Christianity and exposure of Paganism, the first two being devoted to the one, and the remaining five to the other topic. They appeal directly and strongly to the Christian miracles, noticing their salutary and God-like character, their number, their publicity, the circumstances attending their performance, and the transmission of the power to others, and finally, their merits as compared with the miraculous virtues ascribed to the gods: the latter are condemned on the grounds of their being tentative, and requiring a medium. Arnobius is the only Apologist who does not argue directly from antiquity. Dr. Woodham accounts him the keenest of all the Apologists, and in some respects the most apposite to the popular arguments of modern times. It must, however, be confessed that his acquaintance with the Gospel scheme and with the sacred writings, was not very profound, unless we suppose him intent only upon setting forth what might immediately tell upon the Pagan theology. He is called by Vossius the Varro of the early Christians, on account both of his extensive and his minute information; for which, in truth, he will be found well worthy the attention of every philologist and theologian.

ARCHELAUS (Syr.), in his dispute with the heretic Manes, and METHODIUS (Greek), with a fragment *De Resurrectione*, written against Origenism, supply something for our consideration. The last named author is said to have been martyred at Chalcis, in Syria, *circ.* A. D. 303.*

THE APOLOGIES OF THE FOURTH CENTURY.

LACTANTIUS (Lat.), a pupil of Arnobius, at Sikka, was born of Gentile parents, and reared in theh eathen religion. Of the mode of his becoming a Christian we have no account. His great work consists of seven books entitled *Divine Institutes.* It is of a didactic and elaborate character; but none the less apologetic, professing as it does to demolish paganism, to confute philosophy, and to show the indissoluble connection between true wisdom and Christianity. A running comparison is kept up between true wisdom and true religion on the one side, and false wisdom and false religion on the other. Our author argues well for the humanity of the heathen gods and the impiety and vanity of worshipping them. "The first two books expose the Pagan rites, and the third, the hollowness of philosophy; the fourth contains the more apologetic portion of the treatise; and the remainder completes the whole into such a system of Christian ethics as the writer could compose." † There is likewise extant an *epitome* of the above in one book, drawn up, according to Jerome, by the author himself. He just refers

* Smith's *Biographical Dictionary.*

† Woodham's Preface to *Tertullian.*

to the *Octavius* of Minutius Felix, and to the kindred works of Theophilus,* Tertullian, and Cyprian. "This author," says Dr. Woodham, "presents a striking contrast to Arnobius; the latter declining argument, acknowledging mystery, and asserting facts; the former substituting argumentation for everything; thus the one declines to consider the question of the existence of evil; the other says it is necessary to the formation of its contrary, good." Lactantius in another work, *De Ira Dei*, directed against the Epicureans, furnishes some *à priori* reasoning for a future state; though a few of his positions are rash and erroneous. Also in his *De Opificio Dei*, we find a natural argument in favor of the wisdom and beneficence of God, deduced from the wonderful contrivances and adaptations of means to an end, discernible in the structure of the human frame. Lactantius has ever been esteemed the flower of the Latin doctors, the Cicero of Christian writers. Jerome styles him, "most learned and eloquent." He was in favor at court, for we find him patronized by Diocletian before his conversion, and afterwards teaching the young prince Crispus, son of Constantine, (*circ.* A. D. 312,) himself living but frugally the while, as Eusebius tells us. "The Institutes" are dedicated to the father of his royal pupil, and by their deliberate tone mark the epoch at which Christian influence had won its own toleration, at least in head-quarters: the immediate occasion of their appearance is said to have been some insulting attacks made upon religion by Porphyry and others.

EUSEBIUS (Greek, A. D. 315–340), the ecclesiastical historian and bishop of Cæsarea, presents us with several important works on the Evidences of Christianity. His *Præparatio Evangelica*, in fifteen books, is intended to combat the heathen philosophy in the person of Porphyry, and

* *Theoph. ad Autolyc.* by the title of *De Temporibus.*

to demonstrate its irrational character as opposed to the reasonableness of Christianity. In it he collects various facts and quotations from ancient authors, by which it was supposed the mind would be better prepared for the reception of Christian evidence. The *Demonstratio Evangelica* consists of twenty books, in which he refers to his former work, and then, in continuation of his apologetic project, undertakes to show how the prophecies contribute to the demonstration of the truth of the Gospel. He calls the prophets "divine historians in advance of history." This treatise appears, from internal evidence, to have been principally meant for the Jews. I have gathered my materials, however, as furnished by this Apologist, generally out of his *Theophania*, or "Manifestation of Christ," (so faithfully translated from the Syriac, by Professor Lee,) because it is at once the most synoptic, methodical, and direct of all his works. It consists of arguments and evidences to prove the reasonableness and the reality of the incarnation, and dwells with much force and feeling upon the character of Christ, his miraculous powers, and the success of his Church. The same reasoning occurs (sometimes verbatim) in the *Life of Constantine*. Eusebius likewise published a rejoinder to the life of Apollonius Tyaneus, put forward by *Hierocles*, (the Pagan governor of Alexandria and adviser of Diocletian, during a fierce persecution in that southern district) as a rival of the Gospels; in this work he contents himself with a simple review of the biography. Dr. Cave says of Eusebius, "That with incomparable learning he has out of their own writings so baffled the main principles of the Pagan cause, and so strongly asserted the truth of Christianity against the pretences of both Jews and Gentiles, that the Christian world can never be sufficiently indebted to his memory." Of his bias towards Arius rather than Arianism, and of the dishonesty and sycophancy with which Gibbon charges him in an attack too fierce to be fair or effective, I need say nothing.

Traces of these errors doubtless occur, but with regard to all ancient and distinguished characters, we must make due allowance for their day, and judge only upon the whole. As far as contemporaneous testimony is of any avail, it is in his favor : Constantine, a superior and a *pagan* (according to Niebuhr up to his last illness), used to say of him that he was worthy to be the bishop not of one city only, but almost of the whole world.

ATHANASIUS (Greek), Archbishop of Alexandria, his native place, next addresses the heathen in an *Oratio contra Gentes*, "in order that no one should suspect belief in Christ to be irrational, as the Greeks unjustly thought." He shows that the gods are nothing, or only men ; and after inquiring what sort of witness nature bears with regard to the Deity, he confirms his deductions by pointing out the harmony existing between the God of nature and the God of the Bible. Cave says, that he disputes rationally and wittily in his two books against the Gentiles. Of the former, our author himself premises, "having succinctly though sufficiently treated of the idolatry and superstition of the Gentiles, and of its origin in the world, and said something of the divinity of the Word of God, and his universal power and providence, as He by whom God the Father creates, governs and disposes all things, he would, according to his method, proceed to treat of the Incarnation of the Word against the calumnies of the Jews and the derision of the Gentiles." The parents of Athanasius were heathens, but he was providentially brought under the notice and care of Alexander the primate of Egypt. Erasmus admires his didactic powers and the clearness and manliness of his style.

MATERNUS (Lat. A. D. 350) succeeds. He was a convert from Paganism, and being very desirous of turning others to the faith he had embraced, wrote a treatise *De Errore Profanarum Religionum*, dedicating it to the Emperors Constantine and Constans. The object of the essay is not so much to enlarge upon the evidences of the true faith, as to demonstrate the falsehood of the various forms of Pagan belief. All error is traced, step by step, to our falling away from the service of the true God, and then personifying the powers of Nature, and raising men to the rank of divinities. Having thus shown the absurdity and evil effects of image-worship, he is rather urgent upon the authorities to extirpate idolatry at once by the use of the sternest measures; a plain intimation of the position and influence Christianity had by this time attained. Maternus is said to have been of senatorial dignity.

EPHRAIM (Syrian), a Deacon of Edessa, is found disputing with the *Sceptics and Jews.* To the former he represents and opposes the finite capacity of human thought; to the latter the accomplishment of prophecy. The style of his rhythms, which were extremely popular in their time, is flowery and antithetical, constantly reminding the reader of their Oriental source, and thereby accounting in a measure for many hyperbolical expressions. They are said to have been written to counteract the effect of some poems of the heretic Harmonius denying the Resurrection of the body.

GREGORY NAZIANZEN (Greek, A. D. 363), Archbishop of Constantinople, offers two *Invectives* against Julian the apostate, with whom both he and Basil had been fellow-students in early life. They were published just after the death of the Prince, to describe his pernicious principles and projects; they are, however, rather slight for our purpose. The father of Gregory was a Pagan and a fire-worshipper, but his mother Nonna a pattern of Christian piety.

CHRYSOSTOM (Greek, A. D. 380–407) has some fine comments in his Homilies upon the Evidences of Christianity, drawn principally from its success, as likewise in his Sermons, *adversus Judæos*, in which he takes pains to illustrate the prophetical argument. Chrysostom, so called for his eloquence, was born at Antioch. His father, an officer of the Romano-Asiatic provinces, dying early, the education of the youth devolved upon his mother Anthusa, who was a Christian,— another of those noble and excellent females to whom the world and the Church are alike indebted. The exiles which this famous preacher was subjected to, indicate both the remaining strength of Paganism in his day, and the zeal he exerted against it.

AUGUSTINE (Lat.), the bishop of Hippo, closes our list of Apologists with his celebrated treatise *De Civitate Dei*, (A. D. 426), and a work entitled *De Doctrina Christiana*. The latter is directed against the Manichæans: the former against the heathen, to meet the absurd reproach that the gods had sent the Goths upon Rome in consequence of the number of Christian worshippers within its walls.* The first five books confute such of the heathen as think the gods ought to be worshipped for the benefits they confer upon men in this life; the next five consider the subject in regard to a future life. The remaining twelve consist of alternate parallel sketches of the rise, progress, and end of the earthly and heavenly kingdoms. Neander calls the *City of God* an excellent apologetical work. Our author was an African by birth, and had formerly taught rhetoric at his native place as well as at Carthage; he subsequently went to Milan, where he was converted under the preaching of Ambrose, and the instructions of Simplicius, a presbyter.

Besides the above authors, I have only occasionally quoted an apologetic idea as it occurs in a work of the times.

* See also *Retract.* Lib. II. c. 47.

Such are the sources of information at hand, and from this rapid glance at them we may derive a few pertinent inferences, as the most essential to our object.

First, with regard to the *authors*, it is observable that while all the Apostles and some of the apostolical Fathers were born Jews, this was not the case with the apologetic writers. They were one and all Gentile converts, taken, as we should say, indifferently out of every nation. It is found likewise (as I had previously assumed) that most of them were learned men, and had been philosophers, rhetoricians, or the like, in their original condition; and also that they suffered, some of them, imprisonment and death, all of them, persecution for the sake of Christ; which, according to Cyprian, is "the touchstone of sincerity," a proof *ex abundanti* of the truth of Christianity.

Secondly, with regard to the *Apologies*, it will be seen that they are plainly traceable to persecution. They were ever rather extorted than voluntary. Is it not indeed a most striking fact in the history of the Gospel, displaying both the short-sightedness of its enemies, and the overruling power of God, that the very means employed to stay its progress, so often worked out its advancement? This unexpected result of human machinations had already taken place in apostolic times. To the dispersion of the Apostles, at the death of Stephen, Syria and the East owed their evangelization; and it was in consequence of an attempt upon the life of St. Paul, that Rome and the western Gentiles enjoyed his presence and his teaching. In like manner our Apologists were forced to take up the pen in defence of their churches, their characters, their lives. It has been said that the literature of early Christianity is attributable to "the increase of scientific culture;" * but, whilst the conversions of the learned and refined doubtlessly affected its style, they can

* Neander.

hardly be thought to have caused its appearance. It is rather to the malice of men that we are indebted for the Apologies. They were the *first fruits* of general persecution: the wrath of man praising God. Nor is this reflection the less true during those *lulls* in the storm occasioned by policy or indifference. The popular intention was manifestly the same throughout, and merely exchanged an avowed and legal opposition for one more secret and less responsible. Some of the apologetic treatises appeared at such comparatively quiet intervals; but I can see little essential difference between them and the rest, save that they are more methodical and complete, and without that excitement or vehemence which naturally appertain to an extempore production. There is still apparent the consciousness of a host of enemies and the anticipation of danger. The arm of violence was occasionally weary or restrained, but it was only to make way for the ceaseless energy of the *tongue*. And this holds true even down to the end of the period to which our review is restricted. Augustine wrote his *City of God* to repel a verbal slander.* I have not therefore deemed it advisable to separate these writings, as is sometimes done. They were *all* occasioned by persecution in some form; the ethical and hortatory parts are only expansions of the defence; even the retort is but another mode of repulsion.

Thirdly, with respect to the *persons addressed*, or in other words, the *chief enemies of the Gospel* during the times in question, we gather that they consisted of three classes, the Jewish zealot, the Grecian philosopher, the Roman ruler. *These* formed the mainsprings of resistance: these moved the masses; at once the cause and medium of popular excitement. Hence it is we find the Apologies only addressed to *these* the upper or privileged ranks (as it were) of society, and never to

* Ambrose, his instructor, had just (*circ.* A. D. 384) answered a like charge of Symmachus.

the people. The Apologists *preached* to the people; they had to *write* to the elevated and recondite.

The first enemy of Christianity was the *Jew*. "Mine own familiar friend," said the Saviour in prophecy, "in whom I trusted, which did eat of my bread, hath lifted up his heel against me."* With that fatal prescience, of which Caiaphas† had given an example, the Jews foresaw in the ascendancy of the hated sect the degradation of their own. They had therefore opposed the Gospel with their wonted determination, and the deeper they imbrued their hands in guilt, the more insatiable and delirious became their hatred: indeed, had their power equalled their will, Christianity would soon have been swept from the face of the earth. But their ability to injure was checked by the Roman government, and about this time they had suffered the loss of their temple and nationality. Nevertheless out of the midst of their miseries they contended with what energy they could; and though their sun had set in ominous clouds, though forbidden by a penal law to set foot in their own land, though Ælia Capitolina owned an uncircumcised bishop, yet no hour seemed too late or too dismal, and no situation too forlorn, for a people destined to prove by their own fate, that the kingdom promised to their fathers was "not of this world." Perceiving the decline of their civil power, they only endeavored the more to preserve their religious influence. Every occasion was seized for urging the powerful popular opposition which an extended dispersion and commerce, and a general education and acquaintance with the new system, enabled them to wage. Not to mention the intimations in the Acts of the Apostles, and the strong Jewish element against which the apostolical Fathers evidently had to strive, we find the author of the epistle to Diognetus ‡ distinctly asserting that "the

* Psalm xli. 9. † John xi. 51.

‡ In allusion probably to the cruelties of Barchochebas.

Jews make war upon us;" Justin Martyr, that "the Jews regard us with hatred, slaying and persecuting us;" Tertullian, that "the Jews are our enemies through envy," and so on: add to this, that they were not content with open hostility, but condescended to whisper the vilest slanders against the early Church, as those of child-murder, incest, and treason.

Upon the whole, it appears from a perusal of the primitive Fathers that Judaism was the first *felt* enemy of Christianity. At the same time it is equally clear that as the Jewish power became crippled, and as Christianity began her migration, and drew the site of the controversy westward, extricating herself from all fear of identity with and influence from Judaism, by placing her defence in the hands of Gentile Apologists, this first and most implacable foe began to disappear. But it was only to bequeath his place and his spirit to others.

In extending from Palestine to Rome, Christianity must needs pass through Greece, there to stand the test of intellectual criticism, and the sallies of lively wit, as it had already stood the test of inveterate bigotry; the *Greek philosopher* was the next foe to the Gospel. The introduction of the subject at Athens by St. Paul furnished quite a specimen of what was to take place on a wider scale. The gay attack of the Epicureans and Stoics upon Christ's ambassador was the type of others upon Christ's followers; the speech upon Mars hill was an epitome of many an *apology* in after times. To these fashionable and worldly minds, "the cross" was both offensive and foolish. It was offensive, because of the contrast it formed to their licentiousness: it was foolish, because it did not square with their notions of wisdom. By the indulgence of an unrivalled imagination and taste, the Greeks had contrived to throw a halo of glory about idolatry, and to conceal beneath a veil of sentiment the absurdity and grossness of hero-worship. Excessive art had petrified their moral life. Their sculptors had hewn the sacred but amorphous blocks of earlier ages, and transformed what were originally perhaps, mere *memorials*, into elegant and all-but breathing statues; their poets had collected and embodied the false notions of Deity from every land, upon their own sublime Olympus; their musicians had professed to soften the powers of hell, and to bring back "Eurydice" almost to life; whilst their sages had taken care to provide a reserve of plausible theories for the satisfaction of the more shrewd and reflective. Is it any marvel that arts so enchanting, learning so eloquent, religion so accommodating, should be scandalized at the cross of Christ, and at his "form of a servant?" Mental pride and sensual gratification were the moving principles in the one case, humility and holiness in the other: "The darkness comprehended not the light."

Moreover, at the date of our Apologies, Grecian philosophy had spread itself over the world, and leavened all the moral systems of the West. The Roman schools were but reflections of the Grecian schools.* It was this large, combined and intellectual body that now began to turn its attention to the sect just emerging into notice, claiming the only wisdom worth knowing, and challenging the rights of any rival to the proud title of "the schools of glory." Learning, sarcasm, prescription, were kindled into one flame. The philosophers of every party demanded to be either satisfied or silenced by erudition and reasoning powers at least *equal* to their own. In this emergency the *Apologists* arose, and as at first, in a former antagonism, St. Paul, the most effectual opponent of the Jews, came forth from their own bosom; so now, and doubtless with a like design of Providence, the first regular defenders of Christianity were summoned out of the ranks of the philosophers themselves. Hitherto it had been of the utmost importance that the power of God should be strongly

* See Tennemann's *Manual of the History of Philosophy*, p. 161.

contrasted with the weakness and plainness of its instruments; now perhaps it was as necessary to show that religion could influence the greatest as well as commonest minds. Thus its universal adaptation might be proved; thus the most influential men of the day might become interested on its side; thus after being tested by reason and learning, the most exalted would be left without excuse. To these ends the *Apologists* addressed the Greeks in elaborate and spirited discourses, accompanied by the most touching expostulations.

The last great enemy to Christianity we have to follow out, is the *Roman ruler.* It will be remembered in a former quotation from the Epistle to Diognetus, reaching almost to the apostolic period, that whilst the Jews and Greeks are recognized as hostile, the Romans are not named at all. The truth is that at first the Western government, by its destruction of the Jews, by the universal freedom of intercourse it established throughout the civilized world, and by the general equality of its laws, had so far unwittingly favored the spread of the Gospel. For a long time the young Church appeared to be rather protected than persecuted by the authorities of this vast empire. Indifferent Gallios and ambitious Cæsars thought a band of enthusiasts beneath their notice; and so actually sheltered the tender plant until it had taken deep root, and silently sent its seeds on the wings of every wind. No doubt the earnest preachers of the Cross suffered sufficiently, as we have already seen, but it was in a more *private* way. "It took some time," says Paley, "for the vast machine of the Roman empire to be put in motion." At length, however, the movement commenced; the rulers of the earth awoke from their lethargy, and as they had the greater power, so they inflicted the severest calamities that had ever befallen, perhaps ever will befall, the Christian cause. "The days of tribulation" had arrived. From the reign of Nero to that of Constantine the Church was tried by a series of persecutions; the way to heaven was tracked with blood. The grounds of this inconsistent conduct (for the Romans tolerated every other religion) were probably, alarm at a rival kingdom, as in the cases of Claudius,* Vespasian, and Domitian; subterfuge, as in that of Nero; the confounding Christians with rebellious Jews, as of Titus; the misunderstandings founded upon slanderous reports and interested appeals from a sinking priesthood, and their dependants, as of Trajan; malignant and revengeful feelings of apostates; the natural disposition of men to attribute their misfortunes to those they hate, and the general dislike of the human heart to all that is gentle and pure. However explained, the fact itself illustrates the rapid growth of the Christian religion, that it could thus have arrayed *the whole world* against itself; and it is scarcely less a sign of its internal vitality and power that it had already absorbed so much of the intellect of society, as to be able to furnish a succession of authors of sufficient address and courage to defend themselves and their interests before emperors, senates, and the *rulers of the whole world.*

Such were the enemies with whom the Apologists undertook to cope, and as their cause was that of Christianity itself, their writings supply us with the materials we are in search of, viz., the early evidences. At the same time it appears from the nature of the case, that we could not expect any *formal* defence of Christianity. The apologetic portion, which was the original plea for writing, *is* formally arranged; but the evidential portion, though the most important, was necessarily dependent. And be it remembered, this was no choice of the Apologists; in no other way could they have got a chance of a hearing, or a hope of doing good. Still everything is included, we may be sure, that they wished to say. It remains for us, therefore, to select some system, by way of method, on which to display these scattered thoughts

* Suet. Claud. xxv.

and arguments; and I think such a system offers itself, as a fourth and last deduction from the foregoing sketch.

An inspection of the brief notices therein contained of the *substance* of the Apologies, will show that the Fathers chiefly dwelt upon certain arguments and modes of proof, which may be gathered together under seven heads, as those derived from the *antecedent probability*, the *antiquity*, the *prophetical*, and *miraculous* elements, the *doctrines*, the *morals*, and the *success* of the Gospel. And this seems to be the most satisfactory classification that can be adopted. It is true a summary of each Apology could alone prevent the dislocation, in a few instances, of successive arguments well drawn out, and of considerable cumulative force; but such an arrangement would require volumes. Again, there are classifications founded upon certain divisions of arguments, as such; or, on some order of time, locality, antagonism, and the like; but they all appear more or less artificial when compared with one suggested by the *subject matter* of the writings themselves. Upon the whole, therefore, I think, the plan thus suggested will be found natural; adapted to modern expectations, as well as any; comprehensive, covering the whole ground, and so doing thorough justice to the work before us; and yet of sufficient compactness and regularity for the limits and unity of an essay.

Taking with us then the above hints respecting the sources of information, and the situation of our authors, we shall be prepared, I hope, to form a better estimate of the *arguments* about to be considered, albeit they were used long since, in foreign lands and on occasions to us directly unknown. We shall certainly comprehend them better, even if we do not appreciate them more. Where I have thought any point needs special explanation, I have attempted it in a short opening attached to each chapter on the nature and use of the various contents.

I have only further to say that some repetition must be

excused in a work of this kind, where the popularity and supposed value of an argument can scarcely be illustrated without it. I trust, however, that what little of this kind occurs, will be found placed in such various points of light as not to weary the reader. It has been my endeavor, likewise, to avoid isolated passages which have but a slight authority; and those which while they might have some weight with Christian minds as tending to prove our point, were not used for that purpose by the Fathers; also a few of what may be termed apocryphal arguments that have become more worthless than ever, in consequence of later advances in science. And lastly, in attempting to point out the real or relative value of any of the following evidences whatsoever, it should be borne in mind that the Fathers never depended upon any one separately or alone. This needless experiment was left for modern times, and is perhaps the result of that *excessive* systematizing and overstraining the spontaneous suggestions of mind, which was introduced or encouraged by the schoolmen. Origen says, "the faith of Christians does not depend upon a *single* argument, but upon the concurrence and conjunction of several;" and, again, Chrysostom: "If upon the subject of religion we desire to be fully persuaded of the truth, we must consider carefully the *whole* train of things which, like a chain, is composed of different links, bound the one to the other."

I cannot better close this introductory chapter respecting our arguments in general, than by stating the effect they produced in their own day and generation. It certainly adds some importance to an attempt, to know that its object was attained. On this point Dr. Woodham remarks: "After all, perhaps we have scarcely given due credit, or assigned sufficient influence, to the Christian Apologists. We know that Christianity spread over the surface of the known world, and that the Apologies were written to promote its diffusion; we may not be able to trace their insensible operation, or find recorded instances of their power; but it is at least not improbable that the steadfast endurance of a martyr, whose blood was the seed of the Church, might have itself resulted from the patient and private study of such writings as these. Even their perpetual repetition argues an experience of some previous success.*" I think we may add to this, that not only was the cause they advocated triumphant generally, but in the *very direction* in which these Apologies were aimed, viz., the higher classes, always the most difficult to persuade. Surely without derogating from the glory due to God alone, we may attribute to a Nazianzen,† as an humble instrument, some share in extorting the confession from the dying Julian: "Thou hast conquered, oh, Galilean!" And again, it is not to be overlooked that as soon as their work was done, as soon as Pagan Rome was overthrown, and Christ's kingdom fairly established throughout the world, the Apologists ceased as a distinct class, and not before. Both these facts furnish presumptive evidence of the share their writings had in the Gospel triumph.

* Tertull. pref. LX. Ed. Woodham.

† Gregory relates that his brother Cæsarius also, who though a Christian was retained as court-physician by Julian, freely conversed with the Emperor on the subject of religion, defending his cause with equal learning and skill.

CHAPTER I.

THE ARGUMENT FROM ANTECEDENT PROBABILITY.

That which may be known of God is manifest in them; for God hath showed it unto them. For the invisible things of him from the creation of the world are clearly seen, being understood by the things that are made, even his eternal power and Godhead; so that they are without excuse. *Romans* 1:19, 20.

Under this title may be collected such considerations as were adduced by the Apologists for the specific purpose of making Christianity appear plausible. They consist of those abstract ideas which serve to introduce any important subject. That the Fathers had such a class of arguments in their minds, however rarely arranged with system, or carried out at much length, it would be strange to doubt. They were emphatically the philosophers of their day; many of them being deemed, but for their religion, worthy to fill the highest chairs. "Chrysostom should succeed me," said Libanius, the heathen rhetorician of Antioch, on his death-bed, "if the Christians had not stolen him from us." Even as Moses they were skilled in all the learning of their associates, and had almost, as a matter of course, inherited with their mantle, the received and natural methods of discussion handed down from Aristotle. Their writings confirm this reasonable conjecture.

Not only do numerous instances of abstract argument occur (as this chapter will exemplify), but its nature is described and reasons are given for its introduction.

The motives that restrained our authors from a more frequent use of it, were such as control us now; it is somewhat indirect and indefinite, and not always conclusive even to the mind of believers. Wherefore we find Justin, "begging pardon of the sons of truth for urging an extra-scriptural argument;" Clemens Alexandrinus affirming that "he who asks a proof of a Providence deserves condemnation;" and Origen, "doubting whether if left to himself he would interrupt in any way that silence which Jesus maintained at his trial."

Yet as we cannot refuse it altogether in our day, so did not the Apologists in theirs. For its nature is just such that while its presence may not prove much, its absence might prejudice much. It seems that in every imaginable cause that can give rise to a question at all, the first point for consideration is, whether it lies within a certain range of reason, within limits at least not at war with reason, however far they may lie beyond its jurisdiction. Unless this be the case, the whole subject is thrown up as essentially absurd, and not worth another thought. This preliminary examination, I need hardly say, is not always expressed; it may be understood. Indeed it can only be because the idea is so often mental, and almost instinctive to us in the common affairs of life, that it is overlooked, and when applied to religion, even unwelcome. But in important matters there should be no room for misunderstanding. Every witness must be summoned, every plea put in, and the *whole* truth, as well as nothing but the truth, be told.

Further, with regard to the nature of this method of reasoning, it is not only introductory, but incidental. It appeals to any testimony that may be supposed independent of the immediate question, or not constructed with the direct view of favoring it. Its value therefore depends upon a contingency, upon the coincidence without design which it exhibits. Other evidences from argument and testimony we know were *intended* to convince; this had no such original purpose; and thus, slight as it is in itself and worthless alone, it acquires some weight from the circumstance of its being a disinterested witness. In this way we find that not only is a subject introduced, but an air of plausibility and therefore of importance is given to it.

In the present case a question is raised between man and his Maker. God has issued a revelation: man will not receive it. He denies perhaps the possibility of such a thing, to say nothing of doubts quite as signifieant, on the Providence and Being of God himself. The Christian Apologist might well despair. "The law and the testimony," which are to him and to his people an end of all controversy, will not be listened to. A series of satisfactory evidences cannot be entertained for want of a place of *entrance.* It is equally plain that some ground of discussion common to the sceptic and ourselves must be looked for (if the discussion is to be carried on at all) *outside* of the ecclesiastical pale. In this way alone, humanly speaking, can the unbelieving mind be apprehended: and hence it is that the Word of God so often directs and sanctions our appeal to Nature and conscience, God's first witnesses to man, (testimonies that cannot be impugned by an opponent, since he himself forms a part of them,) to the end that we may indicate, if no more, how a God, a Providence, a Revelation, are at least not abstractly improbable. "It hath always been allowed," says Butler, "to argue from what is acknowledged to what is disputed."

Thus we see that the mode of reasoning before us includes appeals to whatever is palpable in this life of ours, considered apart from religion.

And this leads us on to observe its proper province and application, a point by no means to be neglected. For whilst it is introductory and so useful, and incidental and therefore effective, it is also peculiar and limited to certain subjects. These have ever been such matters as other arguments can hardly lay hold of,—the infinite, the future, the physical; things simply assumed or asserted in Scripture. And it is quite interesting, as it is obvious to mark, how closely the Apologists adhered to this rule of propriety; and as they spared no labor, so on the other hand they wasted none, but were careful to confine each argument, and this among the rest, to its own class of subjects.

The above reflections explain why it is we find no modern treatise (of any pretensions) in defence of religion, without some notice of this species of evidence, either by way of introduction or appendage: and I think, therefore, that both the works of the Fathers and this illustration of them, would have wanted completeness without some notice of it also.

The Apologists dwell especially upon four points which we proceed to consider in order, under the heads of Analogies from Nature; Instinctive Suggestions of the Soul; The Example of Heathen Ideas; and Answers to Objections.

SECTION I.

ANALOGIES FROM NATURE.

Before producing the proofs under this section, it is needful to premise two cautions with respect to Analogy. First, to distinguish Analogy *illustrative* from Analogy *probative*. The variety of senses in which the term before us is used, (Mill says "no word in the language more loosely,")* and the

* *Syst. of Log.* Vol. II.

difference of opinion as to some of the identical examples I have to produce,* seem to require an explanation of the grounds on which their authority may be supposed to rest.

Speaking logically, "Analogy is the similarity of ratios or relations."† There must be two ratios, and consequently four terms or objects of comparison. When these terms are all *different*, the analogy is only illustrative; indeed, strictly speaking, it is then a metaphor,‡ *proving* nothing. If used in argument at all, it for the most part *assumes* the proposition which it is brought to bear upon. Its use is therefore merely to aid the apprehension; it cannot prove, though it often suggests, the proof.

But there is another species of analogy. It is *not* necessary that each of the four terms should be different. If there was such a necessity, one of the chief uses of analogy as an engine of argument and discovery of truth, (as remarked by Quintilian long ago,) would be destroyed. All that is required is that there should be two distinct ratios: of what terms those ratios consist is a matter of choice. Frequently the relation in which one thing stands to another being known enables us to discover, with greater or less certainty, the relation which the *same* thing bears to something else which is unknown. Thus the moral government of mankind by the

* The bishop of Lincoln, for instance, asserts in his *Ecclesiastical History* of the second and third centuries: "Tertullian does not seem aware that some of the instances he had alleged for rendering the resurrection of the body credible are nothing to the purpose; such as the changes of day and night, of summer and winter, &c.:" whilst we have Pearson, on the contrary, borrowing these same instances among others, and from the same source, under "a consideration of the things without us, and the natural course of variation in the creature which render the resurrection yet more highly probable."

† Whately and Ferguson, after Aristotle. So *Penny Cyclopædia*, Article "Analogy."

‡ "Metaphors are cases of analogy."—Mill.

Deity in this world, furnishes, as Butler has most ably shown,* a means of conjecturing his religious government, both in this world and in the next, independently of a Divine Revelation. St. Paul even calls a man "a fool" (ἄφρων)† for not perceiving the forcible witness which the processes of nature bear to the possibility and probability of a resurrection.

It is on the strength of this *probative* value of Analogy that the Apologists adduced it. They seem fully to recognize the distinction I have been pointing out. Illustrations constantly occur in their works: as when they endeavor, for the sake of a sceptical or carnal auditory, to clear up some of the mystery that enshrouds the generation of the Son of God, by allusions to the torch that borrows without reducing light; or to the solar rays descending on the earth; or to the indwelling mind, and faculty of speech in man. But such ideas were introduced as mere metaphors, or similitudes: they are not intended to establish, but solely to illustrate the truth. This the frequent and free acknowledgment of their weakness and shortcoming sufficiently shows; while it is equally obvious that sound analogical argument was always considered of weight and value towards conviction.

The other caution to be observed with regard to Analogy is, that it should not be pressed beyond its point. "Perversions of this kind," says Archbishop Whately, "are by no means rare."‡ The similitude is extended beyond its proper limits; and it is supposed that because the two objects are like each other in one respect, they are like in all. As the former mistake may be said to underrate the argumentative value of Analogy, so this consists in overrating it, or expecting from it all the results of a case of *induction or deduction.*

* Butler's *Analogy*. † 1 Corinth. xv. 36.

‡ Also see remainder of the bishop of Lincoln's criticism, quoted above, "If any inference is to be drawn from such physical changes, it would rather be of an alternate dissolution and restoration of the same bodies."

Compared with these it is confessed that our analogies only offer a probability, a fair inference.

From the whole of the above remarks it will be gathered that Analogy is chiefly useful in the absence of other proof, or previous to it; and that it is at all times sufficient to answer objections.*

The cases referred to by the Apologists relate, for the most part, to the unity and power of God, — to the possibility of miracles taking place, — to difficulties in the word of God, — and to the resurrection of the body.

CLEMENS ROMANUS † calls the attention of his brethren to "the resurrection ‡ which is continually taking place: day and night declare it to us. The night lies down, the day arises; again, the day departs, and the night comes on. Behold the fruits of the earth also; the sower casts forth the seed which falls upon the ground dry and naked and is in time dissolved; and from this dissolution the mighty power of the Lord raises it, so that out of one seed many arise and bring forth abundantly."

JUSTIN MARTYR § defends the same doctrine by showing, that it is no more incredible than the first conception and birth of a person would appear to one who had never heard of such a thing. "We pretend not to say," he concludes, "how worthy an estimate of divine power they form who maintain that everything returns to its original state, and that beyond this even God can do nothing: but we plainly see that by the same reasoning they would not have conceived it

* Mill's *System of Logic.*

† I beg to observe that I shall quote the Fathers in the chronological order of the Introduction. Likewise, that I generally use the divisions into chapters, or sections of Caillau's ed. *Coll. select. SS. Eccles. Patr.* Parisiis, 1829.

‡ *Ep. ad Cor.* c. 24.

§ *Apol.* I. c. 25.

possible for beings like themselves, or for the whole world to haveexisted or had their origin."

Again,* he alludes to the generation of mankind, particularly to "the protoplast Adam who was made out of the earth, as a plain instance of God's omnipotence."

ATHENAGORAS† holds that those who doubt the resurrection ought not to do so unless they can show that God is either unable or unwilling to raise up the dead, dissolved body, reanimate the dispersed particles, and restore to life the same men. The want of power,‡ he then contends, cannot be supposed of God, since the generation of men is a matter quite as wonderful as that of resuscitating their dead bodies. In fact the power of primarily producing something out of nothing, evinces God's sufficiency for the renewal and resurrection of all bodies. Again, it requires as great power to order and diversify with various forms rude and shapeless matter, or to unite different elements into one composition, the human frame, as to reunite the scattered parts of it, through whatever process they may have passed.

He further adduces § some of the affections of sleep, as being very analogous to a corporeal resurrection. "Sleep," he says, "has been called the brother of death, inasmuch as many of the same things are common to the dead and to the sleeping. Each is a state of insensibility. If then we call human life a continuous life, though it is full of breaks and pauses, occasioned by sleep, neither should we scruple to admit a life after a dissolution, though it may seem interrupted by the separation of soul and body. Nothing in a seed appears to the eye of its future beauty or magnificence, nor do those qualities exhibit themselves in an infant which future years develop. Thus reason, by just deductions and

* *De Res.* c. 1.
† *De Resurr. Mort.* c. 2.
‡ *Ib.* c. 3.
§ *Ib.* c. 4.

illustrated by *similar* experiments, establishes the truth of the Resurrection."

THEOPHILUS * asks his heathen friend, "Why do you not believe in the raising the dead? Are we not obliged to exercise faith in all the concerns of life? The husbandman trusts to the ground; the sailor to his bark; the sick man to his medicine; the scholar to his tutor; why then should we hesitate to trust God from whom we have received so many and such excellent pledges? He it was who created you and breathed into you the breath of life. Yet, strange to say, you will not believe that he can recall you to life, though you readily believe that manufactured images are gods, and that they work wonders."

He recognizes † other pledges of the Resurrection in the decline and return of the seasons, in the alternations of day and night, in the growth of seeds and fruits, noticing by the way, as an element of the analogy, that these changes all subserve the benefit of man. He then adds, "Let us, moreover, raise our eyes above terrestrial things and look at the continual renewal of the moon, as it waxes and wanes. Consider likewise the resurrection of yourself, perchance, sometime from a bed of sickness, brought about in a way you understand not. Your flesh, and strength, and beauty were lost for a time; but through the mercy and healing power of God, you have recovered them again. As you were ignorant how your body decayed, so you are ignorant how it was restored. Or if you say it was owing to medicine and food, be it so; that also was the work of God who so arranged it."‡

* *Ad Autol.* Lib. I. c. 8. † Ib. c. 13.

‡ The *Stromata* of Clemens Alex. contain many appeals to analogy. One, curious rather than satisfactory, having reference to our own country, occurs in the Sixth Book, Art. I.

MINUTIUS FELIX * demands, "Who can impugn this truth; that man who was at first made by God, can be made by Him again?"

TERTULLIAN † in like manner wonders "why after the mystery of our birth, we might not once more be brought into existence by the will of the great Creator, who made us at first out of nothing. It would be no *new* thing, at least; and as we cannot explain how we were at first made, we cannot expect to understand how we shall again be made. Whence we see that the Resurrection can be readily conceived of. But if any man still doubts respecting the power of God, let him look around and behold! Nature stamped with examples of the resurrection, is a testimony to us. The light dies daily and shines again; the stars fade away and reappear; the fruits of the earth are consumed and reproduced; seeds rise not again with increase unless they are corrupted and die; all things are preserved by dissolution, renewed by perishing. And shall man, the lord of all this universe of creatures which die and rise again, himself die only to perish for ever?"

A like train of thought is observed in this author's more direct work on the Resurrection.‡

ORIGEN,§ calling attention to the writings of the prophets, thus prepares his hearers' minds for any mysteries they may meet with. "If some passages should appear to the unlearned to be above the reach of the human understanding, let it not be a matter of surprise; for in the works of Providence which fill the whole world, there are some things so abstruse and occult that they might seem to afford a handle for doubting whether God really superintends the affairs of men."

* *Octav.* c. 33.

† *Apol.* c. 43.

‡ *De Res. Carn.* c. 12.

§ *De Princip.* Lib. IV. sect. 6.

Wherefore he argues, the divinity of the Scriptures should not be doubted merely because of the difficulties contained in them.

CYPRIAN,* following the footsteps of Minutius Felix (c. 18), points out some analogies in nature implying the unity of God. He remarks that every association must have a superior head, and then proceeds to illustrate this principle by the histories of kingdoms and communities of men. It is even found to be in accordance with the nature of animals. As human societies have their king, so bees and sheep and oxen have their common leader. "How reasonable then for us to suppose that the universe should have *one* Governor, who, by his Almighty Word of wisdom and power, orders, disposes, and executes whatever he wills."

ARNOBIUS,† in reply to a reproach cast upon the Christian system, in consequence of its not explaining the existence of evil in the world, tells the heathen that their complaints would avail more if they themselves had first cleared up some difficulties nearer home; as, for example, whence and what we are, whether the world was made and arranged for us, &c. This subject is reverted to in the second book of the Disputations (c. 24, 25); where, after showing how completely the human mind is baffled in its attempt to explore the depths of nature and the ways of God, our author urges upon his readers the necessity of humility and submission in all matters connected with religion.

Again, to expose the vaunted wisdom of the Greeks, he asks "if there is any one among them who can explain what Socrates was unable to apprehend in his Phædo, namely, the origin and quality of mind; that mind which is called immortal, and by some esteemed a God. Why should it be

* *De Idol. Van.* c. 5. † *Adv. Gent.* Lib. I. c. 4.

dull in sickness, weak in infancy, wild in delirium, wanting in old age?" "And," continues he,* addressing the heathen, "since you are accustomed to sneer at *our* exercise of faith, I beg to know if there is any affair or business of life that does not demand faith? You trade, you marry, you sow, you physic, you fight, in faith; and is not the very identical use of the faculty you ridicule us for exercised by you, whenever you pray to your gods, and as often as you rely upon your philosophers and their writings?"

With equal address he blunts the point of an objection against the lateness of the incarnation, intimating † that nothing is early or late with God; that Mercury, their own heavenly messenger, had not appeared until a certain time; and that the seasons of the year did not return always to a month.

METHODIUS ‡ alludes to the power and wisdom of God displayed in his care of the embryo in the womb, a clearing the way for crediting the divine ability and even desire to introduce our bodies into another state of being.

LACTANTIUS § points out the vanity of that philosophy which supposes God cannot be angry, and therefore will neither judge nor punish the wicked; whilst not only demons but also the very heavens and the earth are trembling at his nod, as the Milesian oracle confesses.

In defence of the unity of God, he remarks ‖ that though there is much diversity of opinion on this important point, it ought not so to be; since reason herself teaches us the truth. "There is one mind," he contends, "governing our body and its many members, one commander in every army, one

* *Adv. Gent.* Lib. I. c. 5.
† *Ib.* c. 32.
‡ *De Resur.*
§ *De Ira Dei*, c. 23.
‖ *Epitom.* c. 2.

sovereign in every empire, one moderator in every republic; and so in the management of this world there can be but one Lord, who is the founder of his own kingdom and claims the whole, and nothing less than the whole, for himself."

EUSEBIUS,* after surveying the wonders of creation, and drawing therefrom an illustration of skilful design and infinite power, hints at an analogy between them and the miracles of Christ: "Who," he asks, "can be the efficient cause of all this, but He, the justly entitled Word of God, that worker of miracles?"

The unity † of the Creator is seen ‡ reflected in "the one sun that warms and enlightens us all, and in the uniformity or harmony to be traced amidst the variety of character in man, and of form and appearance in nature. One and the same effectuating art is found everywhere employed upon the one universe of manifold composition, the workmanship of the one Word, the Maker of the world."

Speaking of the Resurrection,§ this author observes, "If grains of wheat are not wholly subject to corruption, shall man be? Is he not superior to seeds?"

And again, ‖ he argues that as God is beneficent and just, he will care for our bodies and souls as well as for the life of trees, and so on.

EPHRAIM ¶ defends the divinity of the Saviour, and insists that as we cannot comprehend the nature of our own souls, it is in vain for us to expect to understand the generation, human or divine, of the Son of God.

* *Theoph.* Lib. I. c. 6–21.

† See also Dem. *Evan.* Lib. IV. c. 5, on this argument.

‡ *Theoph.* Lib. I. c. 33, 34.

§ *Ib.* Lib. I. c. 77.

‖ *De Resur.*

¶ *Serm. adv. Scrutat.* 1–7.

He then produces* the unaccountable phenomena connected with memory and dreams as mysteries equally difficult of explanation with any in the Christian system. Indeed† he considers it harder to understand nature than Scripture; and to analyze man's word or faculty of speech, than God's Word, the Saviour himself.

AUGUSTINE,‡ having spoken of the Mosaic miracles, warns us against those persons who deny that the invisible God works visible miracles. He asks, "Is not the world a miracle, yet visible and of his making?—nay, all the miracles done in this world are less than the world itself, the heavens, the earth, and all therein; yet God made them all, and after a manner we cannot conceive. Man himself is a still greater miracle; therefore God who made the heavens and the earth scorns not still to work miracles in heaven and earth, to draw men's souls by such means to the worship of his invisible essence."

In refutation of an objection raised against the Resurrection of the body and the torments of hell, he declares § the omnipotence of God to be a sufficient ground for believing in anything he has promised; wherefore he cannot see why God may not cause the bodies of the dead to rise again, ‖ and the damned to suffer and yet not consume, seeing he has filled heaven, earth, air, and water, with innumerable marvels; the world itself being a greater marvel than any it contains.

* *Serm.* 57.
† *Serm.* 65.
‡ *De Civit. Dei*, Lib. x. c. 12.
§ *Ib.* Lib. xxi. c. 7.
‖ See *De Catechizandis Rudibus* to the same purpose.

SECTION II.

INSTINCTIVE SUGGESTIONS OF THE SOUL.

THE next witness independent of Revelation, and invoked by the Apologists, is the soul of man himself. We are supposed possessed of certain intellectual and moral instincts, such as notions of sequence; a consciousness of Deity as well as of a principle of evil; a sense of justice, accountability, &c. It is now generally conceded that the theory of original impressions, as held by the ancients, is not far from the truth. Reason and experience tell us that there are in the nature of man *faculties* whose existence cannot be accounted for by any known action of matter. With as little satisfaction can they be derived from education or tradition; for, as Tertullian observes on this very question, "such explanations still leave the matter short, and it may be asked, Whence were they derived by the man who first used them? The idea must have been conceived in the soul, before it was delivered to others by the tongue or the pen." The truth seems to be, as a modern writer remarks,* that our understanding assents to any proposition only as it agrees with the suggestions of reason,—those laws originally written on our hearts. "We do not say that the mind can know (in the common acceptation of the word) before it observes external things, but that its capacity and tendency furnish evidence of something having been in the mind before it was directed to facts, just as we have had eyes before we used them properly. Thus the mind does not simply reflect the images of things without, but impresses a character of its own upon them." On some such predication the force of our present argument depends. The soul is viewed as a part of nature, God's work, stamped with his own image of what is true; and which if it

* *Small Books on Great Subjects.* Pickering, London.

could be found disengaged (though only to a degree) of its unhappily-acquired prejudice for error, might remember and reveal something of the will of its Maker. With this hope it is seized upon as at unawares, — in the crowd, — on the first waking moment, — under the chastening hand of affliction, — or in a primeval condition to be conceived of rather than found, and is there and then solemnly cited as a witness. The specimens of this kind of reasoning to be met with in the Apologists, form themselves into three distinct subdivisions.

(1.) *Arguments from Cause to Effect.**

JUSTIN MARTYR.† "If any one thinks that God cares not for the human race, such a man must either profess that God exists not at all; or affirm that if he exists, he delights in evil; or else that he remains insensible as a stone; and that vice and virtue are indifferent things in the judgment of men; all which suppositions are full of impiety and injustice."

He further‡ pleads against the stoical doctrine of fatality, that there would be on such a principle nothing laudable in doing right. To be virtuous we must be free agents.

TATIAN.§ "It is from a contemplation of the incomprehensible, self-producing God, that we believe in the resurrection of the body, whereby all things shall be perfect and complete. Not as the Stoics suppose, according to certain cycles or orbits, within which we are ever being born and then perishing again, and all to no purpose; but once only

* For the sense in which the *à priori* and *a posteriori* arguments are here used, I refer to Whately's *Rhetoric*, Part I. c. ii. § 2.

† *Apol.* I. c. 36.

‡ *Ib.* II. c. 9.

§ *Orat. ad Græc.* c. 6.

for the last judgment; when neither by Minos nor Rhadamanthus shall we be judged, but by the Creator himself. I knew not myself before I was born; I know not what will become of my body when I die; fire, the waves, wild beasts may devour it, but I shall still rest in the treasury of a rich Lord, where the worthy and the worthless, yea, even the atheist, lie concealed. God, who alone observes my dust, alone can recall it when he will into its pristine state."

ATHENAGORAS,* addressing the heathen emperors, argues thus: "That there is one God and Maker of all things, you may conceive in this way, and thereby have one good reason of our faith. If there were at first two or more Gods, they must have existed either together in one and the same place, or each separately by himself. They could not exist in the same place, being of the same nature both equal and commensurate to each other; for, if they could, then must two commensurates of the same kind exist in one and the same place, which cannot be. And, on the other hand, if these Gods existed separately, since one God is over all his works, and governs all by his providence, (as nature indicates,) where can the other be? Not in the world, for it is the place of another; nor above it, for our God is also above the world, and comprehends within himself all his works." Wherefore our Christian philosopher concludes that "another God has no place, that is, does not exist at all."

Replying to a technical difficulty in the way of the resurrection of the body,† raised on the supposition of shipwrecked mariners becoming a prey to fish, or of slaves in the amphitheatre being devoured by wild animals, or even of men having been incorporated with the flesh of their fellow-men, (as at the tragic supper of Thyestes,) Athenagoras observes, that the propounders of such objections forget the wisdom and the

* *Legat. pro Christianis*, c. 8. † *De Res. Mort.* c. 4, 5.

resources of God, who could never be perplexed in distinguishing and separating any parts of different natures. This leads to the question how far the matter of different bodies can and does coalesce and yet retain its own qualities. It is not found to follow, as a matter of course, that all food taken into the stomach nourishes or becomes a portion of the organization; and, even if it were so, it is contended that such a circumstance need not affect in any essential way the subject of the resurrection. Food * does not change, but only dilates and augments the limbs; the identity of person remains the same; nay, further, its effects are but temporary, or if they continue through life, being of no further use to bodies raised in glory and incorruption, they will doubtless be dispensed with and dropped hereafter. "Our adversaries," he affirms, "cannot prove that one human body becomes an integral part of another." He then proceeds with his argument to demonstrate that as the resurrection of the body is a work possible to God, so it is equally an object of his will. "For† if God is unwilling, it must be because the thing is unjust or unbecoming his majesty. But it is evident that nothing can suffer injury by the revival of dead bodies; neither inanimate things nor brutes, nor our bodies themselves: and it cannot be unbecoming God's majesty to restore to life and symmetry what he once made, much less to crown it with immortality."

Having thus shown that God can both will and do, he passes on to confirm the truth of the resurrection positively, by the following reasons. First, from the end and design of the creation of the first man and all his descendants. He argues that God must have had an end in view when he created us; and that end was *perpetual* life (the basis of all blessings), and the contemplation of his wisdom and power. Secondly, from the nature of man, as an accountable and religious creature. He shows that God gave this life not to

* *De Res. Mort.* c. 9. † *Ib.* c. 10.

the soul or body separately, but to both together. Their intimate connection in this world; and the ways they affect one another, the body humbling the soul, and the soul restraining the body, illustrate this. Whatever therefore is morally true of the one is true of the other also. The soul is accountable, so is the body. Thirdly, from the justice of God, which must be manifested in the distribution of rewards and punishments. Having proved man to be a responsible creature, he now contends that as God is just, the righteous sentence will be laid on the true actor, which is the united soul and body. "For the soul alone cannot be punished for the sins committed in conjunction with the body, just as the body alone would not be a subject fit for law and justice. A due recompense of good or evil is clearly not received in this life, where the wicked often flourish, while saints suffer. Without a resurrection and a judgment, the practice of virtue (so universally recognized) must be stupidity; and it would especially be impossible to punish *accumulated* guilt, as where a robber or a tyrant commits a succession of murders; a single life being no equivalent penalty for so many crimes." From such considerations it is argued that justice cannot exert itself with full force in this life, and therefore demands a future judgment, to which end a resurrection of the body will be necessary. "In no other way can a just examination of the actions of men take place, and it were impious to suppose that God will not judge justly. Vices and virtues are properties of men as mental *and* corporeal, and cannot be conceived inherent in the soul separately, since God's law could not be obeyed by the soul without the body at all." An *identity* of body will also be required. "But a soul cannot have the same body except it be raised; and when this comes to pass, man will have the end suitable to which his nature was originally framed. For we may presume that the chief end of a virtuous life and a rational nature is to be through all eternity employed about spiritual objects, and in the contemplation of God."

THEOPHILUS* follows the steps of Athenagoras in arguing that moral accountability implies a judgment, and a judgment a resurrection of the flesh, "without which the soul cannot be justly tried." He supposes that the soul could only suffer eternal punishments by the intervention of corpuscular matter.

MINUTIUS FELIX† inquires, with respect to the great coflagration of the world, "what man of any sense can doubt that all things which had a beginning may have an end; that the heavens with all their garniture, as they began, so they may cease to be; for certainly there is nothing so wonderful in this, that He who made, should be able to destroy what he has made?"

ORIGEN.‡ "What can be more reasonable than the plan our Saviour took to teach men who as a mass, partly through the pressure of earthly cares and occupations, and partly through a natural inclination to a vicious life, cannot apply themselves to the study of philosophy? The love of God therefore in sending his Son into the world, plainly appears in accommodating things to the circumstances of human life, that so the Gospel might be of more general advantage; and this is none of the least powerful arguments to prove that our blessed Redeemer had a divine commission. We hesitate not to say,§ that it is *likely* God would send messengers to correct us. Of this kind were Moses and the Prophets; but in doing good to men, Jesus far excelled all who have ever visited this earth."

He contends,‖ that the end of the world and the final judgment are both of them doctrines in harmony with the conclusions of reason.

* *Ad Aut.* † *Octav.* c. 33. ‡ *Cont. Cels.* Lib. I. s. 1.
§ *Ib.* Lib. IV. s. 4. ‖ *Ib.* s. 9.

Speaking* of the authority of the sacred writers, he finds it is "founded on reason, inasmuch as their doctrines are beneficial to mankind; for surely no one will dare deny that the spring of all utility is to believe in the great God and to regard his pleasure in all things, who is to be our judge both of thought and deed! What can be more rational or salutary? And what persuasive so efficacious to this end as the assurance of God's constant inspection?"

With regard to the Resurrection, it is remarked† that "the qualities of bodies may be changed, so that what is sown in corruption may be raised in incorruption. Only admit a Providence over matter, and a power in its Maker to endow it with any quality, and it follows that God can renew our bodies in a more excellent fashion if he will."

Also, "The doctrine of a future punishment" is considered‡ "as useful as it is true; it has ever been handed down, though obscurely, with the greatest profit to men."

CYPRIAN§ holds that Christians are not dependent upon temples, like the heathen, because "any such place is too narrow to contain God."

ARNOBIUS,‖ in several consecutive chapters, argues that the soul is not essentially divine; nor, on the other hand, brutish; but of a middle quality, as Plato likewise conceived. The use he makes of this argument, or rather elaborate discourse, is to point out the necessity of some revelation for the soul's guidance to immortality; and thus by implication, the value of the Christian system, which is just such a Revelation.

He adds,¶ "Christ taught that the souls of men are not of the essence of God, which is clear, or they would not be suffering and sinning here."

* *Cont. Cels.* Lib. I. s. 53. † *Ib.* s. 57. ‡ *Ib.* Lib. III. s 79.
§ *De Idol. Van.* c. 5. ‖ *Adv. Gent.* Lib. II. c. 11, *et seqq.*
¶ *Ib.* c. 18.

He defends* the lateness of the Incarnation, on the supposition that it took place only when the depravity of men and their inability to help themselves were fully established.

ARCHELAUS,† in his dispute with Manes, shows how human responsibility is agreeable to reason, and implies a future judgment.

LACTANTIUS‡ remarks, that "God's mercy, which even the Pagans claim, argues his wrath; for to allow that God can pardon, is to prove that he can punish."

EUSEBIUS§ conceives that "it is quite proper for us to desire some assistance from the heavenly abodes, some messenger to teach us the way of salvation; for by the soundest argument it can be shown that nothing is so fit, as for a physician to heal the sick, for a master to condescend to his pupils, for him who is above to be sent below; but not the reverse, there being then no longer the same plea of necessity and use. No reason, therefore, appears why the divine nature, which is so beneficent and providential, should not hold converse with us. Under the condition of natural providence it benefits our bodies day by day; much more then might it be expected in connection with a Revelation, for the sake of our immortal souls."

It was impossible, on account of our frailty, for us to approach God; kindly therefore did he send a Mediator to unite us to him.‖

After describing¶ the degradation of morals into which the heathen had sunk, he shows from a consideration of God's compassion, that it is *likely* he would manifest himself in some remedial way to mankind; and then that the Incarnation

* *Adv. Gent.* Lib. II. c. 32. † *Act. Disp.* ‡ *De Ira Dei*, c. 20.
§ *Adv. Hierocl.* c. 6. ‖ *Theoph.* Lib. I. c. 5. ¶ *Ib.* Lib. II. c. 35

was an apposite means of communication, as also a wise provision for satiating man's thirst after something visible.

AUGUSTINE* conceives that the mystery of redemption is not essentially obscure, but has been revealed in a reasonable, gradual way to the world as it could bear it.

(2.) *Arguments from Effect to Cause.*

ATHENAGORAS.† "How can we do otherwise than believe in a God, when we see such convincing proofs of a divine nature in that standing miracle — the world; in its order and proportion, in its beauty and grandeur, in the figure and disposition of all its parts? Could we be blind to the light, and deaf to the voice of Nature, we should be deservedly accursed and persecuted."

"The disposition‡ and order of the material world speak the praise of the Almighty architect, God, and not the praise of mere matter. As clay is to the potter, so is all matter subject to His will and operation. It must be confessed that the world is beautiful, and for its size and spherical figure, and the arrangement of all its parts, most excellent and wonderful. The ranging of the stars in the Zodiac, and the adjustment of the North Pole, are of great service to mankind. But these are no reasons why we should worship this great and glorious system, or any part of it; though they are reasons why we should worship their Creator. When any persons petition your majesties, (he writes to the emperors) they turn not aside from *you* to your palace, from your persons to your buildings. So likewise they who dispose of the awards at the public games are not accustomed to crown the

* *De Civit. Dei,* Lib. VIII. c. 32. † *Legat. pro Christianis,* c. 4.
‡ *Ib.* c. 16.

harp and neglect the musician who played upon it. How then can we be expected to adore as Gods, corruptible images made by men like ourselves?"

THEOPHILUS.* "As the soul of man cannot be seen, but only its effects, so God is only known by his works and providence. An earthly king is believed to exist by all his subjects, though rarely seen by any: he is recognized by his power, his laws, his images. And wherefore will you not know God by his works and the effects of his power?"

MINUTIUS FELIX† shows how we differ from the beasts that perish mainly "in having language and reason to conduct us to the knowledge of God. For what is so clear, whether we look above or around us, as that the divine power inspires, supports, and governs all nature?" He refers to "the constant vicissitudes of day and night, as well adapted for the business and needful repose of man; to the stars which direct the pilot and the husbandman; to that care which interposes and moderates the extremes of heat and cold, keeps the ocean within bounds, and so charmingly diversifies the surface of the earth with hill and dale, mountains and plains; which has provided every animal with some means of defence; and, above all, formed man the crowning piece of the whole."

"Were we to go into a house," he continues,‡ "the rooms of which were exquisitely proportioned and furnished, we should not doubt that such a house was under the eye of a master, and that he himself was preferable to all the contents. And thus in this palace of a world, when we cast our eyes upon the heavens and the earth, and behold the admirable order and economy of things, we have as little reason to question whether there is a Lord of the Universe, or to doubt that he himself is more glorious than the stars, and more to be admired than any of the works of his own hands."

* *Ad Aut.* Lib. I. c. 5. † *Octav.* c. 17. ‡ *Ib.* c. 18.

ORIGEN.* "If a man with any sort of religion will acknowledge that the physician who recovers the sick is sent from God, though he cures only bodily infirmities, how much more must we acknowledge our Saviour to have been indeed sent from the Father, seeing that he has recovered so many thousands from spiritual and more fatal distempers, and has improved the faculties of their minds and prevailed upon them to trust to the will and care of God."

Celsus† having reproached the Jews with being simple shepherds, deceived into the doctrine of one God by the arts of Moses, Origen takes the opportunity of asking ironically, concerning the obscure origin of Polytheism. He begs to be informed in what the essence of Mnemosyne, the mother of the Muses, consisted; and of Themis who brought forth the hours; also the substance of the naked Graces, and of that diversity of gods worshipped by the Egyptians. The bare mention of these things sufficing to expose them, he then demands "how such empty fictions can deserve to be compared with that one argument, drawn from the entire harmony of the parts of the spacious universe, in proof of the perfect unity of God. For it is impossible in the nature of things that a piece of such divine architecture, all the parts of which are in such admirable agreement, and in such manifest and constant subserviency to the advantage of the whole, should be made by many hands."‡

ARCHELAUS § argues against ascribing the body of man to the creation of the evil spirit, on the ground that the natural harmony, evident between soul and body, proves them to have had a common author.

* *Cont. Cels.* Lib. I. s. 9. † *Ib.* s. 23.

‡ Palmer, *On Development and Conscience*, p. 13, says, "The Fathers employed the argument from the order and harmony of the material universe, not only to establish the existence of a God against Atheists, but also in proof of the unity of God against the Gentiles."

§ *Act. Disp.*

ARNOBIUS.* "Scarce any one ever denied the existence of God; and if he did, the mute animals, had they the use of speech, the fields, the trees, the stones, would cry out that there is a God—their Creator."

LACTANTIUS† says, "The Creator has given man sense and reason so that he should know him; for the possession of this intelligence (which animals want) is alone a witness, within ourselves, of his existence. Wherefore I wonder at the folly of the Epicureans, who can see no proof of a Providence constructing and ruling the world, but attribute all things to a fortuitous concourse of atoms; even ascribing vice to matter."

Arguing again‡ upon Epicurus' denial of a Providence, he remarks that "the voices of all the Philosophers (with this one exception) agree in declaring the world could not have been made without an artificer, nor preserved without a ruler. And this testimony is confirmed by our own senses. The disposition of the heavens and the earth so wonderfully arranged, so beautifully adorned, and all for the use of man and other living creatures, cannot but prove a present God."

He proposes,§ for the sake of infidels, to consider the Incarnation in the light of probable reason. His first premise is that whoever professes to teach, ought to do himself what he commands; his second, that no one but Christ ever delivered wisdom by word, and also established it by example; he concludes therefore that Christ is the prince of teachers. And again, he lays down the maxims, that a heavenly messenger would necessarily be perfect, and yet have to assume a mortal body; "for a teacher of virtue must partake of the same nature with his disciples, that by conquering in his own

* *Adv. Gent.* Lib. I. c. 9.

† *De Offic. Dei*, c. 2.

‡ *Epitom.* c. 1.

§ *Div. Instit.* Lib. IV. c. 22, *et seqq.*

person, he may show that sin and error can really be overcome." This he applies to the case of the Saviour, and thence infers his divine mission.

EUSEBIUS* argues against the Atheists, that a house cannot be made without contrivance and care, nor a ship without a carpenter, nor a garment without a weaver. "By what estrangement of intellect then," he asks, "is it, that these men do not consider the course of the heavenly bodies, the recurrence of the seasons, the provision of herbs and flowers, and the senses of animal life? How could all this wisdom be the effect of blind chance which acts without object or rule? The Polytheists err on the other extreme, and reduce God down to his works. Surely the worshippers of the elements are no better than those who gave to the palace the praise which is rather due to the architect that built it. They are like children whose admiration is expended upon the lyre and not upon its maker or its master; or like umpires who should neglect the victor in a combat, to adorn his spear and shield. Who ever thought of gracing the body† of a philosopher or his gown with the title of wisdom, much less the common utensils of his house, and not rather the unseen mind within him? Thus let *us* wonder at and admire the invisible God, before all his visible universe."

After repeating‡ much of the above, verbatim, he adds, "how could the elements without intelligence, or their common essence devoid of shape and figure, of life and reason, obtain motion or loveliness? Who is it at the present moment, working ten thousand effects of surpassing wonder, and with an invisible influence, daily and hourly perpetuating the production of them all? No one but the omnipotent Word, the cause of all wonders."

* *Theoph.* Lib. I. c. 1–4.

† Imitated apparently by Theodoret, as also other places of this author. See Græc. *Aff. Cur.* Ed. Gaisf. p. 183; Prof. Lee's note in *Theophania.*

‡ *Orat. Const. Vit.*

ATHANASIUS.* "A workman is known by his works, albeit he is not seen. They relate of Phidias the sculptor, that his statues seemed to declare their author, though he might be absent, by a certain proportion and harmony of their parts. Just so by the construction of this world, the Mighty Maker and Designer is revealed, although he is invisible to mortal eyes." Romans i. 20, and Acts xiv. 14, are quoted in confirmation.

An inference is likewise drawn† from the union of contrarieties into such harmony and order as we perceive in nature, that there must be some superior agency at work. The unity of Deity is also seen reflected in every *part* as well as in the whole of nature. "The universe," says our author,‡ "publishes this truth openly.. For if there had been many Gods, there had been likewise many systems which would not have consisted together. No ship governed by many pilots can be kept long in a straight course. *One* must hold the helm. No harp struck by several hands can send forth perfect harmony. One musician alone is wanted. So when there appears but one order of nature we must suppose there is but one Maker and one Director."

(3.) *Sentiments of Natural Conscience.*

TERTULLIAN § proposes to "leave the collation of historical testimonies (a task of great labor, but one by which the persecutors of Christianity have been condemned out of their own documents) to others. He prefers not to follow in the beaten track, but to exhibit the testimony of the soul itself to the divine and eternal matters of religion. To this end the soul of a heathen man is summoned as a conscientious witness, to say whence and what it is. It is bidden to

* *Cont. Gent.* c. 35.
† *Ib.* c. 36, 38.
‡ *Ib.* c. 39.
§ *De Test. Anim.* c. 1.

speak plainly and faithfully, though its depositions should go against himself, that the man may blush at hating and ridiculing doctrines which his own breast cannot but confirm."

Our author commences* by producing the vulgar exclamations, "Oh God grant!" "If God will;" as natural testimonies to the unity of God. He asks how it is that, instead of naming any one of the numerous deities, the objects of pagan worship, the soul selects the word "God," if it does not thus bear unconscious witness to the truth? In like manner the soul is found evincing its knowledge of the attributes of God, his providence, his power, his goodness, by such expressions as "God is good;" "God does good, but man is evil;" and the valediction, "God bless thee." Tertullian wonders "who taught the souls of the common people these truths also?" Even some knowledge of the author of evil is discovered† under the execrations which men pronounce against demons. "The very name is one of dislike and scorn. Thus we recognize our destroyer as well as our God." The acknowledgment of a future retribution is next traced‡ in the terms of spontaneous language, and in our natural dread of death. "We say," he observes, "of the dead; 'Poor man;' 'he is free from care;' thus declaring at once the blessing of life and the benefit of death: or when stung by the recollection of some insult, we curse the dead, and pray that 'the earth may lie heavy upon him;' or that 'his ashes may be tormented in the shades below;' thus confessing a judgment to come." Again, he asks, "Why fear death, as we all do, if there be nothing to fear hereafter? we should have no care for the future if we had no expectation of it." He likewise detects a hint of immortality in that "innate desire after posthumous fame, than which there is no stronger sentiment in the human breast."

* *De Test. Anim.* c. 2. † *Ib.* c. 3. ‡ *Ib.* c. 4.

These testimonies are confessed* to be simple and trite, but yet "not unworthy of notice, if we consider the majesty of *Nature,* whence the authority of the soul is derived. Whatever we must allow to the mistress, we must assign to the disciple : nature is the mistress ; the soul is her pupil : whatever has been taught by the one has been learned by the other ; and both have received from God, who is the master of the mistress herself. What notion the soul is able to conceive of its first and great teacher we may gather from the soul that is within us. Its forebodings are our prophets, its omens our auguries ; and even though encompassed about by its enemy (a heathen body) it remembers its author, his goodness and his law, its own end, and its infernal adversary. Nor is it strange that, being given by God, it should teach those self-same truths that God has since renewed more clearly to his people." "These exclamations," he adds, "were in use long before books, or even letters, had appeared ; always excepting those of the sacred Scriptures, where indeed the ideas they express are to be found ; but, as these precede secular writings by a long period, we must needs believe that, if the soul has taken its declarations from books, it has taken them from ours and not from those of the heathen ; and then it matters little whether this consciousness of what is right emanates from God or from the writings of God."

In conclusion,† he begs the unbeliever to weigh this matter well, and give credit to his own soul. "Let him observe," he says, "agreement of doctrine even amidst inconsistent conduct ; and that, too, not in Greece or Rome alone, but in every age and country. These are expressions belonging to all languages and nations. 'God is everywhere,' and 'the goodness of God' is everywhere ; 'the demon' is everywhere, and 'the curse upon the demon' is everywhere ;

* *De Test. Anim.* c. 5.

† *Ib.* c. 6.

death is everywhere, and so is the consciousness of death and the witness thereof. Each soul of its own accord proclaims aloud these truths, which Christians are not permitted even to whisper. Thus every soul may be called both a culprit and a witness; a culprit as to error, a witness as to truth. And in the day of judgment it shall stand before the bar of God, having nothing to say to the charge, 'Thou didst preach God and didst not seek him; thou didst detest demons, and yet didst worship them; thou didst appeal to the judgment of God, whilst thou didst not believe in his being; thou didst anticipate punishment in a world below, but didst take no heed against it: thou didst savor of the name of Christ, and yet didst persecute Christians.'"

MINUTIUS FELIX.* "The world is on our side in the acknowledgment of one God. I hear the people when they lift up their hands to heaven say nothing, but, 'The God;' 'The great God;' 'The true God;' 'If it should please God;' these expressions of the vulgar are the voice of nature. Even they who make Jove supreme, mistake indeed in the name, but agree in the thing, the *one* notion of an Almighty God."

ORIGEN.† "It is evident that men in general perceive some difference between good and evil, or they would not punish crimes, as they constantly do. Nor need it surprise us that God should plant in the minds of men those natural principles which the prophets, and especially Jesus, continually urged, so that every one might be without excuse."

Our author attributes‡ the rapid spread of the Gospel, at least in part, to the harmony its doctrines preserve with the sentiments of natural conscience. "Wherefore," he says, "the soul, partaker of reason, reflecting upon nature, which is

* *Octav.* c. 18. † *Cont. Cels.* Lib. I. s. 2. ‡ *Ib.* Lib. III. s. 40.

akin to herself, now begins universally to reject those whom she hitherto accounted gods, and conceives a sort of natural love for the Creator."

CYPRIAN.* "Our common people in many cases acknowledge the unity of God; their souls often spontaneously reminding them of their original. Thus you may hear them speaking in the singular number, 'Oh God;' 'God sees it;' 'I commend you to God;' 'God will make amends,' &c. So that the great fault of the Gentiles consists in this, that they will not confess what they cannot but know."

ARNOBIUS.† "Do not our thoughts seem naturally to rest upon God when we say, 'O God,' or call him to witness, or raise our faces to heaven? Does not a suspicion of the truth sometimes strike you as to the unity of the great God?"

EUSEBIUS,‡ speaking of the excellent nature of man's soul, and having observed how Anaxarchus recognized its immortality when he said to his tormentors, "Bruise my form; me you cannot bruise;" and having accounted for our attachment to this life, by the analogy of a child weeping when it leaves the womb and first comes into the light; he suggests whether it is not "reasonable that such a perfectible mind, being released from a corrupt body, should come forth with the dignity and stature of angels."

He reads§ intimations of the soul's high birth in those capacities for lofty thought; those mortifications of bodily members, and restraints of desires; those attempts at obeying the precepts of wisdom, and hopes of deliverance from all that is vile; those advances in the way to heaven, which make the prospect of death and the anticipation of meeting

* *De Idol. Van.* c. 5.
† *Adv. Gent.* Lib. II. c. 2.
‡ *Theoph.* Lib. I. c. 63.
§ *Ib.* Lib. I. c. 75.

all who have gone before us increasingly delightful. Whence he concludes that from the case of the soul itself, reason with probability indicates that we shall partake of a superior, an angelic immortality.

AUGUSTINE* shows, in contending for the existence of good and bad angels, that even the Pagans believe in the latter, saying, when they would speak evil of any one, "He has a demon."

SECTION III.

THE EXAMPLE OF HEATHEN IDEAS.

In making use of the *argumentum ad hominem* against the Pagan or the Jew, the Fathers not only followed up a natural advantage that presented itself to their hand, but also the pattern of an apostle on more than one occasion. This precedent is alleged by Clemens Alex. (*Strom.* Lib. I. Art. 3). Defending his appeal to heathen philosophers, he quotes St. Paul's reference (in Titus) to Epimenides of Crete, named as one of the seven wise men of Greece. "'This is true,' said the apostle. Thus you see how he allowed something of truth to the prophet† of the Greeks. Nor did he blush, for edification and for discoursing to the conversion of others, to use the Greek poems also. Addressing the Corinthians 'on the Resurrection,' he brings forward a Greek Iambic:

* *De Civit. Dei,* Lib. IX. c. 19.

† That Epimenides was more than a poet, see Clem. Alex. *Strom.* Lib. VI. Art. 1, where he is described as offering or recommending sacrifices for the purpose of preventing a Persian invasion of Greece.

'φθείρουσιν ἤθη χρήσθ' ὁμιλίαι κακαί.' " * Also by Origen, who, in one of his homilies, says: "St. Paul allows the Greeks to have held true opinions; for, in the Acts, it is clear he uses a poetical extract from *Aratus Phænomenes*, by which he approves what the Greeks have spoken rightly."

True it is, such reasoning is adapted for defence rather than conviction, but still it does serve to take off a strangeness sometimes attaching to a new doctrine, and introduce it with less prejudice to its enemies. Having appealed to the testimony of nature and of individual conscience, the only other tribunal, at once manifest to all and apart from Revelation, is the common consent of mankind. This forms the ground of the present section, and differs from the last principally in being collective. It supposes that, in spite of all the apparent discord and instability of human opinions, and in spite of all the errors mixed up with them, there are, (it matters not how they came) and appear always to have been, certain prominent dogmas which resemble those of Christianity sufficiently for the purpose. The adumbration might be faint, but there it was, and none of the Christians' making either. It is argued, therefore, that, if one set of opinions is admitted, the other cannot be refused: they must be accounted orthodox, if not divine. "Give us now," says Justin, "but the same degree of credit you yield to your writers, and we will satisfy you of the Resurrection."

To make out the exact force of this method of reasoning in a country professedly Christian, would not be in place here; but that the ancient opponents of the faith *did* feel the sharpness of this arrow feathered from their own wing, is manifest in the attempts they made to elude it by charging Christianity with plagiarisms from the classics, as we shall find in the next chapter.

* Evil communications corrupt good manners. 1 Cor. 15 : 23. *Am. Ed.* So also Eusebius and Jerome. It is a question whether Menander or Euripides is quoted here.

The examples of heathen ideas brought forward by the Apologists embrace correspondences with certain points of Christian belief; as, the being and attributes of God, — the fall of man, — the flood, — theories of prophecy, mysteries and mediation, — the Sonship of Christ, — his acts, — the common duties of religion, — references to the end of the world, the fact of a future state, &c. I need give but a few out of a multitude of instances under this head.

JUSTIN MARTYR* observes, that Socrates, one of the best heathen philosophers, at the suggestion of right reason, endeavored to bring the truth to light, and to lead men away from the worship of devils.

He quotes† Plato, declaring that Rhadamanthus and Minos will punish the wicked who shall come to them. "The event" he adds, "of which we Christians speak is the same, but we say it will be accomplished by Christ, and that both our bodies and souls *united* will be punished with the eternal torments, and not for a thousand years only." He shows‡ how the heathen credit the resurrection unwittingly, "whenever they deal in necromancy and divination, or applaud such stories as the descent of Ulysses."

"Whilst the Sibyl§ and Hystaspes assert there is to be a destruction of corruptible things by fire, (as the Stoics say to be renewed again) Plato taught,‖ that all things were made by God; many of the poets, that there is also a heaven and a hell: and Menander, that men ought not to worship idols. And when we affirm that Christ is the Son of God, and that he died and rose again; in what respect do we differ from you who believe in the sons of Jove: as for example,¶ Mercury, the messenger from God, Perseus, born of a virgin, and Hercules, who burned himself to death?"

* *Apol.* I. c. 5. † *Ib.* I. c. 8. ‡ *Ib.* c. 4.
§ *Ib.* c. 27. ‖ *Ib.* c. 28. ¶ *Ib.* c. 30.

In his address* to the Roman Senate, the Pagans are reminded that Noah is their Deucalion; and that they themselves ought to be looking beyond this life, since even Xenophon figured vice and virtue, the former full of joy and honor here, the latter clothed in a mean vesture, to be eternally glorious hereafter.†

He illustrates‡ from Homer, the common opinion among the heathen, that all things were possible to the gods.

TATIAN.§ "Admit our doctrines at least as you do the divinations of the Babylonians: listen to us at least as you do to the oracular oaks."

ATHENAGORAS.‖ "Your own poets and philosophers were never charged with Atheism, though they believe in one God. Euripides confesses his doubts as to the gods of the vulgar: yea, he owns that God can only be spiritually conceived of, and any knowledge of him arrived at by the contemplation of his works alone. Sophocles was of the same opinion." Other confessions¶ are cited from Philolaus, Aristotle, and the Stoics; and Plato** and Pythagoras adduced to prove that it is not impossible for these bodies, after a dissolution, to be formed again on the same principles they were at first made.

THEOPHILUS.†† "Many of the poets have foretold, being guided perhaps by some oracle, that those who do wickedly must be punished, thus bearing witness against themselves, and such as are like them." He quotes to this effect Æschylus, Pindar, Euripides, Archilochus, Dionysius, Simonides, and Sophocles.

* *Apol.* II. c. 7. † *Ib.* c. 11. ‡ *De Res.* c. 7.
§ *Orat. ad Græc.* c. 12. ‖ *Legat.* c. 4. ¶ *Ib.* c. 6.
** *Ib.* c. 36. †† *Ad Aut.* Lib. II. c. 37.

CLEMENS ALEXAN.* urges upon the Greeks, that as they have given credit to various fables respecting the power of music, believing that Amphion built the walls of Thebes by the aid of his magical lyre, and that Orpheus tamed wild beasts by the sweetness of his song; thus so long neglecting the fair face of truth, and following after troops of raging Bacchantes with the whole chorus of Gods inhabiting Cithæron and Helicon; so they should now raise their eyes to the sacred mount of God, and the holy choir of prophets, even the heavenly Sion. "*There* is music, not indeed according to the measure of Terpander, but according to the eternal measure of a new harmony, of the new name of God. It is this name alone that has truly tamed those *wild beasts*, men; that has truly of these *stones* raised up children unto Abraham: so that the very dead have revived at the sound of the voice of Him who created them at the first."

TERTULLIAN.† "Your own philosophers coincide with ours in ascribing the creation of the world to the Logos, that is, to the Word or Reason. Zeno called him Fate, God, the mind of the universe: Cleanthes ascribes to him the spirit that pervades all things." Our author further remarks that the heathen ought not to find any difficulty in receiving the Incarnation, since it resembles some of their own fables; nor the Jews either, who are daily looking for a Messiah. "Besides," he adds, "the Jews and the Greeks both have their systems of mediation, the one through Moses, the other through Orpheus, Musæus, Melampus, or Trophonius; while you, Romans, have submitted to the oppressive superstitions of Pompilius Numa. Surely, then, Christ may be permitted to set forth that divinity which properly belongs to him."

He thinks‡ that those who believe in the transmigration of souls into other bodies, cannot consistently deny the possi-

* *Hort. ad Græc.* c. 1. † *Apol.* c. 21. ‡ *Ib.* c. 48.

bility of their being recalled into the same bodies at the Resurrection.

MINUTIUS FELIX.* "The poets plead for one Intelligence, and the philosophers agree with us in the doctrine of one God. So that either the Christians now are philosophers, or the philosophers of old were Christians (thus far)."

"The Stoics,† the Platonists, the Epicureans, have supposed a fiery conflagration of this world. Thus you see your sages philosophize just as we do." Further‡ correspondence is discovered in the testimony concerning "the burning river, the Stygian lake, and the manifold fence of fire about it, prepared for eternal torments; and the heathen are reminded that the most tremendous oath Jove can take, is to swear by the boiling banks and horrid gulf of darkness. So that none but atheists can doubt whether those are to be punished as unjust and impious, who know not God."

ORIGEN§ quotes Heraclytus, saying, "They who pay divine honors to inanimate creatures, do just as if they addressed and invoked the walls; an opinion," he adds, "yet publicly held both by Greeks and barbarians." As to mysteries, he asks,‖ what system of philosophy is without them? and refers¶ those of the Greeks who object to the miraculous conception of Jesus, to their own histories. Out of these he reminds them how Plato was said to have been born of Amphictione by a spectre, and also of the fabulous accounts of Danae, Menalippus, Auge, and Antiope.** He then retorts upon Celsus, and asks how the first man was produced; and against his probable reply, that he was made by the spermatic virtue of the earth, contends that such a birth would be more extraordinary than that of our Saviour.

* *Octav.* c. 19. † *Ib.* c. 33. ‡ *Ib.* c. 34.
§ *Cont. Cels.* Lib. I. s. 5. ‖ *Ib.* s. 7. ¶ *Ib.* s. 37.
** See also Lib. V. s. 2.

After calling upon the heathen* to give credit to the evangelistic narratives of the dove and voice at our Lord's baptism, as they would to their own oracles and miracles, he insists upon the Jew, at any rate, believing them, as they believe similar incidents in the Old Testament. The same line of argument occurs Lib. II. sect. 53, 57, 75.

Again,† "because infidels endeavor to expose the doctrine of Christ's resurrection to profane contempt (on account of its wonderful character,) I shall take occasion here to mention what Plato says of Er, the son of Armenius, who at the end of twelve days arose from his tomb, and related several remarkable transactions that had passed to his certain knowledge in the world of spirits; I might also mention the story (not a little to my purpose) which Heraclytus gives of a woman who returned to life; and many other cases which could be produced from the history of persons who have appeared the day after their decease."

Pythagoras and Plato are adduced‡ as believing in the ascent of virtuous souls to heaven, or some place beyond the skies, there to enjoy the society of the blessed. The latter author appears§ to say, in his *Timæus,* that the earth is to be purged by fire and water. He has something too‖ not unlike the Mosaic account of the "Fall," in the *Symposio de Cupidine,* under the story of Porus, with the garden of Jove and the allurements of Penia.

He further¶ silences Celsus, repudiating the miraculous incidents of Sacred Writ, with the incredible reports of Plato's third eye, with the swan and demon of Socrates, and with the stories related by Pythagoras of himself; adding, "The Greeks looked for such things in their divine men."

Finally,** he argues, that "if Jesus died a miserable death, so did Socrates and Anaxarchus; and as a palliation for

* *Cont. Cels.* Lib. V. s. 42–44, 70. † *Cont. Cels.* Lib. II. s. 16.
‡ *Ib.* Lib. III. s. 80, 81. § *Ib.* Lib. IV. s. 20.
‖ *Ib.* s. 37. ¶ *Ib.* Lib. VI. s. 8. ** *Ib.* Lib. VII. s. 56; VIII. s. 6.

Christian pertinacity in refusing to bow the knee to any but Jesus, he instances the case of the Lacedæmonian legates, who could not be induced, even by violence, to adore the Persian monarch, pleading that "the law of Lycurgus was their only Lord."

ARNOBIUS * meets the objectors to the humanity of Christ in their own way, by hinting at a list of minor gods among the heathen who were carried in the womb. Other objections † to the Cross are turned aside by allusions to "Pythagoras slain in the temple of the Muses, to Socrates poisoned in prison, and to many others, who though famous for their virtues, have nevertheless died the most painful deaths; as Aquilius, Tribonius, Regulus; or to mention deities (since we are charged with worshipping this man) Liberius (torn in pieces by the Titans), Æsculapius, Hercules, and Romulus himself."

On the further difficulty‡ arising out of the death of Christ, notwithstanding his divine nature, our author asks the Greeks "whether when the Sibyl was slain by robbers, Apollo was slain in her?"

"How," he continues,§ "can you who pretend to admire the precepts of your philosophers and teachers, blame our Jesus for uttering the same things? You ridicule us because we reverence and worship God, forgetting that Plato in his *Theætetus* confesses that God is the most powerful of names, and also hints at a resurrection in the *Politico;* while in a treatise, 'on the immortality of the soul,' he more than hints at the fires of Gehenna, in those rivers where the lost are rolled along and consumed."

"If Christianity‖ is to be blamed for introducing new customs," he suggests whether "our ancestors who first ex-

* *Adv. Gent.* Lib. I. c. 12. † *Ib.* c. 14. ‡ *Ib.* c. 24.
§ *Ib.* Lib. II, c. 8. ‖ *Ib.* c. 28.

changed their skins for woven fabrics, and gave up caves for houses; or yet more to the purpose, they who introduced the worship of Hercules into Italy long after Saturn had been worshipped there, are not obnoxious to the same charge?"

LACTANTIUS* says, "Because the prophets have spoken of the wrath of God, this is sufficient testimony for us; but since some will not credit them, we will appeal to witnesses whom our opponents cannot refuse to hear. Many great writers have handed down the opinion that God is angry with the wicked. Among the Greeks Aristo and Apollodorus, and among the Latins Varro and Fenestella." He likewise adduces the Erythræan and other oracles to the same effect. Passing† over the witness of the prophets once more,‡ he proposes to consider the testimony of the poets and philosophers as to the unity of God.§ "From these witnesses," he says, "usually invoked against us, we can prove there is but one God. Not that these ancients had any knowledge of the truth, but that the truth forced itself upon them, and shone so brightly in their eyes, that they had been blind not to see it." Of the poets,‖ Orpheus, Ovid, Virgil; of the philosophers, Plato, Aristotle, Antisthenes, Thales, Pythagoras, Anaximenes, Cleanthes, Chrysippus, Zeno, with the Roman Seneca and Cicero; of the heathen prophets,¶ Hermes Trismegistus, and the Sibyls, are brought in affirmation; some of them** being further called upon to testify to the formation of the world and to there being a spirit, the Son of the Great God, endowed with Creative Power.

In conclusion he quotes Plato on the immortality of the soul, and agrees with him in inferring this grand doctrine

* *De Ira Dei*, c. 22. † *Epitom.* c. 3.

‡ This is given in full in *Div. Instit.* Lib. I. c. 4.

§ A subject previously pursued at length in Justin Martyr's *De Monarchia.*

‖ *Epitom.* c. 4. ¶ *Ib.* c. 5. ** *Ib.* c. 42, 70.

from the constant mobility of mind; from the power it has of grasping the past, the present, and the future; from its incorporeity; from its sense of justice and knowledge of God, by which men are raised above the brutes; and lastly, from the circumstance that man is the only creature that makes use of the arts and fire, "that celestial element."

EUSEBIUS* asks, "why if the oracles of the heathen, as stated by Porphyry, have acknowledged the propriety of worshipping one God, Jesus alone should be called a deceiver, because he commends the practice of this virtue to all mankind?"

"Some of the famous philosophers† also taught that the heavens and the earth were made by God, that the soul was immortal, and admonished men of a final judgment at which rewards and punishments are to be distributed."

From like sources he gathers‡ that "there have been in every country of the world, oracles and places of prophecy. 'The care of the Almighty,' say our enemies, 'has accorded them for the use and accommodation of man;' the only question then between us is, how to distinguish those of the heathen from our own."

GREGORY NAZIANZEN§ tells the apostate Julian, that whilst he despises Christian history, he admits things equally extraordinary in Classic history.

AUGUSTINE.‖ "Will any one deny miracles? He that does so in order to injure the authority of Scripture, may as well say at once that the gods have no regard to men; for they had no way of insuring their own worship but by miracles, in which the Pagan stories show how far they had the

* *Theoph.* Lib. v. c. 3, 4.
† *Ib.* c. 6, 7.
‡ *Demonst. Evang.* Lib. v. præf.
§ *Orat. IV. adv. Jul.* s. 7.
‖ *De Civit. Dei*, Lib. x. c. 18.

power to prove themselves more wonderful than useful. But if the believers in Polytheism give credence to *their* histories and magical (or to please them) theurgical books, why should the Scriptures be rejected because of the miracles they recount, which are as far beyond all others, as He whom our books teach us to adore, is above all other gods?"

"Even Porphyry," it is remarked,* "thought that God's Providence would not leave mankind without a way of deliverance for the soul. He does not say there is no such, but that so great and good a revelation is not yet made to us or to him."

SECTION IV.

ANSWERS TO OBJECTIONS.†

CONSIDERING the loose style of the Fathers, and the want of systematic arrangement in their writings, we are not surprised to meet with a quantity of material among them, which is hard to classify, and yet which being interesting in itself, and distinctly meant (as is evident from its interposition with direct arguments) for the purpose of clearing away the prejudices of the ignorant or sagacious, I have not thought it right to pass entirely by. Origen and Arnobius are particularly full of this kind of apologetic matter. We have only room for a few specimens.

THE AUTHOR OF EPISTLE TO DIOGNETUS‡ explains away the objection to the Christian religion raised on the ground of novelty, by the sensible and perhaps correct reason, that God would have it made fully manifest that we

* *De Civit. Dei*, Lib. x. c. 32. † Explanation. ‡ *Ep. ad Diog.* c. 9.

could not save ourselves, or by our own ability attain the kingdom of God. "This being established by the lapse of time, he showed us a Saviour who observed those laws for us which we could not observe."

JUSTIN MARTYR.* It was urged against the truth of prophecy, that a fatal necessity brought about the event; our author explains that there is no such thing as fate. The variety in the world, of good and bad, and the unequal conduct of the same individual at different times, cannot be consonant with such a doctrine; for in that case fate would be at variance with itself, or else we must give up all distinction between vice and virtue, which it would be impious as well as absurd to suppose.

TERTULLIAN† points out how many public calamities like those for which Christianity was reproached in his time, had happened to the empire and city of Rome long before the reign of Tiberius. He alludes to the flood mentioned by Plato, to the destruction of Sodom and Gomorrah, and to their later representatives, Volsinium and Pompeii.

In reply ‡ to the insinuation, that God permits his own people to be injured with the wicked, it is shown that trouble is salutary and needful both as an admonition and punishment; that it does not really injure Christians, because they have no further concern with this world than how they may quickly depart from it; and lastly, that they rejoice in the fulfilment of whatsoever has been divinely predicted, even though they themselves may be temporarily involved therein.

MINUTIUS FELIX.§ Octavius defends Christians against the implication of Cæcilius that they were plebeian,

* *Apol.* I. c. 54.
† *Apol.* c. 40.
‡ *Ib.* c. 42.
§ *Octav.* c. 16.

saying, "They were not a poorer or more despised people than those who have ever made and delivered rules of wisdom to posterity. It is not the genius of the speaker, but the truth of what he utters, that men should attend to: indeed the plainer the discourse, the more visible is the truth it contains, being divested of all meretricious graces."

ORIGEN* rejoins to Celsus questioning the legality of the Christian love-feasts, that truth is to be preferred to bad laws; for as the inhabitants of a city might fairly defend themselves against a prince who unjustly invades their country, so Christians may warrantably violate the laws of Satan, that great usurper, to free themselves and others from his worse than Scythian tyranny.

Being taunted† with the text, "the wisdom of this world is foolishness with God," as though Christians despised learning, he answers, "By the wisdom of the world I understand that vain philosophy, in a comparative sense, which the Scripture does so justly, so frequently, and so severely condemn. When a person becomes a fool in the estimation of this vain and degenerate world, well it is with him: a most useful thing is folly of that limited kind. For the world that ought to have known God, has forgotten him; and he, in his infinite wisdom, has therefore been pleased to save the world by the preaching of a doctrine *esteemed* foolish."

He argues,‡ that it is no fault of Christianity that the Jews do not embrace it, from the well-known difficulty there is in resigning bad habits rooted in our nature, or opinions in which we have been brought up. We all feel a reluctance to quit only a familiar scene, much more to give up a national religion. You may talk to an Egyptian till breath fails, without inducing him to relinquish his superstitions. The case of the Jews is yet more inveterate.

* *Cont. Cels.* Lib. I. s. 1. † *Ib.* Lib. I. s. 12. ‡ *Ib.* s. 52.

He suspects* that our Saviour taught the Jews in parables that the kingdom of God should be taken away from them on account of their wickedness, and given to others, as a less aggravating form of communicating such unwelcome news.

To soften Celsus' surprise† because Christ did not at once avenge himself upon the Jews, Origen remarks that the Greeks find "much the same difficulty in the fact of the Deity not punishing the insults offered him by the fatalists." This was a sly stroke at his Epicurean antagonist.

Celsus‡ wonders that Christ did not vanish from the Cross; our author explains that such a procedure would have vitiated the design of his mission.

Origen§ again suggests the inconvenience and confusion which must necessarily follow from every nation having its own gods: "What could strangers do?"

On Celsus charging Jesus‖ with robbing Plato of the text, "How hardly shall they that have riches enter into the Kingdom of Heaven," he contends, first, that the "resemblance between the rival passages is not so considerable; Plato's running thus, 'It is impossible for a very rich man to be a very good man;' and, secondly, that it is exceedingly improbable that the son of a poor carpenter, as Jesus was, knowing neither the Greek nor Hebrew letters, should have studied Plato."

He supposes¶ the reason for the subversion of Judaism was, that the Hebrews would never have been a settled people again: politically, they could not submit their theocracy to a foreign yoke; or religiously, their ancient dispensations to evangelical rules.

Finally,** he defends the simplicity of the sacred writings, on the score that they are meant for food and not for display;

* *Cont. Cels.* Lib. II. s. 5. † *Ib.* s. 35. ‡ *Ib.* s. 58.
§ *Ib.* Lib. V. s. 38. ‖ *Ib.* Lib. VI. s. 16.
¶ *Ib.* Lib. VII. s. 20. ** *Ib.* s. 49.

for all mankind, not for a few accomplished individuals. It is remarked, however, that there is a deep meaning and beauty in them, to be attained by reflection.

ARNOBIUS,* after having shown that Christians cannot be accountable for calamities, since they have happened in the earliest ages of the world, inquires† into the nature of physical evil, and questions whether it is not the result of the general benevolence of the Deity. He supports this opinion from Plato.

To the reproach‡ of barbarisms detected by the Greeks and Romans, in the Sacred Writings, he replies that the object of the Scriptures was not to amuse, but to edify; and moreover contends vigorously against any written law, or limitation of arbitrary forms of speech. He asks the hyper-critic by what original propriety *paries* should be masculine and *sella* feminine? He further produces words with two genders as *cœlus* and *cœlum; hoc pane* and *hic panis; hic sanguis, hoc sanguen;* which he shows to be absurd in the nature of things. Thus he thinks the most polite of scholars commit the very solecisms which they complain of, and that too, notwithstanding all their study and all their grammarians.

The heathen having cavilled§ that Christ's promises of the future are not demonstrable, Arnobius allows it; but maintains upon the whole, and taking a fair view of the matter, that it is more rational to believe in Jesus, even though his promises should fail, than in those who can promise nothing at all. For if Christianity *should* prove true, by not believing it we incur the loss of salvation, the greatest of all losses.

EUSEBIUS ‖ observes, that the synchronism of the establishment of peace throughout the world by means of

* *Adv. Gent.* Lib. I. c. 1. † *Ib.* c. 2. ‡ *Ib.* c. 22.
§ *Ib.* Lib. II. c. 3. ‖ *Theoph.* Lib. III. c. 2.

the Roman arms, with the advent of our blessed Lord, the Prince of Peace, is a great marvel to those who reflect upon it.

He accounts* for some obscurity in the Prophets by supposing that a veil was purposely cast over certain passages, in order to conceal the predictions concerning the ruin of the Jews, lest that people should have destroyed even their own writings, or attempted in some way to have prevented the accomplishment of prophecy. "History," he says, "as it is, gives us intimations of such attempts."

AUGUSTINE† argues that of invisible matters, such as the creation of the world, man's creation and the like, which no human being could possibly have witnessed, none but God can inform us; and therefore infers that "since the prophets profess to furnish us with a divine account, which profession was accompanied by consistent and holy lives, we are bound to give them credit."

* *Dem. Evan.* Lib. VI. præf. † *De Civit. Dei,* Lib. XI. c. 3, 4.

CHAPTER II.

THE ARGUMENT FROM ANTIQUITY.

Stand ye in the ways, and see, and ask for the old paths.
JER. 6 : 16.

THERE are three points to be observed in estimating the proofs arranged under this chapter: the *claim* of the Fathers to the books of the Old Testament; the *sense* in which they appealed to antiquity; and the *use* they made of the argument.

The first need not detain us long. None can now doubt that the Fathers laid a fair claim to the books, and so to the authority in question. Various sayings of our blessed Lord and his Apostles, with the entire succession of Christianity to Judaism as a matter of fact, and the further thought that this argument, itself so popular with the Apologists, was never disallowed,* will render any lengthened demonstration unnecessary. The right, even if it be not asserted in some cases, is clearly implied in all. I shall therefore produce an authority or two at once. Origen asks,† "Why should we think it strange that the Gospel is founded upon the law of Moses, when our Saviour, addressing those who refused to believe in him, said, 'If ye believe Moses, believe me also;

* Chrysostom names both Celsus and Porphyry as witnessing to the antiquity of our writings.—*Hom.* VI. ep. to Cor.

† *Cont. Cels.* Lib. II.

for he wrote of me;' and when Mark the Evangelist opens his history, as if intimating to us that the Gospel is based on the Scriptures of the Old Testament itself?" And he elsewhere reminds us that "Celsus* thought he could not more effectually overthrow Christianity, than by his assaults upon the Jewish system, on which the doctrine of our Saviour is acknowledged to be built." Again, Archelaus, bishop of Kaskar, grounds his complaint against the Manichæan heresy upon its attempt to dissociate the two Testaments, by attributing them and the institutions they represent, to different authors. Lactantius† also says, "The Jews use the Old Testament, we use the New; but still the two are not diverse, for the New is the completion of the Old, Christ being the common testator." Lastly, Eusebius and Augustine, as others before them, in explaining why they adopt the books of the Jews but refuse their ceremonies, insist that the Prophets belong to Christians because they wrote concerning them; "in truth, rather against the Jews and in favor of the Gentiles." Nothing can explain more clearly than these statements and reasonings do, the claims which the early Fathers laid to the Old Testament Scriptures.

Having thus appropriated the material to their use, and ranged themselves in the line of spiritual Judaism, the next step was to prove the antiquity of the common religion. And in doing this the Fathers have exhibited that spirit of fair and fearless discussion, which is of itself a mark of sincerity. They have appealed (1) to profane authors, as far back as they extend; and upon their failure, (2) to their own books, the books of Moses.

With regard to the former of these tests, I am bound to say that the Apologists were not the first to make use of it. Profane history had already been cited for this purpose. The Jews themselves were obliged to check the towering pride of

* *Cont. Cels.* Lib. I. s. 22. † *Div. Instit.* Lib. XIV. c. 20.

Paganism, by references to its own memorials; and to say to the Gentile (with better reason than Eliphaz to Job,) "With us are the grey-headed and very aged men, much elder than thy father." Josephus, about 100 A. D., in his two books against Apion, had demonstrated, by the direct testimony of general literature, the great age of the Hebrew race and institutions.* The Fathers duly acknowledge their obligations to the noble Jew, for his hint and for his researches. Perhaps, however, the commencement of such a discussion at all, is still more justly due to Christianity itself, and to that catholicism and freedom of inquiry it introduced among men. Yet, be that as it may, the Christian Apologists have the credit of continuing and considerably enlarging this species of evidence, until, as one converted philosopher after another brought in the spoils of foreign lore from the east and from the west, and thus increased its *substance*, whilst the experience and sifting of three or four centuries had fully tried its *value*, it stood forth an irrefragable argument against all superstitions.

This appeal to antiquity is made on the strength of a natural sentiment. Other things being equal, antiquity will ever insure veneration. It is the ground of all prescriptive right, and its influence is taken for granted in the commonest affairs of life. But without entering upon general questions, we can perceive a peculiar propriety in appealing to the past on matters of a sacred nature. "With respect to religious topics that have long occupied the attention of mankind, the novelty of an opinion is *primâ facie* a presumption against its truth."† The facts with which important opinions are ushered in, must be expected to stand the test of constant as well as severe criticism. Truth is the daughter of Time; and the more serious the truth, the more needful and honorable will be the trial.

* Flavii Jos. *contra Apoinem et Manethonem*, libro duo.

† Bishop of Lincoln's *Just. Martyr.*

With such a view the Apologists seem to have been impressed. All of them, with the exception of Arnobius, make use of this argument. That they undertook at all, long and elaborate collations of events and dates, is enough to show the importance they attached to their production, an importance that can only be based upon the principle above stated. But Tertullian distinctly gives this as his ground of argument, in the *Apologeticus:* "Our records," he says, "have the greatest claim to attention by the authority of their high antiquity. For even among yourselves (the heathen), it is as it were a part of your religion, to pay regard to any observance according to its age." The first idea then of the Apologists under this head, was to show the superior antiquity of their own records by an appeal to profane history.

This was well as far as it went, but it only constituted a negative proof, and left Christianity short of its divinity. As soon therefore as *heathen* literature ceases to furnish any evidence, we find them appealing to their own literature. They turn from comparative to positive antiquity. And so far is this proceeding from being unfair or injurious to their cause, it was clearly the only course they could adopt; indeed the very necessity for it affords a strong affirmation in their favor; it proves, if it proves nothing else, the superior antiquity of the Mosaic traditions. But to proceed; by the aid of this new witness our authors were led beyond the bounds of a mere opposition or superiority to Paganism. The argument began to assume an absolute value, to exhibit a more refined and divine quality. It could now be carried on across the Flood and up to the very gates of Paradise. What could be adequate to describe such sublime, yet rational details, but the eye of God and the pen of inspiration?

The principle of this appeal appears to be equally natural with the other. It is that as God is of one mind and all his works are perfect, and that since the circumstances that first called forth his pity towards our fallen race, have ever continued the same in their agency and effects, we should expect, from first to last, but *one* Revelation of the divine Will, but one plan for our Redemption. Modification, adaptation, revival, development (in form), might be called for, but still the system, the substance would be the same. A promise given the moment it was needed, and completed the moment it was fit. Under some impression of this sort, the Fathers recognized their unity with the Mosaic and patriarchal dispensations, and hence raised to a yet higher estimate the documents by which so venerable a unity was warranted. But, besides expecting that a Divine Revelation would be one and continuous,* we might also expect it, from the nature of the case, to exhibit a clear pathway up to God himself, and so prove the perfection of its golden chain. Thus, with a divine source and an uninterrupted continuity, not merely the superior antiquity and value of the Sacred Writings would be attested, but even their inspiration might be inferred. This was the legitimate end of the argument from antiquity.

How far the different Fathers came up to it, will be seen in the sequel. Some were content with the lower and more definite ground. Their main desire was to settle the question of antiquity in favor of the Old Testament, and for this purpose they were content to follow up the Sacred Chronology out of the reach of profane hands. So long as Homer yielded the palm of years to David, and Cadmus to Moses, this was enough; Abraham and Job were yet in reserve.

Others saw and went further. Theophilus says, "It is necessary, in a perfect history of the world, that mention be made of all things from the beginning. Even of those things

* It is curious to notice how men of all religions and times have respected the idea of historic continuity. Greece was content to receive her theology from Egypt or the East; Italy from Greece; whilst, since Christianity became established, there has been no heresy and no antichrist that has not endeavored to tack itself on to her chariot-wheels.

that happened beyond the Flood, such as the origin of the earth and of mankind. These subjects the prophets of the Egyptians and Chaldæans ought to have explained, if indeed they spake under the influence of a pure and divine spirit, and announced that which was true." Even Arnobius suggests that, "if the antiquity of authors be required, ours is that of God himself." Thus, that marvellous opening of our Sacred Books: "In the beginning God created the heavens and the earth;" and that unique genealogy, traced with mercantile exactness, from "Adam, who was the son of God," to Jesus himself, which they contain and certify, were shown to be auxiliary evidences for the truth of Christianity. And whilst the records of heathen Mythology were soon lost amidst the clouds of Olympus, or the darkness of Egyptian tombs, the true religion was found uniting itself (as the works of Nature do by a different law) to the creation of all things; and without a doubt, a fable, or a lapse, deducing its pedigree from a Divine original.

The whole material of this chapter forms an argument of some weight with a candid and reflective mind. It implies in fact a superhuman knowledge of the past, and points out an element in the Bible which is not of this world. It likewise illustrates that love of order so apparent in all that is divine; and the practical character of Christianity, which is ready to abide by the lowest tests of truth.

I have in the third place to mention the account to which the Apologists turned this argument. The claim they maintained to the Old Testament, gave them a powerful handle against the Jew; and the appeal to profane authors acted with equal force against the Pagan. Of the Jewish discussion nothing need be said; it explains itself. But with regard to heathenism, we must observe that this argument was an answer to a double charge. Having appropriated and proved this antiquity, the Apologist could now repel the charge of novelty. It was constantly urged to the disparagement of the

Gospel that it was but of yesterday. In one sense this was true, and therefore we find Arnobius replying, "So much the better; its facts can be the more easily tested;" or Eusebius, saying, "So much the greater marvel since it has already subdued the world." But in another sense, and as the heathen employed it, the objection had a force which I conceive the Apologists could only meet as they did meet it, by counteraction. Besides, by acknowledging the principle of this sacred prescription, they gained and took for the service of God, all the credit which had been misapplied to idolatry. The natural sentiment of men and the heathen's own principles, went over to the side of truth; and, may we not hope, carried some thoughtful minds along with them?

Again, reference was made, in the last chapter, to a charge of plagiarism, brought by the heathen against the Sacred Scriptures. They asserted that the coincidence of opinion between the Christian and heathen writers was no cause of wonder, no ground for an *argumentum ad hominem*, because doubtless our prophets had borrowed from their poets and philosophers. The Apologists returned this charge upon their opponents, and by a fearless appeal to historical data, undertook to show that all the probability lay the other way, inasmuch as our sacred witnesses extend ages further back than any other records, monuments, or even reasonable traditions. And thus as before, the natural veneration that time and fame had given to the sages of Greece, was seen transferring itself to the cause of Christianity.

The hypotheses of the Fathers for explaining these correspondences, were, (1) that the ancient poets had borrowed directly from the Scriptures, purposely obscuring their citations through jealousy or fear; or (2) that they were indebted to the assistance and suggestion of Satan through the mouth of oracles. It was thought that our spiritual enemy might have foreseen the advent of Christ, and endeavored to anticipate his doctrines and confuse his actions. The first supposition, though probable, is not proved. The other yet more crude, is only one of the characteristic and fanciful speculations of the day.* But those theories, whether right or wrong, form no part of the argument before us: they are quite gratuitous explanations. Passing them by, therefore, we find enough of the sensible and certain, to show that the object of the Apologists was accomplished; the false charges were rebutted. And in doing this a far more substantial advantage followed. The religion defended, was necessarily and materially enhanced. As it quietly rose above the ruins of all human systems, the question naturally suggested itself, whence this superiority? The indirect argument that had won for it a hearing and an unrivalled character, gave place to the more direct argument in support of its claims to divinity: abstract antiquity supplied it with one of the attributes of a Revelation from Heaven. And all this had been effected at the expense, and very much by the concessions of enemies. Truly might it be said, to borrow a fine figure of Origen on a kindred topic, "the Israelites had spoiled the Egyptians, and taken their ornaments for the decoration of the tabernacle."

Another use of the plea of antiquity to be gathered from these writings has been almost anticipated. One of the distinguishing traits of the early theology, is the honor it paid to Christ as "the Word" from everlasting. The results of this argument were therefore in the highest degree welcome to the Apologetic cause. They afforded the heathen an illustration of that marvellous nature which, while it appeared on earth as "a man of sorrows," could be traced absolutely to a period before the world was, and to an elevation only compatible with the majesty of Godhead. They were in truth an

* A singular conjecture of this kind is hazarded by one of our authors, that the two thieves were crucified with Christ, at the instigation of the Devil, who hoped thereby to confound the identity of the sacred person.

exegesis of the text, "In the beginning was the Word, and the Word was with God, and the Word was God."*

I cannot dismiss the entire subject without observing that whilst the Apologists could not with any propriety have overlooked the advantages of this argument to Christianity, I do not see that they abused it. They never depended upon it solely, or supposed it to be more that what Warburton says it can but be, "a thing relative." Their maxim was not that a doctrine was true because it was old, (rather would they have said it was old because true,) but that it was *authoritative*. The age and preservation of the Scriptures, (and so of religion,) afforded a presumption in favor of their heavenly inspiration; an absolute title to respect and authority. And as the Apologists did not exaggerate, so they did not misapply this argument. With one exception only, I believe, they restricted its use to the single subject just named — the antiquity of the Bible. The exception is that of Tertullian (after a germ of Irenæus possibly) in his controversy with the heretics, a discussion and a principle quite apart from our present one, but which Mosheim† has, I think unfairly, made to tell against the whole patristic body.

JUSTIN MARTYR.‡ "We desire also to make it fully apparent to you that those things only which we affirm and have learned from Christ and the prophets are the truth, and more ancient than anything recorded by other writers."

Defending the freedom of the will, he remarks,§ "When Plato said, 'the fault lies with him who chooses, but God is blameless,' he took it from Moses, who was more ancient than all the writers of the Greeks. And so everything the poets and philosophers have said concerning the immortality

* John i. 1.
† *Eccles. Hist.* Cent. II. Part II. c. 3.
‡ *Apol.* I. c. 31.
§ *Ib.* c. 57.

of the soul, or of punishments after death, or of the contemplation of heavenly things, they conceive and explain as they first derived them from the prophets."

"It is not therefore* that we hold the same opinions as others, but that all others speak in imitation of us."

Having surmised† that evil spirits might suggest the misinterpretation of prophecies concerning the prince Messiah (whence Bacchus was said to have been born of Jupiter, Perseus of a virgin, Hercules a ruler, and Æsculapius a healer of the sick), our author endeavors to trace many of the heathen ceremonies to a like source; such as the offering of libations, the sprinkling with water, the loosing the shoes in the vestibule of a temple, and some of the mysteries of Mithra. "Whatever‡ the philosophers and legislators of antiquity said or thought that was at all worthy, they had elaborated out of the Word of God. But because they knew not everything concerning the word, that is, Christ, they have often said and done things inconsistent with themselves." In this way he concludes that Christ is superior to them all, and his doctrine more sublime than all human doctrines.

Endeavoring § to persuade the Greeks to forego the teaching of their own sages, he adduces as one argument, the greater antiquity of Moses and the prophets. This point he engages to prove, "not out of our own divine histories (to which as yet you may not assent on account of your errors,) but even from profane historians themselves. Thus some professing to be of the time of Ogyges and Inachus, mention Moses as the leader and chief of the Jewish nation. So also Polemon in his first book of Grecian history. Again, Apion, in his work against the Jews, as likewise in the fourth book of his histories, relates that whilst Inachus reigned in Argos, the Hebrews revolted from Amasis, king of Egypt, under

* *Apol.* I. 78.

† *Ib.* c. 8.

‡ *Apol.* II. c. 10.

§ *Exhort. ad Græc.* c. 9.

their leader Moses. Ptolemæus, also, writing of the affairs of the Egyptians, assents to this. Add to these testimonies the writers on Athenian history, Hellanicus and Philochorus, Castor and Thallus, and Alexander Polyhistor, together with the best Jewish writers, Philo and Josephus, all of whom commemorate Moses, the oldest and most venerable Jewish leader. The very title of Josephus' famous work, *The Antiquities*, is something for our proposition. Then there is Diodorus, the most celebrated of your own historical writers, who in his first book distinctly says that he has heard from the Egyptian priests that Moses was the first and most ancient of legislators. Such* is the witness, oh Greeks, that you yourselves bear to our antiquity. But it is needful to go a little more into detail, and inquire in what ages your philosophers lived, that you may perceive their recent date and the greater antiquity of our Moses." He proceeds thus: "Socrates was the master of Plato, Plato of Aristotle; now these men flourished in the times of Philip and Alexander of Macedon, contemporaries of the great Athenian orators, as the orations of Demosthenes against Philip prove. Wherefore it is plain, how much older Moses must be than any of them. Moreover, there were no records kept by the Greeks before the Olympiads, nor are there any ancient monuments of their deeds before that time. The only history of those early periods now extant, is that of our Moses, written in the Hebrew character before Greek letters were invented. Your grammarians themselves allow this when they say that Cadmus first brought the alphabet from Phœnicia, and taught it to the Greeks: which alone proves the lateness of your literature; for all your poets, however ancient, your legislators, historians, philosophers, and orators, have composed and spoken in the Greek character." An account† of the Septuagint translation follows, to explain the appearance of the

* *Exhort. ad Græc.* c. 12.

† *Ib.* c. 13.

Old Testament in Greek, after which he presses his conclusion upon the heathen: "It seems,* therefore, that beholding the judgment (rendered) not only by believers, but also by those without us, you ought not to adhere so heedlessly to the errors of your ancestors, or suppose that to be necessarily true which they have handed down. Consider the danger of a mistake in such a momentous concern, and carefully examine whatever has been spoken by your so-called teachers. In such a research you will find that they were compelled by divine providence to say much, however unwillingly, that makes in our favor. Especially is this the case with those who travelled into Egypt, and there profited by the religious teaching that Moses and our ancestors left behind them." He gathers from the history of Diodorus, &c., that Orpheus, Homer, Solon, Pythagoras and Plato, with many others, in this way visited Egypt, where they met with the Pentateuch;† for it would seem "thenceforth‡ they changed their incorrect opinions concerning the Deity, and began to speak of one and the only God;" darkly § it is true, but then perhaps "Plato was deterred from expressing his full belief by the fate of his master Socrates." He gives ‖ as his reason for mentioning these things, the hope of drawing off the Greeks from their confidence in "those who did not write what was original, but what they took from Moses and the prophets,¶ concealing their theft under various figures."

"It is now time,** therefore," he adds, "that you being persuaded by extraneous accounts, of the far greater antiquity of Moses and the rest of the prophets above all those whom you account wise, should depart from the fatal errors of *your* predecessors, and learn what is true from *ours*."

* *Exhort. ad Græc.* c. 14. † *Ib.* c. 15. ‡ *Ib.* c. 19.
§ *Ib.* c. 20. ‖ *Ib.* c. 34
¶ For coincident passages see *Exhort. ad Græc.* c. 22, 25–27, 31–33.
** *Ib.* c. 35.

TATIAN.* "It is right I should satisfy you that our philosophy is older than any of the Grecian systems; and let us begin by comparing Moses and Homer, each being the oldest on his side. We shall find by this means that not only can we date farther back than any of your schools, but than the invention of Greek letters themselves. For the purpose of proving this, I will not bring forward our own witnesses, but yours; the Greeks themselves shall testify. Indeed I know that any other witnesses would be useless, because you would not admit their testimony; but then it will be a greater victory for us if we can convince you by arguments not to be impugned, and thus fight you with your own weapons." He commences by allowing that the notices concerning Homer are both many and ancient. Theagines Rhegius, who lived in the reign of Cambyses; Stesimbrotus, Herodotus, Thasius, Antimachus, Collophonius, Dionysius, and others, both Peripatetics and grammarians, all name him, but "all agree in placing him after the Trojan war." Yet even granting† "that Homer was contemporaneous with Agamemnon at the siege of Troy, or, if you will, lived before the invention of letters, it is still evident that our Moses is the more remote, preceding as well the building of Troy, as the very origin of the Greek and Trojan races." To verify this statement, he proposes to make use of the Chaldean, Phœnician, and Egyptian writers. Berosus, of Babylon, is found mentioning Nebuchodonozor's expedition against the Phœnicians and Jews, which exactly tallies with the account of the circumstance given by our prophets, many ages after Moses. Now this furnishes a date seventy years before the foundation of the Persian empire. From the Phœnician authors,‡ Theodotus, Hypsicrates and Mochus, he gathers that the following events occurred under their kings: "the transference of Europa, the advent of Menelaus into Egypt, and the acts of

* *Orat. ad Græc.* c. 21. † *Ib.* c. 36. ‡ *Ib.* c. 37.

Chiramus, who gave his own daughter in marriage to Solomon, and supplied him with every kind of wood for the construction of the temple, as is confirmed by Menander of Pergamos. Now the age of Chiramus was near that of Troy; but Solomon was his contemporary; wherefore the above-named events were of much later date than Moses."

Ptolemy* the priest, furnishes our author with Egyptian testimony, to the effect that "the Jews went out of Egypt under the direction of Moses, in the reign of Amosis, coeval with Inachus. This Apion confirms. But the time that elapsed from Inachus to the destruction of Troy was twenty generations, as is seen by examining the list of the Argive kings (which is given) down to Agamemnon, in the eighteenth year of whose reign Troy was taken."

A parallel list† of the Attic sovereigns follows, beginning with Ogyges (of the same age with Phoroneus, son of Inachus, under whom the first deluge is said to have happened), and including Actæus, who gave Attica its name, Prometheus, Epimetheus, Atlas, and Cecrops (during this reign occur the burning of Phaethon, and Deucalion's flood), and others whose eras include the facts or fictions of Grecian History; such as the landing of Danaus on the Peloponnesus; the fable of Proserpine; the building of the Eleusinian temple; the narrations concerning Triptolemus, Cadmus and Minos; the Thracian and Athenian wars, &c., down to the time of Agamemnon again; thus establishing the general fact, that Moses was older than the most venerable and ancient of the Grecian heroes.

The date of Cadmus' entrance into Bœotia is next ascertained to have been many generations later than Inachus; and lastly,‡ our author is at pains to show that Moses is likewise older than any sages before the time of Homer; as Linus (called the preceptor of Hercules, whose son Triptolemus was engaged in the Trojan war), Philammon, Thamyrides,

**Orat. ad Græc.* c. 38. †*Ib.* c. 39. ‡*Ib.* c. 41.

Amphion, Musæus, Orpheus, Demodocus, the Sibyl, Epimenides, the Cretan who went to Sparta, and so on, the catalogue of worthies being completed by the addition of the legislators and sages from Minos downwards.

"And now," he concludes,* "I, Tatian, a Christian, have composed these things; born in Syria, initiated into your mysteries, I have turned to those I herein recommend; for as soon as I knew God and his works, I felt a desire to exhibit to others the result of my own examination, which offers beyond all denial a sound reason for thus worshipping God (as Christians do)."

ATHENAGORAS.† "It is necessary in this Apology to show that the very names of the heathen gods are modern, and that their statues were but of yesterday. I need scarcely remark that some of your writers, such as Orpheus, Homer, and Hesiod, were almost contemporaneous with your gods. Herodotus testifiesto this when he says, 'Hesiod and Homer, I am of opinion, were not above five hundred years more ancient than myself.' They first formed a Theogony for the Greeks, gave names to the several divinities, distributed their honors and occupations, and described their sex, form and other characteristics. Pictures and images were not invented for many years after this. The invention of drawing is due to Saurias of Samos, who traced a horse from a shadow in the sun; of painting, to Crato making a colored picture of a man on a board; and of wax-images to Core, whose father relieved in wax an outline of her lover, which she had sketched upon the wall of her chamber, the original being still preserved in Corinth. Dædalus and Theodorus the Milesian, long afterwards began to sculpture, and indeed of so recent a date are the statues of the gods, that we can name the very persons who carved them; for example, Endyus, a scholar of Dædalus,

* *Orat. ad Græc.* c. 42.

† *Legat.* c. 17.

made the famous statue of Diana of the Ephesians, and that of Minerva or Athena. The Pythian Apollo is the work of Theodorus and Telecles. The skill of Angelion and Smilis, made the Juno of Samos; Praxiteles, the figure of Venus the lady, in Cnidus: Phidias, that of Æsculapius in Epidaurus; in fine, there is not any celebrated statue the author of which is not known. Now if these are the gods, how came they to be made by men's hands? How is it they did not exist from everlasting? How came they to be younger than their authors?"

THEOPHILUS.* "The future punishment of the wicked was predicted long ago, by the prophets from whom your poets and philosophers, posterior in point of time, have borrowed in order to give authority to their opinions."

Our author subsequently shows,† that "both Jupiter and his father Saturn were born later not only than matter, but even than the formation of the world, and a multitude of men."

Referring‡ to the generations from Adam, he says: "They are clearly pointed out in the sacred Scriptures, as the Holy Ghost inspired Moses and the other prophets, so that our writings are proved to be more ancient than any others. Many have fancied that Apollo was the inventor of music, or that Orpheus derived it from the singing of birds, but our books trace this art beyond the Deluge. We have also § a rational account of the first building of cities and the rise of monarchies, with names and sketches of the races that sprang from the three sons of Noah." A tabular view follows, of the Assyrian kings; such as were coeval with Melchisedec, Abimelech, &c., being pointed out.

* *Ad Autol.* Lib. I. c. 14.
† *Ib.* Lib. II. c. 6.
‡ *Ib.* c. 30.
§ *Ib.* c. 31.

Thus* he finds that all the narratives of human transactions are but recent when compared with that of the Sacred Writings, and urges his friend, on the strength of such a discovery, not to trust those who were so much later in date, and who have introduced a host of false gods, born many years after cities were built, and nations established.

Having remarked † that the enemies of Christianity reproach it for its novelty, he calls attention to the actual dates of the systems under discussion. He shows how uncertain all the early heathen Theogonies and philosophies are: that some account the world unproduced, thus plunging into infinity, whilst others who allow its creation have antedated it by myriads of years. The reckoning of Plato, for instance, is criticised, as found in his book *De Civitate,* concerning the ages that have elapsed from the flood to the time of Dædalus. With these he confronts the well-substantiated dates of Moses,‡ whom our author (with Josephus) supposes to have lived near a thousand years after Noah; of the building of the temple, § five hundred and sixty years from the Exodus, whilst Hiram was king of Tyre, (as furnished by Menander); and lastly, of the foundation of Carthage, which he sets at a hundred and forty-three years and eight months subsequent to the building of Solomon's temple.

In like manner ‖ the times of the legislators are investigated. Solon is found to synchronize with Cyrus and the prophet Zacharias; and with reference to Lycurgus, Draco, and Minos, Josephus' authority is produced to show that our books are much more ancient than any of the laws of these men. "Yea, our divine law," it is added, "was prior to the reign of Jupiter in Crete, or to the Trojan war; and our books even recount events that happened before the flood, relating to the creation of the world and the formation of the first man."

* *Ad Autol.* Lib. II. c. 32. † *Ib.* Lib. III. c. 16. ‡ *Ib.* c. 20.
§ *Ib.* c. 22. ‖ *Ib.* c. 23.

Upon the whole, from a comparison* of the histories of the Persian, Roman, and other dynasties, Theophilus calculates the lapse of seven hundred and forty-four years, from the reign of Cyrus to the death of the emperor Aurelius Verus; or five thousand six hundred and ninety-eight years from the beginning of the world to his own time.

CLEMENS ALEXANDRINUS,† after an exordium, demonstrates that the Christian discipline is older than any of the schools. He commences with an account of the rise of the Grecian Philosophy for the purpose of exposing "its recent date when compared with the Hebrew writings, from which in truth it seems to have been borrowed." He extends the same remarks to the arts and sciences of which the barbarians, as the Greeks designate them, were the inventors. "In this respect," he says, "the philosophers may be called thieves and robbers, because before the coming of Christ, they stole and appropriated to themselves, portions of truth from the Hebrew prophets (without clearly understanding them,) which they adulterated or disfigured with ignorant diligence."

He then passes on to a long chronological detail, tracing the succession of poets, sages and sibyls down to the death of Commodus, by which he manifestly proves that Moses and the prophets lived long anterior to the period of the rise of philosophy.

This emboldens him to try and show further, that the Greeks derived even their strategical skill from the Jews; and that Miltiades, in his night march against the Persians, imitated the tactics of Moses in conducting the children of Israel out of Egypt. By a like fanciful and unsatisfactory process of thought, he traces the first idolatrous columns

* *Ad Autol.* Lib. III. c. 26-28. † *Strom.* Lib. I. Art. 2, 3.

of the ancients to their hearing of the fiery and cloudy pillar, the guide of God's people in the desert.

In the opening of the second book,* we find Clemens returning to his favorite topic, the plagiarisms of the Greeks. He asserts that their philosophers have stolen from the Sacred Scriptures, all they have delivered respecting the divine nature, the existence of matter, the first principle, the providence of God, the immortality of the soul, &c. These things he supposes them to have learned by a sort of circumlocution; and hence deduces that the literature of the Greeks can only be studied profitably in connection with the Hebrew Scriptures, the source from which it flowed. He conceives that the heathen may have been allowed to cull their philosophy in this way, to prepare them for the preaching of the Gospel.

TERTULLIAN † observes that as he has shown the antiquity of the Holy Scriptures above all profane literature (this is done much as usual, in cap. xix.), it will readily be conceded that they constitute the treasure, whence all real wisdom has been extracted. And he thinks it no wonder that the ingenuity of the philosophers has thus perverted the Old Testament, since men sprung from them (the heretics) have perverted the New, and cut many oblique and intricate paths from the one only way.

He concludes that since there is no doubt about the superior antiquity of our books and of the heathen plagiarisms from them, they ought to be believed much more than their imitations.

MINUTIUS FELIX ‡ conjectures that Thales drew his notion of water being the principle of all things, out of the Genesis of Moses; and,§ speaking of the resemblance which

* *Strom.* Lib. II.

† *Apol.* c. 4.

‡ *Octav.* c. 19.

§ *Ib.* c. 33.

the heathen opinions generally bear to Christian truths, he asserts, "the philosophers have taken their sketches from the divine discoveries of our prophets, disguising the theft." So did Pythagoras and Plato, especially concerning the immortality and metempsychosis of the soul. Or* "else these doctrines must have been gleaned from the confessions of demons."

ORIGEN † refers Celsus, who has omitted to reckon the Jews among the ancient nations of the earth, to the Egyptian annals, where the Jews are represented as a peculiar people; adding, "I might also adduce the Assyrian records, which represent their nation as engaged in long and bloody wars with the Hebrews;" upon which he asks, "why the Jewish writers who furnish accounts to the same purpose, should not be equally credited? How much more,‡ then, does Numenius the Pythagorean deserve to be preferred before Celsus! This learned author, in his work *De Bono*, speaking of those nations that hold God to be incorporeal, has named the Jews among them, and likewise gives some passages from the prophetical writings, giving them, however, an allegorical sense. It is reported also on the authority of Hermippus, that Pythagoras borrowed his philosophy from the Jews, and taught it to the Greeks; and there is still extant Hecatæus' history of the Jews, wherein he so highly commends the wisdom of that people, as to make Herennius Philo doubt whether he was not a convert." Origen § thinks it "needless to produce Egyptian, Phœnician, or Grecian testimonies, since any one may read them by consulting Josephus' works, where is a long catalogue of authors, who confirm the truth of this matter by their concurrent testimonies." The perusal of "Tatian's learned discourse against the Pagans" is recommended on the same grounds, as containing

* *Octav.* c. 34.
† *Cont. Cels.* Lib. I. s. 14.
‡ *Ib.* s. 15.
Ib. s. 16.

an abundance of references to the ancients who have written respecting the Jews in general, and Moses in particular.

The Epicurean Philosopher* having further charged the Israelites with borrowing the right of circumcision from the Egyptians, our author points out that Moses attributes its origin to Abraham, whose great antiquity as well as identity he proves, by citing the formularies of Egyptian magicians, in reference to the God of Abraham.

He thinks† it strange that a man of so much reading as Celsus professes to be, should omit to notice Moses among his worthies, though many of the Grecian writers themselves place him about the time of Inachus (the father of Phoroneus), whom the Egyptian and Phœnician authors declare to be the most ancient chief recorded in their histories.

Respecting the tower of Babel and the confusion of tongues,‡ Celsus throws out an insinuation, that the Scripture account is but a version of the story of the Aloidæ. Origen replies, that no mention is made of the sons of Aloeus prior to the time of Homer, but that *our* account of these things was written by Moses, who not only preceded Homer, but also the invention of the Greek letters.

Phaethon's fable is disposed of in the same way, and its writers are shown to have been as much posterior to Homer, as Homer was to Moses. It is likewise observed § that the Hebrew genealogy was never disputed for many ages.

Again,‖ to Celsus' bold assertion, that the Christian doctrines concerning the Evil Spirit, are extracted from Heraclitus and Pherecydes, and that others relating to heaven, are but expansions of Homer's "isles of the blessed," and "the Elysian fields," or of Plato's "pure earth under a pure sky," Origen as boldly opposes the historical fact, that Moses had declared these truths long before either of the above-named authors was born.

* *Cont. Cels.* Lib. I. s. 22. † *Ib.* Lib. IV. s. 11. ‡ *Ib.* s. 21.
§ *Ib.* s. 35. ‖ *Ib.* Lib. VII. s. 28.

Upon the whole, he conceives* that if an opinion is beneficial, and the intention of the projector good, it can matter little whether it arose among the Jews or the Greeks, only it must be remembered that the former have the fairest claim to originality because their writings are the oldest.

LACTANTIUS.† "I must say a few words about the prophets whose testimony is now about to be used, which I have refrained from doing in my former books. Before all things, he who would understand the voices of the prophets, must diligently inquire not only into the animus that prompted them, but also into their times. This is requisite in order to an appreciation of the fulfilment of their predictions; nor is there any difficulty in collating these dates. It is well known under what kings they prophesied; and many persons have written works on the sacred chronology, commencing with Moses who preceded the Trojan war at least seven hundred years." Our author then gives a sketch of the judges and kings of Israel, confirming his statements by reference to Jewish, Greek, and Roman authorities; pointing out in passing, the eras of the several prophets down to Zacharias, whom he calls the last, and places in the second year and eighth month of the reign of Darius; and concludes by stating, that the "fact of the prophets being proved more ancient than the Greek writers, should serve to convince those of their error, who endeavor to disparage the Sacred Scriptures, as if they were but lately penned."

EUSEBIUS ‡ institutes a comparison between the Hebrews and the notable men of Greece and Rome, and invokes history to attest the superior antiquity of the schools of the prophets, over those of the Academy, the Lyceum, or the

* *Cont. Cels.* Lib. VII. s. 59. † *Div. Instit.* Lib. IV. c. 5.
‡ *Præp. Evang.*

Portico. He argues that the ancient Hebrews, of whatever rank or sex, walked in the light of divine wisdom during many centuries in which the rest of the world lay in the deepest barbarism: that the science of the Greeks is wholly borrowed from extraneous sources; that its earliest teachers were foreigners by birth, and that their successors with ingenious subtlety perfected the stolen knowledge; in brief, that Plato was an Attic imitator of Moses. In comparing the discipline and institutions of these great rival leaders, he points out such a resemblance between them, as he thinks could not have been the result of accident, but of a deep and well adjusted imitation.* He farther † shows that Pythagoras borrowed from Moses.

AUGUSTINE ‡ traces some of Plato's ideas to his reading the prophetic books during his sojourn in Egypt, or to the light of his own conscience. He refers to remarks on this subject, made by Justin, Clemens, Eusebius, Ambrose, and Lactantius; and then § takes up the progress of the earthly state, through the respective epochs of Assyrian and Egyptian history, corresponding to the times of Abraham, Moses, &c. He next ‖ proposes to prove that the prophets were more ancient than the Gentile philosophers. "In *our* prophets' time," he says, (he has just run through their works) "there were no philosophers stirring as yet. The first being Pythagoras the Samian, who flourished at the end of the captivity, so that all others must needs be later than that event. Socrates, the chief of the moralists, lived after Esdras, as chronicles record; and immediately after him came Plato and his scholars; and if the seven sages of Greece and the physical philosophers who succeeded Thales, viz., Anaximander, Anaximenes, Anaxagoras, and others

* Vid. Street's *Leaves of Eusebius*. † *Const. Vit.* c. 17.
‡ *De Civit. Dei*, Lib. VIII. c. 11. § *Ib.* Lib. XVIII. c. 2–5. ‖ *Ib.* c. 37.

who professed philosophy before Pythagoras, are added, we shall still find that not one of these was anterior to the prophets. For Thales, the oldest of them all, was only coeval with Romulus, who flourished long after the stream of prophecy had been flowing from the fountains of Israel. The theological poets therefore alone remain to be considered, as Orpheus, Linus, Musæus, and others (if any) who can be called prior to the canonical prophets. But not even they were as ancient as our divine Moses, who taught them concerning the one true God, and whose books appear at the head of our Scripture. Wherefore though the learning of Greece warms the world to this day, yet it cannot be boasted that it is as excellent as ours. We allow indeed not that the Greeks, but that some other nations, may have had peculiar doctrines, before the time of Moses, or it would not have been said, for example, that he was learned in all the wisdom of the Egyptians, but at the same time I would have it remembered that even the wisdom of these men was posterior in point of time to our prophet Abraham. For we find that Isis, the reputed goddess of Egypt, taught her people letters. But this Isis was the daughter of Inachus, king of Argos, who reigned in the time of Abraham's grandchildren."

CHAPTER III.

THE ARGUMENT FROM PROPHECY.

Who spake by the Prophets.

NICENE CREED.

WHILST it would be quite out of place here, to furnish abstract discussions on the various methods of reasoning adopted by the Fathers, it certainly seems proper to define and occasionally explain terms, or to harmonize an ancient with a modern sense. Such explanations, however, should be brief.

The object of prophecy is to exhibit a superhuman knowledge of the future. We have been considering in the last chapter how far Christianity answers to an ordeal as regards the past: we have now to apply a yet stronger test of divinity. It has to look *forward* as well as backward.

An essential relation to the future is *the* great characteristic of prophecy; that which distinguishes it from other knowledge and other miracles. And this definition seems necessarily to include the idea of an extra-human source: for what can any but God, know of the future? "Of all knowledge this is that which man has the greatest desire and the least ability to attain to."* We may surmise and judge with some confidence, but all is alike speculative; especially in regard to remote regions of time, whose distinctness seems to decrease incal-

* Horne's *Introduction*.

culably with the distance. "Such then being the contingency, and our ignorance of what concurs to produce any event, we may be sure that certain and infallible predictions are of heaven and not of earth; and therefore by what means we are assured of a prophecy, by the same are we assured of its divinity."*

Of the value of such an argument in any age of the Church there can be no doubt; but it derived additional virtue from certain circumstances of the parties we are concerned with. I cannot illustrate this better, than by referring to a question often mooted as to the comparative worth of the prophetical argument. In no case can comparisons be so odious as in sacred things; and yet they have been made. The different evidences of religion have been arrayed one against the other, in different ages, and in consequence of the partial views of men. *Here*, prophecies have been preferred, owing to a misinterpretation† of the text, "We also have a more sure word of prophecy;" *there*, miracles especially of late, have been estimated out of all due proportion, so that the judgment of the Apostles as well as of the Apologists, not to say the truth of the Gospel itself, has been called in question, because of the less exaggerated importance that was anciently attached to them.‡

But without troubling ourselves with the propriety or merits of such a discussion at all, we hasten to make use of an explanation to which it gives rise. The Fathers, in offering a reason for not availing themselves of the evidence of miracles so much as they might and would have done, inform us of two opinions of their day. First, the universal belief in magic or demoniacal agency, by which the force of miracles

* Pearson *On the Creed*.

† An Exposition, says Sherlock, which all commentators reject as contradictory to the general sense of mankind on this point, and inconsistent with other places of Scripture.

‡ Paley's *Evidences*, Part III. c. 5.

was weakened, and a doubt cast upon their origin. This will be noticed more at large in the next chapter. At present we need only observe, that in refutation of this notion, Justin Martyr, Irenæus, and Lactantius appeal to the prophecies of the Old Testament, showing how improbable it was that those deeds should be performed by magic, which had been foretold, ages before, by God himself.* Secondly, the belief quite as universal among the heathen, that the prophetic spirit was a sure sign of divinity. This is the opinion to which I would now call attention, as preparing the way for the testimony of the prophets.

The reverence which the Gentile world have ever attached to prophecy, is abundantly manifested in their literature and practices. Justin Martyr, addressing the Emperor Adrian and his sons, hesitates not to say, "I suppose your majesties will concede that those who prophesy, are inspired by nothing else than the divine word." And Origen tells Celsus, that "even the Greeks confess it is a God who speaks by the mouth of the Pythian priestess." The fact also of ten oracular sites in Greece alone, each claiming the inspiration of a god, and proving their popularity by enormous revenues, speaks for itself. The heathen therefore could hardly refuse to listen to the Hebrew oracles, and, if they were shown to be verified, even to recognize their divine source.

The case was yet stronger when this evidence was turned towards the Jew; and I need hardly remark, that it constituted the *point* of the controversy with him in the first centuries, as it continues to do in our own. Here the child of Abraham was at home; himself deeply involved and interested. He with the Pagan acknowledged the Divine source of all prescience, but more than that, he firmly believed in the authenticity, and bowed to the authority, of the particular afflatus in question. The whole ground was common to

* Palmer, *On Development and Consc.* c. 1.

the Christian and himself; the only dispute was as to accomplishment and other matters of fact.

Another value of prophecy occasionally noted by the Apologists, is that of its being present and growing evidence. So Justin Martyr:* "In prophecy there is this advantage to us over miracles, that while we have to depend on testimony for any knowledge of the latter, the fulfilments of the former are taking place daily under our own eyes." Eusebius has the same idea.†

The purposes to which the Fathers turned the witness of prophecy were, to establish the doctrine of our Saviour's divinity, and all that is dependent upon it, against either Jew or Gentile, and at the same time to disprove the blasphemous pretensions of other claimants. Justin says, "We are not like those who compose fables concerning the supposititious sons of Jupiter, asserting what they cannot prove; for how should we believe of Him that was crucified, that he was the first-born of the unbegotten God, and will himself one day be the judge of all the human race, unless we found testimonies of these things, delivered before he became incarnate, and saw also that they so came to pass?" Next, to argue from what is a matter of fulfilled to what is a matter of unfulfilled prediction; such as the general resurrection, final judgment, &c. Thus Theophilus:‡ "Once I believed not in the resurrection of the body, but now I believe, after having more attentively considered these things in connection with the accomplishment of prophecy." Lastly, to confirm and console themselves in the truth.

There is one subject under this argument demanding a particular notice here. Some of the Apologists (Lactantius especially) appeal not only to the oracles of the Old and New Testament, but also occasionally to the sibyls and other legendary authorities. Neander considers it a sound and healthy

* *Apol.* I. c. 37. † *Theoph.* Bk. IV. s. 1. ‡ *Ad Autol.* Lib. I. c. 14.

feeling that induced this assumption of a prophetic spirit in Paganism as well as in Judaism, and this appeal to it, after the manner of St. Paul at Athens, when he appealed to the sentiments of the poets concerning the unknown God. He laments, however, that, owing to the want of critical skill among the early Christian writers, they should have been imposed upon by spurious and interpolated matter, which presented itself in the search after ancient testimonies; such as "the writings passing under the name of that mythic person of antiquity, the Grecian Hermes, or the Egyptian Thoth; also under the name of the Persian Hystaspes, and of the sibyls." These general statements need a little qualification. That some of the Fathers were actually deceived by the theory of demons possessing the power and abetting the practice of oracular deception, no careful reader of their works can doubt; but that *as a body* they were so deceived, or attributed to Paganism any reality of prophetical power, can never be shown. In fact, Neander himself subsequently says, "it is far more probable to suppose that they revolted *à priori* at the very hypothesis of anything like prophetical power having existed among the heathen:"* wherefore we have Theophilus telling Autolychus that "the prophets of the Egyptians and Chaldeans furnish us with no evidences of truth."

Nor, on the other hand, is there any sort of proof, that disbelieving this profane delusion, the Apologists yet employed it for the purpose of intentional deceit. They took what they found at its reputed valuation. Finding that such ideas influenced the minds of their heathen auditory, they used them as an *argumentum ad hominem:* but while they did this, they did not attempt to conceal their own convictions. Hear Origen, for example; after quoting a response of the oracle to Laius, he says, "By the way, I shall here take it for granted

* Neander's *Church History.*

that the oracle was true, since I think I may make the supposition without the least prejudice to the subject in hand."*

One reason for this partial concession may be surmised, viz., that our Apologists feared to disturb the accepted rules for the admission of evidence, lest in denying the authenticity of pagan authorities, they should excite an equivalent prejudice against their own.

But after all, the apologetic allusions of this kind are but rare, and these rather appendages than anything else. With this explanation, and considering that the materials referred to, are of still less interest now, I am sure I shall be pardoned for omitting them in the substance of my proofs.

The only subdivision it has been thought advisable to make in this chapter, is that between the portions of evidence from prophecy, which are addressed to the Gentile and Jew, at least as nearly as it could be done. The purpose of this, is, to exhibit the different methods of pressing the argument upon the attention of these respective parties; and so to account for some matter which otherwise might appear elementary or superfluous. Thus we find the Gentile alone presented with a glance at the Old Testament history; because with him, it was the part of an Apologist's business to show the probable authenticity, &c., of the prophetical books; or with an account of the Septuagint translation, to prove that the prophecies were delivered before the events they predicted, a premise the Jew would readily allow; or with a reference to any profane authority a Pagan might value: whilst towards the Jew, there is too often manifested a kind of bitter spirit, that cannot be justified at all, but which would appear yet more inappropriate than it is, if supposed to be indulged in towards the heathen. This separation will serve likewise to show that the preponderance of matter, and so of weight, attached to the evidence of prophecy over that of miracles, is

* Origen, *Cont. Cels.* Lib. II. c. 20.

not so great (with regard to the *Pagan* controversy at least) as has been supposed.

The extracts I have to offer, will be found to embrace, first, predictions concerning the Messiah, the time of his advent, the place and manner of his birth, his miracles, life, death, resurrection, &c.; and secondly, those uttered by himself with regard to the destruction of Jerusalem, the final spread of the Gospel, &c.

I beg to suggest whether our authors, when they occasionally omit to point out the accomplishment of a prophecy, do not take it for granted, as being sufficiently notorious.

SECTION I.

ARGUMENT FROM PROPHECY ADDRESSED TO THE GENTILE.

JUSTIN MARTYR.* "Our teacher, the Son and Apostle of God the Father, even Jesus Christ, from whom also we have obtained the name of Christians, has forewarned us of these persecutions. Wherefore we cleave steadfastly to all things which were taught of him, since whatsoever he before declared should happen, hath indeed been fulfilled. For this is the work of God only, to declare events before they happen, and manifestly to bring them to pass even as they were predicted."

"There were† among the Jews certain men, prophets of God, by whom the prophetic Spirit proclaimed future events before they came to pass. And the kings who were over the Jews in those days, possessed and preserved with great care the predictions of these men, as they were first delivered in

* *Apol.* x. c. 14. † *Ib.* c. 38.

books composed by the prophets themselves, in the Hebrew tongue. These were translated by order of Ptolemy into Greek, and this being done, the books have remained with the Egyptians to this day, and are also to be met with in the hands of the Jews in every place. Now* in these books of the prophets we find it predicted, that Jesus our Christ should come, should be born of a virgin, and be made man; that he should heal every disease, and all manner of sickness, and raise the dead; that he should be enviously treated and not be known; that he should be crucified and die, and rise again and ascend into heaven; that he should be the Son of God, and so be called; that some should be sent by him to preach these things to every nation of mankind, and that men of the Gentiles should especially believe on him. Some of these prophecies respecting him were delivered five thousand years before his appearance, some three thousand, some two, and some one, and some eight hundred years; for in the course of successive generations different prophets succeeded one another." Our author† then enters into details, quoting and applying particular predictions. He shows how that of Jacob, "A prince shall not fail from Judah, nor a ruler from between his feet, until he shall come for whom it is reserved," was completed "by the Romans having possession of Judæa ever since Christ came, who has also become actually the expectation of the Gentiles, some out of all nations looking to him." He quotes‡ and points out the fulfilment of the predictions, of the star by Balaam; of the virgin mother by Isaiah;§ of the place of nativity by Micah,‖ and of the circumstances attending the crucifixion by David,¶ contained in the texts, "they pierced my hands and my feet, and cast lots for my vesture." "That these things were accomplished," says he, "you may learn from the records of what took

* *Apol.* I. c. 39. † *Ib.* c. 40. ‡ *Ib.* c. 42. § *Ib.* c. 43.
‖ *Ib.* c. 44. ¶ *Ib.* c. 45.

place under Pontius Pilate." Other predictions* then follow from Isaiah and the Psalms, chiefly relating to the unbelief and malice of the Jews, to the progress of the Gospel, and to the general amelioration of the state of mankind. In confirmation of the last point, he adds, "Wherefore we who formerly killed one another, now refuse not only to fight our enemies, but are ready to meet death with cheerfulness, confessing Christ rather than lie and deceive those who persecute us."

He recognizes† in the agreement of Herod, Pilate and the chief priests, at the trial of Jesus, the application of the verse, "The kings of the earth stood up, and the rulers were gathered together against the Lord, and against his anointed." "That Jerusalem‡ is laid waste," he reminds the heathen, "according to prediction, ye have good proof, for ye yourselves have forbidden any Jew to dwell therein, denouncing the punishment of death, against those who shall disobey."

The rejection§ of the Jew and the calling of the Gentile, are seen to be completed in the evil entreating of Jesus by the former, and in the joyful trust placed in Him by the latter, together with their renunciation of idols. The result‖ is, he thinks, that "what has now been so fully seen, is sufficient to cause a reasonable belief and persuasion in those that love the truth, and are not vainglorious nor governed by their passions; whereas they who teach the mythology of the poets, offer no proof to their disciples." The same idea, to show the rational grounds of Christian faith, and the want of evidence in Paganism, occurs elsewhere¶.

THEOPHILUS.** "When therefore those things that were predicted happen, they demonstrate the truth to me, and I am no longer incredulous, but believe, complying with God.

* *Apol.* I. c. 47. † *Ib.* c. 51. ‡ *Ib.* c. 62. § *Ib.* c. 63.
‖ *Ib.* c. 70. ¶ c. 68. ** *Ad Autol.* Lib. I. c. 14.

Believe thou also, lest thou hast to believe when stung with eternal torments."

Our author* contrasts the uncertain and fallacious inspiration of the heathen poets, with the manner and effects of that which filled the prophets of God. He observes first, that the latter were holy and just men, and, as it were, worthier of such an honorable distinction; in the next place, the wars, the famines, the pestilences they predicted, did not occur once or twice only, but at various times among the Hebrews. Thirdly, they always spoke in harmony with one another; and in the last place, "their revelations related to all times; some to things done before they lived, or during their life, and some to what has happened in our own times, or will happen hereafter."

Commenting† on the Biblical account of the Fall, he asks, "Is it not right to consider those sorrows which women suffer in parturition, and their subsequent joy, together with the condemnation and degradation of the serpent, as evident fulfilments of God's threatenings, so that by this argument the truth of what we said is confirmed?"

CLEMENS ALEXANDRINUS,‡ in describing the true Gnostic, says incidentally, "one of the evidences for the divinity of our Saviour is the prophecy that preceded his appearance:" and, speaking of the prophets, he alludes to those among the heathen who pretended to the spirit of prophecy, remarking that the latter foretold future events either from observation and probable conjecture, as physicians and fortune-tellers judge by the countenance, or from the instruction of demons when under the influence of some inhalation or drug; but that the former foretold events by the power and influence of the Spirit of God.

* *Ad Autol.* Lib. II. c. 9. † *Ib.* c. 23. ‡ *Strom.* Lib. II.

TERTULLIAN* shows how the accomplishment of prophecy in the Holy Scriptures, proves them to be of divine authority; "and thus," says he, "their majesty and authority can be established, as well as their antiquity. The grounds of this proof are obvious in the history of all periods; whatever is now done, was foretold; earthquakes, floods, wars, famines, pestilences, changes in the social order of men, monsters, prodigies, all have been predicted by God. While we suffer calamities, we read of them, and when we recognize the objects of prophecy, the Scripture that predicts them is proved. The daily fulfilment of prophecy is surely a full proof of Revelation, and hence we have a well-grounded belief of things yet to come to pass. There are† the Jews, dispersed and vagabond, wandering like exiles from their native soil throughout the whole world, without either man or God for their King, and not permitted even as strangers to set foot upon their own land. Now all the sacred Scriptures with one voice foretold that such would be their condition, and that in the last days, God would gather together a more faithful people for himself."

ORIGEN.‡ "We hesitate not to say that it implies a knowledge more than human, to have taught as Christ did, with the utmost confidence, that his doctrine would be opposed, but never overcome, speaking thus to his disciples: "Ye shall be brought before kings and councils for my name's sake, for a testimony to them and to the Gentiles:" and again, "in my name shall you cast out devils." Now if such things as these had been accidentally pronounced, they might have taken place without exciting much wonder; but when we find that they were uttered with authority and distinctness, and then came to pass with the greatest exactness, it is clear that God alone caused the whole of this doctrine of

* *Apol.* c. 20. † *Ib.* c. 21. ‡ *De Princip.* Lib. IV. s. 2.

salvation to be delivered. Our author then proceeds* to quote the prophecy of Jacob (Gen. xlix.), and insists, upon the authority of history, that since the time of Christ, there has been no king of the Jews, but that all their affairs have lain in disorder; whilst the destruction of their temple, their priesthood, and their sacrifices, has served to exemplify another prediction (Hosea iii. 4). It is further observed, that the Jews to this day anticipate a Messiah in consequence of the promise through Jacob; and it is considered marvellous that they should not perceive its due accomplishment already, together with those relating to their own punishment and dispersion, and the calling of the Gentiles; the last being clearly established, in the multitudes of people, who believe in God through Christ.

It appears† that in the third book of *his* work, Celsus had thrown aside his Jewish disguise, and assumed the more natural character of an Epicurean sophist. Origen, following the track of his adversary, commences the third book with a particular reference to heathen objections. In reply to a profane jest, he endeavors to prove that the religion he professes is something more than a shadow. For this purpose he takes up the prophets one by one, and points out how they indicate the exact place and time of our Saviour's birth, the signs and wonders he performed, and notify his death and rising again, and the universal extension of his Gospel. He asks why the prophets should have thought these cogitations of theirs worthy of record, and how they happened to have been preserved with such care, especially by a people who frequently discriminated true and false prophets; adding,‡ that it is not only by the prophets that the incarnation is to be proved, but also by the Gospels and Epistles which have been carefully handed down to us.

* *De Princip.* Lib. IV. s. 3.

† *Cont. Cels.* Lib. III. s. 1, 2.

‡ *Ib.* s. 15.

Again,* "the testimony of the great God and his holy messengers, as well before as after the advent of Jesus, ought to satisfy men; for that he was announced, the Jews themselves are witnesses, who were awaiting the Messiah just at the time he came, and indeed were divided into two parties in consequence. The Christians† only go a little farther than the Jews, and believe that he who was to come, is come."

He remarks,‡ in demonstrating the genuineness of the prophets, that "passages out of them" are to be found in the works of Numenius the Pythagorean, (together with a notice of Moses in connection with Jannes and Jambres,) as also in other books; see, for example,§ "the dispute of Papiscus and Jason,"‖ in which the Christian has clearly shown, from the Jewish Scriptures, that the prophecies appertain to Jesus, though his adversary strenuously contradicts him and well sustains his own cause.

Finally,¶ "It is an essential mark of Divinity to foretell future events, so that the reason of the prediction should exceed human ability, and the event decide whether its author really has the Spirit (of God). But** Jesus is the only person whose appearance and influence throughout the world, as the Son of God, have been matters of prediction. Simon Magus, though once called the Great, has no followers now. Dositheanus, who claimed to be the Son of God, has scarce thirty of his sect left; and the like may be said of Judas Galileus and Theudas (Acts v. 35–37)! We have not therefore to choose between sons of God, as Celsus insinuates."

* *Cont. Cels.* Lib. III. s. 28. † *Ib.* Lib. IV. 4. s. 2. ‡ *Ib.* s. 51.

§ *Ib.* s. 52.

‖ This work is also quoted by Jerome (Lardner II. p. 310). It is ascribed to Aristo of Pella, in Hadrian's reign.

¶ *Cont. Cels.* Lib. VI. s. 10. ** *Ib.* s. 11.

LACTANTIUS* proves that the passion and death of Christ were foretold by the prophets, quoting Isaiah l. 5, 6, on the sufferings and silence of our Lord; Psalms xxxv. and lxix. on the cruelty of the Jews, particularly in offering the vinegar; and Moses, in Deut. xxviii. 65, and Numb. xxiii. 19; with Zech. xii. 10, and Amos viii. 9, 10, on the Jewish troubles, &c. "Nor," says he, "were these things spoken in vain; for in no long time after (the death of Jesus), the Emperor Vespasian made war upon the Jews, and having devastated their land, and subdued Jerusalem by famine, he completely overturned it, and led some of its inhabitants away captive, while he interdicted the rest from ever setting foot again on their native soil. These things were done by God, on account of that cross of Christ, as Solomon had testified in his dedication of the temple." (2 Chron. vii. 21, 22.)

He then† proceeds to illustrate the fulfilment of Psalm xvi. 9, 10, and of Hosea vi. 2, and xiii. 14, from the evangelistic account of the resurrection of Christ. Illustrative of the ascension, Daniel vii. 13, and Psalm cx. 1, are quoted; and of the disinheriting the Jews, &c. Jer. xii. 8; Malachi i. 11; Isaiah xlii. 6, 7, and lxvi. 18.

The inference is,‡ "When all these things were predicted by the unanimous voice of the prophets, it can no longer be doubted but that all hope, and life, and salvation, are to be found alone in the religion of our God."

Our author§ explains the opening of the Scriptures to the disciples on their way to Emmaus, as meaning the revelation of those prophecies which had not before been perceived, announcing the passion itself; and which he thinks, as part of a Testament, could not be known until the death of the testator.

* *Epit.* c. 46. † *Ib.* c. 47. ‡ *Ib.* c. 73.

§ *Div. Inst.* Lib. IV. c. 30.

EUSEBIUS* asks, "Who of those that taught in ancient times became known, established, and declared by the announcement of prophets many ages ago? Who declared in writing, the place, the time, and manner of his birth; the power, the words, the deeds of his life? Observe, likewise,† the execution of vengeance upon the Jews — their temple and their sacred institutions being destroyed in consequence of their wickedness. This Christ had foretold, as also the establishment of his own church. On the one hand,‡ hear him saying, 'your house is left unto you desolate,' 'nor shall stone remain upon stone in this place, that shall not be thrown down;' and on the other, 'upon this rock will I build my Church, and the gates of hell shall not prevail against it.' Notice § particularly his foretelling the disciples that he would make those who had been fishermen, teachers of all nations; and that they should come before kings and governors, and be punished, and undergo grievous torments. Let any one,‖ therefore, who will take up the true faith, together with the proof of the revelation of our Saviour's divinity, judge from the fact that he openly foretold the spreading of his doctrine throughout the world, as also that he himself would accomplish it; and then, on such a foundation as this, let him place faith in the other promises (of Christ)."

In the parables¶ of the husbandman and of the marriage feast, are recognized the announcements of the rejection of the Jews; Matt. xxiii. 37, and Luke xiii. 34, being cited on the destruction of Jerusalem. "And just as the prediction was," our author adds, "so are the results. The whole temple and the beautiful buildings within its precincts, remain desolate from that time to this, whilst its inhabitants wander about in lands not their own, without a prince and without a nationality." He points** out how various minutiæ connected

* *Theoph.* Lib. III. c. 25. † *Ib.* c. 26. ‡ *Ib.* c. 27. § *Ib.* c. 28.
‖ *Ib.* c. 41. ¶ Lib. IV. c. 3-15. ** *Ib.* c. 19.

with the siege of Jerusalem, hinted at in Luke xix. 41, &c., xxii. 20, &c., were literally fulfilled. This is done on the authority of Josephus, himself a Jew, who mentions "the distresses and straits, the famine and flight of the people, in his sixth book; and we ourselves know how truly they are scattered still, and their city, newly called Elia, supplied with inhabitants from foreign places."

It is next* shown, that according to prediction, the Gentiles were to be first moved by Jewish teaching, which is found realized in the fact, that beginning with James, there were fifteen Jewish bishops of Jerusalem, who had been the means of establishing a Church of many thousands of Gentiles, as well as of their own countrymen, at the time of the desolation in the reign of Hadrian: Peter also, it is remarked in this connection, was a Jew.

Our author then† dwells with astonishment upon the words "For my sake," Matth. x. 18. His comment runs, "It was not enough that Christ should know and forewarn of persecution, but he would also name the very cause; and in truth it was so, for not on account of any evil practice, nor for any other reason, but as he had previously testified, every affliction should befall them 'for his sake.' The Christians suffered only for confessing the name of Christ. Never did any teacher previously determine such specialities as these.‡ And all these proofs of the divine manifestation of our Saviour, are also demonstrative that both his doctrine and deeds were divine."§

The emperor Constantine is introduced‖ saying, that "the coming of Christ was predicted by the prophets, to be the overthrow of idols and of idolatrous cities. Assyria and

* *Theoph.* Lib. IV. c. 24. † *Ib.* Lib. III. c. 26. ‡ *Ib.* c. 37.

§ Several prophecies on the Advent, apostolic labors, fall of Jerusalem, &c., will be seen in Origen's *Philocalia*, c. 1, Ed. Spencer, and in *Dem. Ev. Vide* Prof. Lee's note.

‖ *Constant. Orat.* c. 16.

Egypt were full of such places; in which even human sacrifices were offered up to images of brass and clay. Wherefore these nations have received a recompense worthy so foul a worship. Memphis and Babylon, it was declared, should be wasted, and I myself have been an eye-witness of their ruin."

GREGORY NAZIANZEN* states, that out of hatred to the Christians, Julian had permitted the Jews to attempt the rebuilding of the temple; but that they were prevented from carrying it on, by miraculous interference. This was all in fulfilment of prophecy.

CHRYSOSTOM† observes that the establishment of the Gospel, was not a matter of chance, but of clear prophecy; and in order that the predictions might not be suspected, we receive them through the Jews themselves who crucified Christ, so that it is from the testimony of our enemies taken from the books they themselves preserve, that we draw this truth.

AUGUSTINE,‡ in his progress of the heavenly state, comes down to the eras of the prophets. He first alludes to the temporal promises to the Jews, literally fulfilled in the land of Canaan, and then passes on§ to the times of Samuel and Eli, noticing the various predictions, with their accomplishments, which distinguished each period. Advancing yet farther, he takes the predictions relating to the Messiah; shows‖ that the promises to David were not fulfilled in Solomon, but in Jesus; and points out¶ the prophecies in Psalms xxxix., xlix., l., li., the tropes and figures** in Psalm xli. concerning Christ and his Church, with references†† to his priest-

* *Orat. adv. Jul.* c. 3, 4.
† *On the Divinity of Christ.*
‡ *De Civit. Dei*, Lib. XVII. c. 1.
§ *Ib.* c. 5.
‖ *Ib.* c. 12.
¶ *Ib.* c. 16.
** *Ib.* c. 17.
†† *Ib.* c. 18.

hood in Psalm cx., and to his passion in Psalm xxii. Our Lord's resurrection is found* plainly set forth in Psalms iii., xvi., xli., lxviii.; and the obstinate infidelity of the Jews, in Psalm lxix. Having descended to† the prophets at the period of the decline of the Assyrian empire, he traces the predictions of the Gospel, in Hosea and Amos; of Christ and his people,‡ in Isaiah liii. 1–12, and liv. 1–5; others concerning the world's salvation by Christ,§ as furnished by Micah iv. 1–3, by Jonah ii. 1, by Joel ii. 28, 29, by Obadiah, Nahum, Habakkuk; and what Jeremiah, Zephaniah, Daniel, Ezekiel, Haggai, Zechariah and Malachi have foretold of Christ, of the calling of the Gentiles, and of the permanency of the Church. He says,‖ that whilst the Jews refuse to credit *our* Scriptures, their own are being fulfilled on themselves. "The leaves of the sibyls¶ may be doubtful, but here we have books preserved by our very enemies the Jews, and that too, it would seem, against their own wills; and dispersed as far as the Church of God extends, even to the remote corners of the earth, just as the Psalm (lix. 10, 11) which they themselves read, foretells."—And in this appears one reason for the dispersion of the ancient people of God, that they might be a witness coëxtensive with the Gospel, concerning their own prophets, who prophesy of Christ.

In the 20th book of the *City of God*, Augustine makes use of the prophets, whose veracity he has thus established, to prove a day of judgment and a future state.

* *De Civit. Dei*, Lib. XVII. c. 19. † *Ib.* Lib. XVIII. c. 28.
‡ *Ib.* c. 29. § *Ib.* c. 30–35. ‖ *Ib.* c. 46.
¶ Augustine had referred in the twenty-third chapter of this book, to the oracle of Sibylla Erythræa, concerning Christ, citing Lactantius' previous allusion to the same.

SECTION II.

ARGUMENT FROM PROPHECY ADDRESSED TO THE JEW.

Justin Martyr* commences his dialogue with Trypho, by premising, "that from those things which Jesus foretold were to happen to them that should believe and confess him to be the Christ, we are sure that he did know what would come to pass after his departure out of the world; for instance, the sufferings of Christians,"&c. It is then† remarked that Psalm xc. cannot be interpreted of Hezekiah, nor Psalm lxxii. of Solomon: it is also proved, that Christ was called the Lord of Hosts, and ought to be worshipped, according to David. Our author next‡ shows how the types of the law prefigured Christ alone; how John was his forerunner,§ in fulfilment of the prophecies of Isaiah xxxix. and xl.; how he was born‖ of the tribe of Judah, after the promise of Jacob (Gen. xlix.); and how he entered Jerusalem¶ in humble triumph according to Zechariah. He then** observes, that there are more persons in the Godhead than the Father, is evident from†† Abraham's communion with the angel called the Lord; from Jacob's visions; and from‡‡ Moses' wonderful interview at the bush, even upon the Jews' own showing; also§§ that the Wisdom or Logos must be a person, even he who was recognized in the creation of man. This person, or God, is proved in conclusion to have been promised in the flesh by the prophets, and particularly to be born of a virgin, which thing was accomplished in our Christ alone.

Our author‖‖ reminds Trypho, that the very cross which is such a stumbling-block to him on account of the curse

* *Dial. cum Tryph.* s. 33–35. † *Ib.* s. 36–38. ‡ *Ib.* s. 40.
§ *Ib.* s. 50. ‖ *Ib.* s. 52. ¶ *Ib.* s. 53.
** *Ib.* s. 56. †† *Ib.* s. 58. ‡‡ *Ib.* s. 59.
§§ *Ib.* s. 61. ‖‖ *Ib.* s. 89.

attached to it, alone proves that Jesus is the Christ, cursed for us, because crucified for us. He finds hints of the Cross in the Old Testament, as the spreading of Moses' hands, the brazen serpent, &c.

The several incidents* connected with the death and burial of Jesus, are brought into view, as matter of prophecy in Psalm xxii., and as realizations in the Gospels; thus, the piercing the hands and the feet, the withdrawal of God's countenance, the parting of the raiment, the resurrection; the last being also foreshadowed† in the history of Jonah. Lastly, the conversion of the Gentiles,‡ quoted from Micah, is shown to be in part accomplished already, in the spread of Christianity; and a consideration of the whole subject,§ should warn the Jews "not to speak evil of Him who was crucified for them, nor to laugh at His stripes by which all may be healed, as we have been healed. For it would be well for you, if you would assent to the Scriptures and receive the circumcision of the hardness of your heart; not that which you have such an opinion of and fondness for, which was given for a sign, and not for a work of righteousness, as the Scriptures evidently declare."

TERTULLIAN first shows‖ how God promised to Abraham that in his seed should all the families of the earth be blessed; and that he should be the father of two nations, the Jews and the Gentiles. He next¶ explains the true nature of the sabbath, of circumcision,** of sacrifices and offerings; and points†† out where the prophets foretold that the old law would cease in favor of a new law, at the coming of Christ and His kingdom. This latter point‡‡ our author thinks is "clearly seen accomplished in the extension of Christianity among the Moors, the Spaniards, the Gauls, the Britons, the

* *Dial. cum Tryph.* s. 97-99. † *Ib.* s. 107. ‡ *Ib.* s. 109, 110, 130.
§ *Ib.* s. 137. ‖ *Adv. Jud.* s. 1. ¶ *Ib.* s. 3, 4. ** *Ib.* s. 5.
†† *Ib.* s. 6. ‡‡ *Ib.* s. 7.

Samaritans, the Germans, and Scythians, with other nations, isles and provinces, too numerous to name."

Then* follow the predictions of the birth and passion of our Lord, and of the destruction of Jerusalem, taken† from Daniel ix. (the weeks are applied historically;) from Isaiah xii.; Zech. xiv. 14, (the magi); and Psalm lxxi. &c., all of which have received their confirmation in the Gospel.

On the subject‡ of our Lord's sufferings and death, he adduces Isaiah lviii. 1, and xxxv. 5; Deut. xxi. 23; and Psalms xxiv., lxviii., and xxi.

In Ezekiel he discerns § the fate of the Jew, and ‖ in Psalm ii. 7, and Isaiah xlix. 6, the calling and healing of the nations; and finally,¶ discriminates the two advents, one in humility and the other in glory, as foretold by the prophets.

HIPPOLYTUS,** addressing the Jews, bids them lend their ear; "You often boast," says he, "in that you have condemned Jesus of Nazareth, and because you gave him vinegar and gall to drink. Let us consider whether this is a just boast, or whether that little drop of vinegar and gall has not brought upon you the most terrible denunciations and calamities." To establish†† this, he cites David, "who predicted the true Christ, and sang praises to our God through the Holy Spirit. This man clearly announced all those things that were done by the Jews at the passion of Christ, when he humbled himself and took upon him the form of his servant, Adam. In one of the Psalms, Christ is heard, as though in our stead, invoking his heavenly Father thus: 'The waters have come in unto my soul; I sink in the mire.... For thy sake I have endured hatred (that is, the cross) .... therefore thou wilt not suffer my body to see corruption,' (that is, in the sepulchre.) And again, complaining of the desertion of his disciples: 'I looked for some to comfort, and found

* *Adv. Jud.* s. 8. † *Ib.* s. 9. ‡ *Ib.* s. 10. § *Ib.* s. 11.
‖ *Ib.* s. 12. ¶ *Ib.* s. 14. ** *Ib.* s. 1. †† *Ib.* s. 3.

none.' But mark what follows, O Jew: 'They gave me gall and vinegar to drink!' Now these indignities he has suffered at your hands, as you yourselves confess and boast. Hear then what a price the Holy Spirit declares shall be paid for that drop of vinegar: 'Let their table become a snare unto them, and a retribution.' (Ps. lxix. 22;) and what does that mean? Manifestly the miseries with which the Jews are now overwhelmed, when according to the same prophet, 'Christ would speak to them in his anger, and vex them in his fury.'" (Ps. ii. 5.)

ORIGEN* incidentally alludes to a discussion he once held with some Jewish Rabbis, before a large and learned company. He begged to know of his opponents on what grounds they believed *their* Moses to have written his history (seeing that it is called an illusion by the Egyptians), whilst they disbelieve *our* Jesus who wrote nothing himself, but was testified of by sincere disciples. A still further resemblance between the two cases under dispute is seen in that the authority of both leaders is supported by a respectable and immense body of followers. "Now Christians," he continued, "do not repudiate Moses, but tend to confirm him: if therefore you want a justification of our conduct in trusting the blessed Saviour, do you first assign some reasons for believing in Moses, who came into the world many ages before the Incarnation of Jesus, (and therefore may be called a more indistinct character,) and then it will be time for us to acquaint you with the rational grounds on which our faith is built." The Rabbis having nothing to say to this, he proceeded to prove that Jesus is the Messiah, from their own law and prophets, observing by the way, that "though it may seem strange, the same argument proves Moses and the prophets themselves, to be inspired persons."

* *Cont. Cels.* Lib. I. s. 45.

Our author* charges Celsus, while he personates the Jew, with "purposely or ignorantly overlooking one of the most cogent arguments that can be brought in favor of our blessed Lord, namely, his being foretold by the Jewish prophets, by Moses, and even by some who lived before him." "I suppose," he adds, "he knew that he could return no reasonable answer to a proposition in which the Jews, as well as the greatest heretics, agree with us. For my own part, I firmly believe that the person, of whom there are so many predictions in the Sacred Writings of the Jews, is the Son of God." He shows that these predictions apply to no one else. "For† all and each of them must tally with the history of the individual to whom they are applied." By means of this rule‡ of interpretation, he gets rid of various imposters or false Messiahs, who are proposed by Celsus as answering the expectations of the Jewish people. It is found, for example, that none of them were born in Bethlehem; whilst that Jesus was born there is notorious, since the cave is still shown, and it was confessed by the chief priests and teachers, in reply to Herod's inquiry.

Next,§ he touches upon the yet older prediction of Jacob (Gen. xlix. 10). "Now any one who reads this ancient promise, cannot but wonder how Jacob could foreknow that the rulers of the nation should come of a particular tribe, as also that they should fail at a certain period." Yet both these events have exactly taken place; the Jews have derived their very name from the tribe of Judah; and that "the desire of nations" is come, the vast number of persons who flock to him abundantly proves, making good the words of the prophet, "They shall feed in the ways, and their pasture shall be in all high places." I must add because of

* *Cont. Cels.* Lib. I. s. 49. † *Ib.* s. 50. ‡ *Ib.* s. 51.
§ *Ib.* s. 53.

Celsus' reproaches, that the prophets foretold Christ's sufferings, and the reasons why he underwent them, and that they would conduce to the advantage of all mankind. The references here, are Isaiah lii. 13–15; liii. 1, 2.

Speaking* of the 53d chapter of Isaiah he relates, that in another disputation with the Jews, one of them asserted that these prophecies are to be referred to their whole body, whose dispersion and other calamities were means to gain proselytes to their religion. In answer to this, Origin says he quoted the passages, "He hath borne our griefs and carried *our sorrows," and "by his stripes we are healed," to show* that such a sense could not be entertained, for they evidently refer to persons cured of spiritual diseases; adding, "but what most perplexed them was that expression, 'For the transgression of my people was he smitten,' which *must* be understood of some single person, and not of the whole nation."

Our author states† that the Saviour's foreknowledge‡ of the reception his doctrine would meet with, was a divine proof of its future happy effect; and this he explains afterwards to be the more remarkable, because the events were so unlikely, and because hostile governors and kings have been made to bring them about against their will. Wherefore he can see no stronger evidence for the truth of any doctrine.

§ Of the rejection of the Jews, he says, "we see the prophecies (relating to this subject) remarkably fulfilled in our own age; for the modern Jews, not rightly understanding the Scriptures, abound in extravagant fancies, while Christians are led into the spiritual knowledge of the truth, which can alone enlighten and elevate the mind; and do not live after the manner of the Jews, as members of an earthly republic, but like worthy and honorable citizens of that

* *Cont. Cels.* s. 55. † *Ib.* s. 62.
‡ See also *Hom.* on Matth. ix. 37. § *Cont. Cels.* Lib. II. s. 5.

heavenly Jerusalem, of which the pompous worship and external grandeur of Judaism is but a very imperfect emblem. It is, moreover,* a matter of fact that since the incarnation of our blessed Lord, the Jews have been left by God, so that the beauty and glory of their religion is entirely effaced, and there is no sign of the divine power among them, except in the way of severe judgments: they are at this day the most miserable people on the face of the earth; for what nation is there beside, that is banished from their metropolis, and denied the liberty of serving God on their native soil? In truth their calamities are only surpassed by their wickedness in torturing that blessed Being who came to save them from sin and hell."

CYPRIAN† shows that the rejection by the Jews of the offers of grace, was foretold by their own prophets, and illustrated in the saying of St. John, "He came unto his own, and his own received him not."

He alludes‡ to the destruction of Jerusalem, and the dispersion of the Jews, as predicted by Christ; to the abolition§ of carnal circumcision in favor of a spiritual dispensation; to the cessation‖ of the law of Moses; to the New Law¶ that was all along intended, and to that Messiah who was to promulgate it (recognized as Christ by Matthew in these words, "This is my beloved Son"); and to Christ** taking the place of the temple, on which Mark xiv. 58 is quoted; and, finally,†† to the promise of Moses, that a prophet like unto himself should arise, which the Saviour is found appropriating to himself, in John v. 46, "Moses wrote of me."

The prophecies‡‡ concerning the divine nature of the Messiah, are seen completed in Christ, and hinted at by St. John xvii. 3–5, and in Coloss. i. 15–18.

* *Cont. Cels.* Lib. II. s. 8. † *Adv. Jud.* Lib. I. c. 3. ‡ *Ib.* c. 6.
§ *Ib.* c. 8. ‖ *Ib.* c. 9. ¶ *Ib.* c. 10. ** *Ib.* c. 15.
†† *Ib.* c. 18. ‡‡ *Ib.* Lib. II. c. 1.

He points out* how correlative are many of the expressions of the New Testament with those of the Old, respecting the Messiah; for instance,† that he was to come of the seed of David, plainly agreeable to Luke i. 30; be born‡ at Bethlehem, confirmed in Matth. ii. 2; in a humble character,§ noted in Philipp. ii. 6–11; that he ‖ whom the Jews should kill was to be a just person, recognized in Matth. xxvii. 3, 4; that he¶ was to be called the sheep and the lamb, literally accomplished in the words, "Behold the Lamb of God;"** that he was to be called†† a stone, referred to by St. Peter; that the Jews were to crucify him, which they notoriously did;‡‡ that there should be darkness at mid-day when Christ suffered, as Amos (viii. 9, 10) and Jeremiah (xv. 9) had foretold, to which agrees the event related by the holy Evangelist, who tells us that from the sixth to the ninth hour, there was darkness over all the land; and, to conclude, that the Christ§§ was not to continue under the dominion of death, but that at his resurrection he should receive all power from his Father, in fulfilment of which Jesus said and proved after he was risen, "All power is given unto me in heaven and in earth."

EUSEBIUS,‖‖ having treated of the divinity and humanity of the Christ of God, and of his connection with man as the Logos, in the 3d and 4th books, now cites some prophecies, which he selects as being perfectly unambiguous. They relate to the advent of Christ and to the calling of the Gentiles. The Psalms,¶¶ the first of Kings, and Micah are adduced for this purpose, and their consideration, as well as*a the extent of their accomplishment, is left to the meditation of the reader. Other passages †a are then brought forward

* *Adv. Jud.* Lib. II. c. 6. † *Ib.* c. 11. ‡ *Ib.* c. 12. § *Ib.* c. 13. ‖ *Ib.* c. 14. ¶ *Ib.* c. 15. ** *Ib.* c. 16. †† *Ib.* c. 20. ‡‡ *Ib.* c. 23. §§ *Ib.* c. 24–26. ‖‖ *Dem. Evan.* Lib. VI. ¶¶ *Ib.* s. 12. *a *Ib.* s. 13. †a *Ib.* s. 14–20.

from Habakkuk, Zechariah, Baruch, and Isaiah,* of a more general cast, which he supposes to be partly fulfilling now, and certainly to be consummated in the glories of heaven.

After this,† he narrows the circle of prophetical evidence, and endeavors to concentrate the attention of his hearers on a few facts, such as the sign of Ahaz, describing the manner of the Messiah's birth; Micah's testimony, as to the locality; and that of the prophet Nathan in 2 Chronicles, and of Jeremiah, Isaiah, and Jacob, as to the tribe and family. These predictions are collated with the Gospels, and found confirmed in the history of Jesus.

He devotes himself,‡ in the next place, to expounding the times of Messiah's appearance, hinted at by Jacob and David. These predictions give rise to an elaborate historical investigation, in the course of which appeals are made to the Evangelists, and to the works of Josephus, for proof of their exact fulfilment. Micah, Zechariah, and Isaiah furnish additional materials, relating to the Messianic epoch. A further correspondence § is traced between the Old and New Testaments, in regard to certain circumstances of the Saviour's life; Balaam's announcement of the Star, is recognized as completed in Matth. ii. 1; Christ's going down into Egypt (Matth. ii. 14), is found referred to by Isaiah (xix. 1); Hosea x. 1, on the return of the holy family, appears to be directly cited by Matth. ii. 15; the preaching of John in the desert (Isaiah xl. 3) is confirmed in Luke iii. 1; a foreshadow of the temptation is seen in Psalm xci. 13, and of the walking on the sea, in Job ix. 8; Galilee, so frequently referred to in the Gospels, is evidently predesignated in Isaiah ix. 1; the same prophet having many allusions to the Christian miracles, see ch. viii. 16, xxxii. 1, lxi. 2, &c.; and the entry into Jerusalem, mentioned by Zech. ix. 9, is traced in Matth.

* *Dem. Evan.* Lib. VI. s. 25.
† *Ib.* Lib. VII.
‡ *Ib.* Lib. VIII.
§ *Ib.* Lib. IX.

xxi. 2, with the acclamations of the children on the same occasion, directly illustrating the Psalms.

Finally* he notices the prophecies concerning Christ's passion. The traitor Judas is discovered, in Psalms xli. 9, liii. 12–21, cix., and his thirty pieces of silver in Zech. xi. 13; the eclipse of the sun, in Amos viii. 7, and Zech. xiv. 5, and many of the circumstances of the crucifixion seriatim, in Psalm xx. These prophecies are all aptly confirmed out of the Gospels, and in conclusion our author "calls upon every person to obey the command of Christ, and 'search the Scriptures' for himself, concerning these matters."

EPHRAIM† (on a Palm Sunday) after a rapid survey of various prophecies relating to Christ's triumphal entry into Jerusalem, calls upon his congregation to examine the Scriptures of the prophets, and see if these things have not been fulfilled. He quotes Jacob's promise, and asks the Jew whether there is a sceptre in Judah, or an interpreter between his feet? He entreats all to observe the present commemoration of Christ on the colt, and the scattered condition of Israel among all nations. How truly has the stone which the builders refused become the head of the corner!

CHRYSOSTOM‡ first insists that the Jews are not to be honored any more, and that their synagogue is scarcely to be preferred before the theatre; while their company ought to be avoided so long as they rail against Christ. He thinks that in place of venerating them on account of their having the Scriptures, we should on that very account be afraid of them.

He produces the prophecies of our Lord concerning the ruin of the temple, pointing out how they have been fulfilled; "which," says he, "is a proof that he is risen from the dead, and now lives in heaven."

* *Dem. Evan.* Lib. x. † *Adv. Jud.* s. 16. ‡ *Orat. adv. Jud.* s. 1.

Next* he instances the promise made by Christ to the woman with the alabaster box of ointment. "There have been," he argues, "queens and noble women, whose names, however they may have blessed their people and country, have long since perished; but here is an abject woman in the presence of a few witnesses, in a common house; and yet neither the humbleness of the person, nor the paucity of the witnesses, nor the obscurity of the place, has prevented the memory of this action from being handed down to posterity. Is not this the work of God?"

With respect to the destruction of Jerusalem,† he remarks, that though so many years have now elapsed, the temple has never been rebuilt. He relates‡ the vain attempt under the direction of Julian; observing, that § if these Jews did not believe this, the very stones of the ruins will cry out against them.

In conclusion,‖ he applies the different allusions in Isaiah, touching Christ's life and death, and the typical qualifications of the high-priesthood in Leviticus, to the atoning sacrifice on Calvary.

JACOBUS NISIBENUS (Syriacus) in his 18th Oration (it is against the Jews), refutes the assertion that the synagogue, &c. will ever be restored, by appeals to the prophets.

* *Orat. adv. Jud.* s. 2. † *Ib.* s. 3. ‡ *Ib.* s. 7.
§ *Ib.* s. 10. ‖ *Orat.* 6.

CHAPTER IV.

THE ARGUMENT FROM MIRACLES.

"Certum est quia impossibile."

TERTULLIAN.

In commencing this chapter, it should at once be stated, that the reader must not expect to find the Apologists offering any regular proof of the reality of the Christian miracles, or of the authenticity of the writings that narrate them. This strange task has fallen to the lot of modern apologists; and has been called for by our doubting critics, who under every disadvantage, have thought fit to question facts, which a Tiberius, a Celsus, a Porphyry,* a Julian, a Hierocles,† a Symmachus did not deny. The heathen were only asked to receive our books, as they received any other credentials; that is, for their intrinsic worth as *historical* or *rational* matter. Up to this mark, it seems the constant endeavor of the Christian writers to keep their opponents; and, though there is a large amount of scattered reference to contemporaneous and foreign testimony, — to Josephus, to the acts of Pilate, to every monument and roll of antiquity, by Justin, or Tatian, or Theophilus; and to the necessities of the case, by all the apologists, — it had evidently not yet entered into the minds

*Chrys. *Hom.* VI. † Lact. *Div. Instit.* V. 3.

of either Christian or Pagan, Jew or Gentile, at the only proper time, seriously to doubt the reality of such a body of facts as Christianity presented. The historical testimony to the miracles was considered on all hands sufficient and conclusive. Any set attempt therefore to confirm it would have been worse than superfluous; it would have introduced suspicion into the very grounds of the controversy. It was enough for Cyril of Alexandria, in his refutation of Julian, to find his adversary allowing, however he might try to disparage, "the healing of the lame and blind," as the deeds of Jesus, together with references to "exorcising demoniacs, and walking on the sea."

While then demanding *so* much credit for the facts of Christianity, our authors did not, humanly speaking, expect more. They knew that however a historical faith might come of evidence and good sense, a belief in spiritualities, in the inspiration of words and divinity of deeds, could only come of the Holy Spirit's teaching; and for this upon their unenlightened hearers, they had rather to pray, than to contend. In short, the great *signa* of Scripture were allowed by the one party, to have taken place; and by the other, were thought sufficient as matters of fact, (with other evidences) to support the truth of religion, and to do all that man can do, towards convincing the understanding.

But there were other questions peculiar to that day, and which grew out of the existing state of things. One of these has been already alluded to, in the opening of the last chapter; that of the Pagans endeavoring to evade the force of the Christian miracles, by explaining them away as the effects of magic. This is the reason given by some of the Fathers themselves, for not insisting more upon this species of evidence. It was the prevalent opinion of early times, that a miracle, though ever a proof of power, is not necessarily a proof of *Divine* power. It might emanate from below, as well as from above. This notion, Origen attributes to the Jews, conceiving that it grew out of the collision between Moses and the magicians of Egypt. The tendency of the present age has decidedly set in against any theory of the sort, and all parties agree in allowing that a miracle, if it can be proved authentic, is one of the strongest evidences any cause can possess. But the apologists had to meet the difficulty; and this they did, not by relinquishing so valuable a proof, but by associating it with other criteria, especially with morality. If then it be found that they have said less upon this topic than we could have wished, we may be sure that what they have afforded, has been well guarded and sifted, and comes down to us with more than the usual value of tradition.

Another peculiar form of opposition the Fathers had to grapple with, was the attempt to confuse the Christian miracles with the prodigies of marvellous men. Numerous examples of this occur, and were always carefully answered. Pythagoras was thus put forward by Porphyry, and Jamblichus and Apuleius, by others; but the most considerable effort of the kind was made by Hierocles, who had the boldness to compare the miraculous accounts of Jesus and the apostles, with a life of Apollonius Tyaneus, written a hundred years after his death, and full of the most ridiculous inventions. Eusebius replies to this indirect attack of Hierocles, and considers it quite sufficient to expose the various incidents related by the original biographer Philostratus, as in strange contrast with the want of authority, and even of pretence of the hero himself during his lifetime. He allows the substance of the history, but disputes the extraordinary parts. It is a curious circumstance noticed by Mr. J. H. Newman, that the only case in the entire document, which would fall under the modern denomination of miracles (the raising of a dead youth), is explained away by the philosopher's own friend, on the ground of natural causes.*

* *Essay* on the Life of Apollonius.

There is one more particular to be noticed, ere we enter upon the proofs of this chapter, on account of the references made to it by the Apologists; viz., the subject of post-apostolic miracles. Gibbon having taken an argument against *all* miracles from the silence of ecclesiastical history respecting their cessation, the bishop of Lincoln replies, that a *gradual* withdrawal would account for the uncertainty which has prevailed respecting the period of their cessation; while the alleged silence is as reasonably referred, "not to the insensibility of Christians to so important an event, but to the combined operation of prejudice and policy; of prejudice that made them reluctant to believe, and of policy that made them reluctant to acknowledge their own loss."* On the appeals and expressions of confidence, used by the Fathers with respect to miraculous powers having extended to their own day, the bishop further explains "that the narrations of such occurrences being couched in general terms, and rarely going so far as to instance any particular case, must needs be open to question." These reflections are as judicious, as they are warranted by the state of the case. The positive assertions of patristic miracles may be met and cancelled by assertions as positive on the other side, and, what is still more significant, by *arguments* built upon them. What, for example, can be more explicit than Augustine's statement in his work *De Doctrina Christiana*,† and repeated in his short discourse, *De Utilitate Credendi*; "since the establishment of the Church, God does not wish to perpetuate miracles even to our day, lest the mind should put its trust

* I find a remark of Origen (*Cont. Cels.* Lib. VII. s. 8,) analogically in favor of the gradual withdrawal theory of Dr. Kaye. Speaking of the inspiration of the prophets, he says, "signs of the Holy Spirit were shown at the preaching and after the Ascension of Jesus, but have gradually departed since; and if any traces are now to be found, it is among Christians."

† c. 25.

in visible signs, or grow cold at the sight of common marvels?" In the latter work, after reciting the miracles of Jesus, it is asked, "Why say you, do not those things take place now? Because they would not move except they were wonderful, and if they were usual they would cease to be wonderful."* Again, we have Chrysostom, urging the superior value of morality over the extraordinary gift of working miracles, in these terms: "Wherefore that this gift of grace is no longer bestowed on men, can neither be to our prejudice, nor will it afford us an excuse when we shall be called upon to render an account of our actions;" and, "We should not indeed require, in an equal degree, the assistance of the word, if we possessed the power of working miracles. But now that no vestige of that power remains, and enemies press us on all sides, we must defend ourselves with the weapons of the word."†

Moreover, from a consideration of all the works of the primitive Fathers, it would seem a much greater miracle than any claimed for their age, how they have all so contrived to leave us bare of those particularities, even of one (if it be true they witnessed any), which are required alike by the common expectations of mankind, and by the example

*The qualification of this in *Retract.* B. I. c. 14, 5, "this I said, because not so great miracles nor all take place now, not because there are none wrought now," cannot, I think, with fairness, be said to include or affect any of the *species* of miracles he had previously enumerated; and among them are "healing the sick," and "curing the lame!" But really, after the above unmistakable and sensible remarks, one is disposed to question the genuineness, as well as the authenticity of a list of miracles, passing under this Father's name, and appended to his *City of God.* Take, for instance, the 10th. A virgin is dispossessed of the devil by anointing herself with oil mixed with the tears of the priest who prayed for her: and if the rest are examined, it will appear that Augustine was present at only one, and that, the healing of a fistula in the course of the night.

†Neander's *Life of Chrysostom*, pp. 64, 71.

of the Scriptures, and which they themselves never neglected in other matters.

Granting, however, that the Apologists must mean *something*, by their positive appeals and assertions respecting the subject in dispute; and also that they were upright men, of which there can be still less doubt, a further explanation offers itself, and one, it appears to me, of a satisfactory nature. It is that they did not mean miracles in our strict sense of the term. This is evinced by their calling and accounting the establishment of Christianity, or the moral change in individuals, miracles, interchangeably with miracles proper. And yet more to our purpose is, what cannot have escaped the notice of any student of ancient theology, viz., that almost every instance of the miracles in question, implies *a demoniacal possession*. Now this is rather an equivocal expression. It had in our Lord's time, doubtless, a distinct and express meaning, but by the time of Chrysostom, it is to be met with in a wider signification. This writer, in an epistle to Stagirius, a youth who had fallen into a nervous malady, addresses him as one "possessed by the devil;" and yet there is no allusion to any power of relief extant; but the Christian hope of comforting and extinguishing "his great grief," is entertained and supported by such advice alone, as a discipline of holy thought and Scripture examples. Cyprian also, in his epistle to Donatus, confesses that "the whole transaction (of exorcism) passes indeed invisibly, and the wounds we give the evil spirits, are not apparent, only their effect is manifest,"* &c. We gather the same idea from "the Constitutions." They allow that the cure of demoniacs was a work of time, and that it did not always succeed. In Const. VIII. 7, the patients are seen being instructed in the faith, but not receiving the communion unless near death, which leads Jortin to ask, "Is it not

* *Ad Donat.* cap. 4.

probable that the ancient Christians accounted mad, and melancholy, and epileptic persons to be *possessed*, at least for the most part, which would greatly increase the number of demoniacs ?"*

Another hint may be thrown out here, in explanation of these references to post-apostolic miracles. The Fathers *copied* one from another. A case just in point occurs, where Cyprian borrows from Minutius Felix, almost verbatim, the following words:† "Even the worshippers themselves (of the demons) may hear them (on the occasion of an exorcism) confessing whence they came and whither they are going. Either they depart immediately, or gradually quit their hold, in proportion either to the faith of the patient, or to the measure of grace conferred on the manager of the cure." Again, as there can be little doubt that Cyprian has drawn this, together with other passages, from the *Octavius* of Minutius Felix, so Mr. Holden traces some of the *Octavius* to the *Apologeticus* of Tertullian; ‡ and thus with other writers,§ and in other cases, it may be that language which properly belongs to an eye-witness, has been transcribed and handed down from nearly apostolic times.

I cannot do better in closing this digression, than refer to the bishop of Lincoln's summary and judgment upon the case. His opinion, after a careful view of the subject in every light, is, that "the power of working miracles was not extended beyond the disciples, upon whom the Apostles had laid their hands."‖

* Jortin's *Remarks*, Vol. I. p. 161.

† Compare Cypr. *Van. of Idols* with Min. Fel. *Octav.* c. 27, or p. 164 of the present dissertation.

‡ See Holden's *Pref. to Minutius Felix.*

§ Euseb. after Athenag. (compare pp. 75 and 79 of this work), also Irenæus, *verbatim* from Justin's *Apol.* (see Iren. Lib. II. c. 56, and Lib. III. c. 2), whilst Justin's *Apol.* itself is said to have been in imitation of one of Aristeides not extant, are instances of a general kind.

‖ Jortin, likewise, "would not engage for the truth of any miracle after A.D. 107." So also Le Clerc and Moyle.

It is refreshing in turning to the main body of this argument, — the Scripture miracles, — to know that such a collateral, doubtful matter as that we have just glanced at, is but occasionally or slightly appealed to; and that even such casual expressions as do occur, admit of some psychological explanation, or only (if they must be taken in full literal force) serve to set off to greater advantage, the splendid and positive miracles of our Lord and his immediate disciples.

QUADRATUS.* "The works of our Saviour were always conspicuous, for they were real; both the healed and those that were raised from the dead were seen not only when they were healed or raised, but for a long time afterwards; not only whilst he dwelt on this earth, but also after his departure, and for a good while after it; insomuch as that some of them have reached to our own times."

JUSTIN MARTYR† says, "Christ healed those who from their birth were blind, and deaf, and lame, causing by his word, even one to leap, another to hear, and a third to see; and having raised the dead also, and made them live again, he by his works excited attention and induced the men of that age to know him; some of whom, however, seeing these things done, said that they were magical appearances, and dared to call him a magician and a deceiver of the people."

Or,‡ addressing the heathen: "Hear also in what manner it was predicted that our Christ should heal all kinds of diseases, and raise the dead (Isai. XXXV. 5, 6;) and that he did these things, ye may learn from the records of what was done under Pontius Pilate."

* Euseb. *Hist.* Lib. IV. c. 3. † *Dial. cum Tryph.* s. 69. ‡ *Apol.* I. c. 63.

In proof that Christ came to save us from the devil, allusion* is made to the wonderful influence which his name has over the demons, "so that many vexed in this way in the whole world, and in your own city, have been relieved by Christians in the name of Jesus Christ crucified."

Lastly,† arguing for the power of God to restore the body, he says: "It is evident that if Christ on earth cured all diseases, and made the body whole and perfect, how much more will he, in the general resurrection, raise it complete and perfect."

ATHENAGORAS.‡ "To confirm the assertion that the images of the gods are divine things, we are told of the miracles performed by them. Let this matter be thoroughly investigated." He then§ supposes that "if the accounts of these supernatural deeds be true, they must be ascribed to evil spirits, making use of the statues." He explains ‖ that by evil spirits he means fallen angels, who delight in tempting men to idolatry. But he would "rather¶ take these said effects not to be real, but the results of some senseless reveries of the mind concerning certain opinions; which occasion men to form of themselves, ideas partly of things existing, and partly of things imaginary; these wild emotions of the mind producing idolatrous imaginations, especially if the soul be pliable and devoid of the true knowledge of God."

THEOPHILUS.** "Our Scriptures teach us with one consent, that God made all things from nothing by means of his Word. And his spirit likewise it was, that descended into the prophets, and enabled them to describe the creation of the world." Expounding the Mosaic account of the origin of things,†† he notices the dignity of the description; and

* *Apol.* II. c. 6. † *De Resur.* s. 1. ‡ *Legat.* c. 18.
§ c. 23. ‖ *Ib.* c. 24. ¶ *Ib.* c. 27.
** *Ad Autol.* Lib. II. c. 10. †† *Ib.* c. 12.

declares that though men had a thousand tongues they could not explain any more, and that when they attempt it, they only weaken the truth by the addition of insipid trifles.

He tells* the Pagans that they will credit the stories of Hercules, living after he was consumed by fire, and of Æsculapius, after he had been scathed by lightning; it is only those things which are said to have been done by God, they will not believe; yea, though he should show them the dead raised to life, they would not believe it.

IRENÆUS† intimates that our Saviour's miracles were admitted for facts not only by Christians, but by others also; adding, "But if they shall say that the Lord performed his miracles by an illusory appearance, we can resort to prophecies."‡

CLEMENS ALEXANDRINUS.§ "Our Saviour has adopted various ways of exhibiting himself to men; he spake out of the bush, because men needed signs and wonders, and by the pillar of fire and cloud. Afterwards, for that the human body is more noble than a column or a bush, he spake by the prophets; and lastly, because some might not even believe them, he humbled himself to be born of a woman; the merciful God, the Word, communed openly with men, in order that he might save the human race, and shame them out of infidelity."

Again,‖ among the evidences for the divinity of Christ, he places the "testimonies that accompanied his visible generation, and the powers that were announced and openly displayed by him after the resurrection."

* *Ad Autol.* Lib. I. c. 13. † Lib. II. c. 57.

‡ Speaking of heretics he says "*their* signs were not beneficial to mankind, nor wrought in the name of Jesus." Lib. II. c. 56.

§ *Hortat.* c. 1. ‖ *Strom.* Lib. II.

TERTULLIAN* advances as an incidental proof of the reality of Christ's miracles, the fact of Tiberius the Emperor proposing some commemoration of him, founded on the intelligence received from Palestine; and though thwarted by the senate in his project of a statue, yet persisting in it; also of his threatening those with punishment who should accuse the Christians.

Speaking† of the Jews denying the divinity of the Saviour in consequence of his humble appearance, our author remarks: "It naturally followed that they should regard him as a magician: they had no other alternative when they witnessed his preternatural powers, how he cast out devils by a word, gave sight to the blind, cleansed lepers, restored the palsied, raised the dead to life, ruled the elements, and walked upon the sea." "At his crucifixion," he continues, "he voluntarily gave up the ghost, while at the same moment the mid-day was deprived of the light of the sun. Some who were ignorant that this also was predicted concerning Christ, thought, doubtless, that it was a natural eclipse; and when they could not account for it (the moon being full,) they denied the fact, although it is related in their own annals."

In giving an account of the resurrection and ascension of Christ, he remarks that "Pilate sent a full account of all these transactions to Tiberius Cæsar; whilst the disciples confirmed the truth of all they had seen with their sufferings and blood."

He next‡ appeals to the power of Christians over those possessed of the devil, as a matter of fact and a proof of the truth of Christianity. He proposes that "any one who is confessedly under the influence of a demoniacal possession should be brought before the tribunal, and if the spirit when commanded by a Christian shall not truly confess himself to be a demon, then let the blood of that impudent Christian

* *Apol.* c. 5. † *Ib.* c. 21. ‡ *Ib.* c. 23.

be shed upon the spot." "What" he exclaims, "can be more impartial than such a mode of proof, where there is no room for suspicion, and no effect of magic, as your own eyes and ears can testify?"

MINUTIUS FELIX.* "Most of you know very well that the demons are forced to confess all things of themselves as often as we command them by our simple word, and expel them from the bodies they possess; for Saturn, Serapis, and Jupiter, or whatever other demons you worship, are not able to endure the pain, but proclaim their true nature even in the presence of those adoring them. When we adjure them by the name of the true God, the wretches, sore against their will, fall into horrible shiverings, and either spring forthwith from the bodies they inhabit, or vanish by degrees according to the faith of the patient, or the grace of the physician."

ORIGEN,† having considered the nature of the Son of God, claims as "one of the greatest proofs of his divinity, and one of the strongest motives to our admiration and love, his having laid aside the preëminent majesty of that nature, and become man, conversing with us; and that even in his humility he was not without witnesses of his divine nature. The grace diffused into his lips was a testimony of the Father concerning him; the signs, wonders, and various miraculous powers which followed him, were all confirmations of his dignity. Prophets were his forerunners, and the messengers of his advent, before he appeared in the body; and after his ascension to heaven, there were in like manner holy Apostles, replete with the power of his own dignity, and whom, though but publicans and fishermen, unskilled and unlearned, he caused to circumvent the whole earth, that out of every race he might collect a people, believing in his name. But‡ of all

* *Octav.* c. 27. † *De Princip.* Lib. II. c. 6, sect. 1.
‡ *Ib.* sect. 11.

the miracles and mighty things relating to Him, that which most taxes the admiration of the human mind, as far as its weakness will permit, is to conceive how that power of the divine majesty, that Word of the Father, that wisdom of God, by whom all things, visible and invisible, were created, could have dwelt within the limits of the man who appeared in Judæa."

"If we consider," says he,* "the journeys of the Apostles to publish the Gospel through the whole world, the affair will appear greater than human, and indeed to have been undertaken at the command, and carried through by the power of God alone. If we weigh well the strange agreement of men to hear a new and foreign doctrine, how they flocked to the Apostles, not to ensnare them any more, but to learn what they should do to be saved, none can doubt but that these Apostles performed miracles, and that God gave testimony to their discourses by signs and wonders and various powers."

In answer† to an imputation that the powers possessed by Christians, were owing to demoniacal agency, our author asserts that they are not due to any kind of enchantment, but to the use of the name of Jesus, with a becoming disposition of mind and a most lively faith. Yea, the name of Jesus has exerted such influence over demons, that sometimes it has proved effectual though pronounced by a wicked person,‡ as Jesus himself foretold in his day.

Again, Celsus having accused Jesus of working miracles by the help of magic, Origen replies, that though we cannot tell in what way the Saviour performed his miracles, we know that his followers only wrought them by repeating his name.

"It is seldom § that any one person is celebrated for a combination of many things at once; but our Saviour was very remarkable for the best sort of wisdom, for authority, for miracles, and for other innumerable excellences."

* *De Princip.* Lib. IV. s. 5.

† *Cont. Cels.* Lib. I. s. 6.

‡ Acts xix. 13, et seqq.

§ *Cont. Cels.* Lib. I. s. 27.

"The effect* of Christ's doctrine, far from depending on the assistance of learned men, was owing to that divine and miraculous power that accompanied the Apostles in their sacred ministrations;" for, as he says elsewhere, "if † the ministry of Jesus and his Apostles had not been accompanied by miracles, they would never have been able to prevail with their hearers to forsake the religion in which they were born, and take up with a new and persecuted one."

He further‡ begs to ask the Greeks, "whether they can show that either Perseus, Inachus, or Minos did any extraordinary service to the world, or performed any exploit to induce future ages to believe the truth of those fables which represent them as having a divine origin? Or which of their fabulous actions can be compared to what our Saviour did; unless they would have us believe their stories rather than our own, of the truth and importance of which we have all the evidence we can reasonably desire?"

Celsus has acknowledged § the reality of some of the miracles, such as the healing of diseases, the raising the dead to life, and feeding the multitude; but chooses to compare them with the performances of the Egyptian magi. Origen points out an essential difference between the two cases. "One," he says, "is a vain show of calling back departed souls, or representing to the deluded sight a table spread with imaginary dainties; the other as real as it was public. The design of the first is not to reform morals, for such amusements have not the slightest tendency to beget in persons a true sense of God, or to regulate their actions, and prepare them for the great day of judgment; whilst the design of Jesus is just to do all this, and to affect mankind with a sense of the will of God." In connection with this contrast, he hints at the immoral lives of magicians and necromancers generally, and then at the bright example of unaffected virtue

* *Cont. Cels.* Lib. I. s. 62.

† *Ib.* s. 46.

‡ *Ib.* s. 67

§ *Ib.* s. 68.

and piety which Jesus gave us all in his own personal conduct; and concludes by giving it as his opinion, that "genuine miracles must be connected with morality, and have for their chief end the converting of those who see them, to a sincere and sacred regard for the honor of God and the interests of the Redeemer."

"Our blessed Saviour* abundantly discovered that his power was nothing less than that of God, by the frequent and incontestable miracles which he wrought even in presence of the Jews; and which they did not deny, but tried to evade on the plea that they were done by the aid of the devil, as Celsus now ascribes them to magic. But our Saviour refuted this absurd conceit, by showing that the kingdom of Satan was thus suffering a most violent shock, as evidently appears to those who read the Gospels with any share of judgment."

Again:† "Is it any wonder at all that he who in the whole course of his life, did so many actions which nothing short of a divine power could have possibly enabled him to perform; who wrought in attestation of his doctrine, miracles so surprising and open before his implacable foes, that Celsus himself has not the face to deny their reality; — is it, I say, any wonder that such a person should have something extraordinary about his death?"

In reply‡ to the challenge, "what did Jesus ever do that was truly great and worthy of a God," Origen refers to the Evangelistic account of the earthquake, the rending of the rocks, the opening of the tombs, the rent veil, and the darkness of the sun at noonday. Touching the last phenomenon, "which happened while the Sun of Righteousness was suffering a darker eclipse," he affirms that "it is well known to have taken place in the reign of Tiberius; and also that the earth trembled when the God of Nature groaned, we have the

* *Cont. Cels.* Lib. II. s. 9. † *Ib.* s. 16. ‡ *Ib.* s. 33.

concurrent testimony of Phlegon, if I mistake not, in the 13th Book of his Chronicle." The dream of Pilate's wife, and the confession of the centurion at the cross, are not overlooked.

He says* the Jews are to be condemned, "because they refuse to believe the miracles of Christ, which, though so evidently stamped with divine authority, they assign to Beelzebub, the prince of devils;" and presently asks, "what excited the rage of the chief priests and elders and scribes, but the consideration of the vast numbers of people who followed Jesus, charmed with the sweetness and heavenly expressions that dropped from his lips, and convinced by the miracles that he wrought."

Next,† he obtains a highly probable argument against the hypothesis of miracles having been done by legerdemain, or of the evangelists having forged the accounts they give of some raised from the *dead*, from the idea that had they practised the invention of falsehoods and delusions, they would have supplied more frequent instances of that striking nature, and also of the resurrection of such as had been dead for a longer period, than we meet with in the Gospels.

It is added, "the disciples performed more miracles than Jesus did, according to his promise (John xiv. 12.) For the eyes of the spiritually blind were frequently opened by them, the ears of those who were once deaf to all the awakening precepts of religion were unstopped, and many spiritually lame were cured by the Gospel, so that they leap as the hart; they could immediately tread on serpents and scorpions, and were effectually fortified against vice from within, and the malicious attempts of demons from without: events, which Jesus foretold some distance of time before their fulfilment.

* *Cont. Cels.* Lib. II. s. 38. † *Ib.* s. 48.

He shows* that false miracles are indications of true ones; that the miraculous resurrection† of Christ is not to be compared with the Greek fables of heroes; concluding upon the whole, that "the glorious miracles‡ of the Gospels were realities, and that Jesus was raised from the dead by the immediate power of the Godhead. His resurrection is all in harmony with the prophecies and miracles, indeed crowns and completes the whole."

An argument is drawn§ from the old dispensation. "The Jews would have renounced their religion long ago, unless they had had especial signs of God's favor. The firmness of this people in adhering to their institutions during their captivities and dispersions, is a testimony in favor of the truth of their histories. So in like manner,‖ Christianity is not indebted either for its origin or progress to human influence, but to God, who has manifested himself by means of various miracles, founding his religion thereon."

He points¶ to the destruction of Jerusalem forty-two years after the crucifixion of Christ, as a circumstance implying something sacred about his person, connected as that place was with his history.

Finally,** he asks "how, if Jesus had been a mere phantom since his resurrection, he could have enabled his followers to perform such great marvels, to convert souls, and to induce men to govern their actions according to the will of God, their judge? How could a spectre chase demons, or work miracles, pervade the entire world, and attract to himself by his own divinity whosoever wishes to be virtuous?"

CYPRIAN.†† "Wherefore when Jesus, according to what the prophets had foretold, cast out devils by the word of his power, cured the sick of the palsy, cleansed the lepers,

* *Cont. Cels.* Lib. II. s. 49. † *Ib.* s. 56. ‡ *Ib.* s. 62. § *Ib.* Lib. III.
‖ *Ib.* s. 14. ¶ *Ib.* Lib. IV. s. 22. ** *Ib.* Lib. VII. s. 35.
†† *De Idol. Van.* c. 7.

restored the sight of the blind, caused the lame to walk, raised the dead to life again, compelled the powers of nature to minister to him, and the winds and waves to obey him, the Jews were surprised at the mighty works he wrought among them; and though the humility of his flesh represented him only a common man, yet the power of his miracles made them think him a dealer in magical arts. He also appeared to his disciples after the resurrection just in the form and manner wherein he had conversed with them, and their senses proved the reality of his appearance."

ARNOBIUS* answers those who ask if we can prove that Christ is God, by holding up "the variety of his powers, as the greatest proof; which things," he says, "they themselves dare not convict of falsity." But "it may be replied, he was a magician, and did all his works by secret arts stolen from Egypt." In contending with this objection, our author "begs to know whoever in former ages did a thousandth part of what Christ did, and that too, as is worthy of notice, without any observance of sacred rites, sacrifices or seasons, but all by the power of his own name?" Yet this is what Jesus did, and it is consistent with the character of the true God. There was nothing hurtful in any of his deeds; but he gave his salutary assistance to man when it was needed, with all the marks of a munificent power. But,† you say, "He was a mortal and one of us." Was he a mortal and one of us, at whose voice sicknesses and diseases fled away? whose presence the race of demons, hid in the bodies of men, could not endure? who caused the lame to run, and those borne on the necks of others to carry home their own beds? Whose light touch stayed the issue of blood, restored the withered hand, a 7 əgavedn eyes evto those born blind, so that they might see the light of heaven? who healed hundreds vexed with

* *Adv. Gent.* Lib. I. c. 15.

† *Ib.* c. 16.

divers diseases? who calmed the sea, walked on the waves, and raised those who were dead and buried? Was he one of us, who after he had delivered the precepts of a true religion to his followers, has suddenly filled the whole world; so that what and who he is, is manifest by the unveiled greatness of his name? Was he one of us, who when his body had been laid in the tomb, raised himself, in the sight of men? whose name since, has silenced oracles, destroyed the business of augurs, and caused the spells of arrogant magicians to be of no avail? Which things indeed were done by Jesus, not to exhibit himself with vain ostentation, but that hardened and incredulous man might know that what he promised was not false, and perceive from the beneficence of his works that he is the true God."

Our author further observes that the fact of Christ's overcoming difficulties like dumbness and blindness, which the heathen conceived to be indissoluble bonds of fate, was a proof clearer than the sun, that he was more powerful than their idea of necessity.

He insists* strongly upon the circumstance, that Jesus wrought his miracles without the intervention of any instrument. "Christ was known," he says, "to have healed by the application of his hand, and the sound of his voice; whilst the gods are said to have used the medium of medicine or food; which is no great thing to do, seeing that physicians perform such cures every day. But is it not degrading and indecorous for a God to be unable to heal without the help of some material means?" Again he tests the miracles of Christ, in order to show that they were not tentative, and asks his readers, "How many thousands do you wish to be shown of your sick and afflicted, consumed by diseases, who have received no cure though they visit all the temples in turn, prostrate themselves before the very faces of the gods,

* *Adv. Gent.* Lib. I. c. 17.

sweep the threshold with kisses, and fatigue Æsculapius, the restorer of health, forsooth! with their prayers, so long as life remains? How many of these unfortunate creatures have grown old in their malady, and become worse instead of better, for their days and nights spent in appeals for mercy! What then does it profit to show us one and another cured by chance, when no one comes to the help of the multitudes, and every temple is full of poor and miserable beings? Christ,* on the other hand, relieved the evil and the good; none were repulsed by him: this is worthy of a God and a King. Was he not kind and gentle, easy of access, familiar in his address, pitiful towards any who were oppressed by grief or any bodily evils? and did he not with singular benignity restore and heal them; even permitting others also to heal in his name; so that what the gods could not effect with all their appliances, was continually done by the command of rude and simple Christians?"

He shows† how much more reason the Christian has for reposing faith in Christ, than the heathen have in their philosophers, "because we follow those most magnificent works, those extraordinary exhibitions of power, which Jesus displayed in a variety of miracles; by which any one ought to be brought to the necessity of believing that those things were not done by a man, but by divine and inscrutable assistance. But what can your philosophers exhibit," says he, "that it becomes you to trust to them, rather than to Christ? It is useless to produce their beautiful compositions and treatises on Music or Numbers; such matters are nothing to the present purpose; he is not to be accounted the good author who speaks well, but he who fulfils his pledges and assures us by divine works."

ARCHELAUS‡ assures the heretic Manes that he could not turn Christians from their faith, though he were to do

* *Adv. Gent.* Lib. I. c. 18--24. † *Ib.* Lib. II c. 6. ‡ *Act. Disp.*

signs and wonders, raise the dead, or even summon the image of St. Paul: and the reason given is, that his life is not that of a virtuous man. He is nevertheless challenged to say what miracles he has performed. "Has he raised the dead, stanched blood, opened the eyes of the blind, &c.?"

LACTANTIUS* having spoken of the birth of Christ, next proceeds to discuss the power and works of his life. "The Jews seeing his miracles," he says, "supposed they were done by magic, forgetting that everything he did had been foretold by their own prophets. He forthwith healed the sick, and those that had been long languishing, by the power of his words, and without the use of any instrumentality, he recovered the weak, raised up those who were bowed down, gave eyes to the blind, tongues to the dumb, ears to the deaf, cleansed the lepers, restored to a right mind those in whom demons had dwelt, and recalled the dead and buried to light and life. Five thousand men he satisfied with five loaves and two fishes, walked on the sea, stilled the tempestuous wind; all which wonders had been long predicted by the prophets. Indeed it was on account of the popularity which these miracles gained him, that the chief priests were filled with envy and rage, and at length condemned him, as if he had been an unjust man."

Finally, it is observed that the Jews charged Jesus with "healing on the sabbath;" and also that at the crucifixion, "there was an earthquake and a great darkness, just as Jesus gave up the ghost."

EUSEBIUS.† "Who ever allowed others, even such as are pure and sincere and arrived at the knowledge of God, to cast out evil spirits from persons by calling upon him? Every one‡ may hear the words and deeds of Jesus; how he

* *Epit.* c. 45. † *Theoph.* Lib. III. c. 14. ‡ *Ib.* c. 40.

taught publicly and healed every sort of disease and infirmity; and how ready he was to good works; and how those things which eye hath not seen nor ear heard, he delivered in mighty deeds, and caused his disciples to approach the very summit of excellence with God, and made them wise through the power which cannot be described: how he healed those whose souls were corrupted by every sort of sin, rebuked others, instructed all, calmed the storm, and fed thousands with a few loaves. To whom does this not appear astonishing? and does it not likewise challenge inquiry with regard to his invisible power?"

The Chiliarch's son healed* is adduced as a proof of the effect of Christ's word.

"If it be said† he was a magician and deceiver, how came he to be taught without a teacher or a book? Observe his knowledge, his wisdom, his miraculous works: surely the matter is divine, and such as exceeds all human endeavors! Besides, had he received his learning from the Egyptians or any one else, how is it that his teachers were not known as well as he? their praise proclaimed like his? And moreover what eye-witnesses of miracles have ever so sealed the truth of their testimony by the trial of fire and sword, as the disciples of the Saviour have done; who indeed suffered all things for the sake of what they had seen, and submitted to every species of torment, still declaring to the last that he was the Son of God?"

Again‡ he asks, "How could he be a magician who neither used libations nor enchantments of any kind, nor was in league with demons, as he proved by destroying them; and yet § all our writers have attested with one mouth, his cleansing of lepers, his casting out devils, his raising the dead, his restoring the sight, and many other instances of cure?"

* *Theoph.* Lib. IV. c. 2. † *Ib.* Lib. V. c. 15, 16. ‡ *Ib.* c. 18.
§ *Ib.* c. 27.

"Indeed,* how could he have attached to himself so many, both of Jews and Gentiles, unless he had made use of miracles, and astonishing deeds, and of doctrines till then unknown? The book of Acts fully goes to show how he, the Christ of God, did, by means of these wondrous works which he performed, reduce many of all classes to his power. Nor could† his disciples have undertaken their enterprise at all without divine aid; but in attestation of his resurrection, not by mere words without proofs, but by power and deeds, did they persuade and show forth the works of the living God; for‡ the multitudes, that witnessed them, must have thought it impossible for those acts to have been brought about by men, though they might not all have acknowledged the truth. This § it was, then, and nothing else, that explains how the disciples of the Saviour gained credit from those who had from the first heard them; and how they came to persuade both barbarians and Greeks, to think of Christ as the Word of God, and set up in the midst of the cities and villages, houses appropriated to the doctrine and worship of the Supreme God."

Our author‖ in following out a comparison which Hierocles had instituted between Jesus and Apollonius Tyaneus, says he will not allude to the Christian evidence of ancient prophecy, nor to the mighty results of the Saviour's teaching throughout the world, nor to the sufferings of his disciples in testimony of the truth, nor to the excellence of Christ's personal character, nor to the fact that he alone of all men being opposed in every way, has nevertheless prevailed; these things speak for themselves; but he will proceed to weigh well the incidents in the history of Apollonius as furnished by his friends, by which means, he thinks, "the authors will be shown to have indulged more in imagination

* *Theoph.* Lib. v. c. 45. † *Ib.* c. 49. ‡ *Ib.* c. 51. § *Ib.* c. 52.
‖ *Cont. Hieroc.* c. 4.

than in truth." He begins* by allowing that Apollonius was a philosopher, but nothing more: he does not seem to have been bad enough for a magician; but he denies altogether that he had any divine communication of power. Laying out of the question,† the mere rumors that a Protean spectre begot him, and that a thunderbolt and a chorus of swans announced his birth, as well as of his understanding the languages of animals,‡ &c., as monstrous and equally inconsistent with reason and the character of Apollonius, he runs over the biography and finds it laden with more absurd tales than even the writers of ancient fiction pretended to. He takes occasion by the way, of reminding Hierocles that these stories sound yet more strange, when put forward by those who charge Christians with credulity. He cites, for instance, from Apollonius' Eastern journey, the detection of an Empusa,§ who was seducing a youth into marriage; his meeting among the Brachmans‖ with a female, the lower part of whose body was white, the rest black; and with dragons having flames on their heads; also, on his return from India to Greece, his declaring men's thoughts, and holding discourse with the absent Emperor Titus; and, finally,¶ his making a satyr drunk. By such ridiculous stories as these, our author thinks that Philostratus does the Pythagorean philosopher no justice, making him out to be a base man, besides flatly contradicting himself, and showing that as a biographer he is not to be compared with our Evangelists. If, says he in conclusion, some of these narrations *were* true, we should attribute them to the assistance afforded by demons. But he contends they never were true: they are essentially fabulous, because they are useless and absurd, and make out of a harmless philosopher, a most wicked magician. Books** of this kind, therefore, are pronounced deserving of abhorrence and contempt.

* *Cont. Hieroc.* c. 5. † *Ib.* c. 8. ‡ *Ib.* c. 10. § *Ib.* c. 13.
‖ *Ib.* c. 18. ¶ *Ib.* c. 34. ** *Ib.* c. 48.

CHRYSOSTOM* observes † that the Apostles did not introduce or spread the Gospel by force of arms or wealth, but their words, simple in themselves, were sustained by miracles. "In proclaiming a crucified Redeemer, they produced miraculous effects, and so subjugated all the earth. Was there ever anything more wonderful than to see a poor fisherman, a publican, a tent-maker, raising the dead by a simple command, casting out devils, confounding philosophers and orators, overcoming princes and kings, and conquering barbarian, Greek, and all other nations by their laws?‡ How could the Apostles have undertaken to convert the whole world unless they had received some guaranty from heaven, some indubitable marks of the divine aid? and how could they have persuaded men to receive their doctrine, without miracles? That they did persuade them, as certainly is the case, is alone a proof of divine power. For it would have been a still greater marvel to have produced such an effect without any cause, that is, without a single miracle. What could have induced these men to expose themselves to so many dangers, if they had not been convinced of the resurrection of Jesus Christ? and how could they have expected to succeed in their enterprise, if it had not been true that Christ was raised from the dead? Is it not evident to the most short-sighted, that if they had not been filled with a strong and celestial influence, and if they had not had certain proofs of the truth of the resurrection, they would never have thought or conceived of, much less carried out such a design?"

AUGUSTINE § argues that a true religion must be founded upon miracles; and that it is our plain duty to choose and follow those doctrines which lead us to adore one

* See *Homily on* 1 *Ep. to Cor.*

† On the Divinity of Christ.

‡ *Tabl. des Peres*, Vol. II. p. 41.

§ *De vera Relig.* c. 25.

God, and not many, and that worship which is rendered certain by a series of visible miracles, credited in past ages and handed down to us. He adduces* the miracles of Jesus, as being more than unusual events (against the Manichæan heretics who set up reason in the place of faith:) "the sick were healed, the lepers cleansed, strength restored to the lame, sight to the blind, hearing to the deaf, water was turned into wine, multitudes fed with little means, seas traversed, the dead raised;" and then concludes, "that *thus* a vast number of believers having been gathered together, and afterwards spread abroad, the authority necessary to cure men of evil habits, and enforce new morals, was obtained and applied."

* *De Utilit. Cred.*

CHAPTER V.

THE ARGUMENT FROM THE REASONABLENESS OF DOCTRINE.

Quare oportet, in ea re maxime, in qua vitæ ratio versatur, sibi quemque considere, suoque judicio ac propriis sensibus niti ad investigandam, et perpendendam veritatem; quam credentem alienis erroribus decipi, tanquam ipsum rationis expertem. Dedit omnibus Deus pro virili portione sapientiam; ut et inaudita investigare possent, et audita perpendere. ......Quare cum sapere, id est, veritatem quærere, omnibus sit innatum; sapientiam sibi adimunt, qui sine ullo judicio inventa majorum probant, et ab aliis pecudum more ducuntur.* †

LACTANTIUS.

THIS argument chiefly consists of a comparison between the heathen and Christian systems of doctrine. In urging it, as well as that of the next chapter (on Morality,) the question may be asked, What authority or standard the Apologists used? Who was the judge of the respective merits? With what sense or hope could they charge the heathen to

* *Inst. Div.* Lib. II. c. 7.

† It is the duty of every man to form independent opinions, especially in relation to the general conduct of life; to rely upon his own judgment and reason in investigating and weighing truth; for whoever blindly accepts the errors of others, confesses himself destitute of reason. God has given wisdom to all as the heritage of manhood, that new opinions may be scrutinized, and old opinions be sifted. And as wisdom, or the searching for truth is natural to all, they deny their own intelligence, who accept without scrutiny, the discoveries of their ancestors, and follow leaders like sheep. *Am. Ed.*

renounce the one and adopt the other, as the more rational system, the purer rule of life? We answer, The heathen themselves were the judges, even in their own cause. Conscience was to be the balance, reason the umpire for every man. Not that these faculties of ours were considered less prone to evil in their way, than our wills; but it was thought, there was enough light left amid all the darkness, to compare things by, to distinguish, *quo virtus, quo ferat error*, though not to rectify or save. And to these faculties the Fathers appealed all the more confidently, because of the example of the Holy Scriptures, the first and best of Apologies. There we discover the use of certain terms without any definitions; a common understanding being presumed, between God and man, between man and man, as to their meaning, and as to the value of rational or irrational deductions, and of moral or immoral qualities. They suppose, for instance, that piety, humanity, justice, and their opposites need no explanation; that Pilate's question, "What is truth?" was indeed a fruitless one: all men will agree as to the general sense of such terms. "The ideas in fact which they represent, had words to express them for many ages antecedent to the introduction of Christianity into the world: the realities must therefore have preëxisted also; and not only existed, but been admired (or despised.) The Scriptures recognize the competency of man to estimate the right and the wrong, the lovely and the unlovely in character* (Rom. i.)" In like manner our Apologists refer to this tribunal in the breast of each man; to those principles of feeling and action, by virtue of which, he knows, however little he may practise, what is just and right. "If there be a willingness," says Justin, "to hear the reason of this thing, it will be shown that we have not been in error, &c." They hoped that men might be brought in thoughtful hours, notwithstanding the distraction caused by a false

* Chalmers's *Discourses*, Vol. I. p. 3.

education, to render homage to truth; and that so, under God,* by discovering the follies of Polytheism, the absurdities of heathen philosophy, and the immoralities of idol worship, their understanding if not their heart might be affected. "Although difficult," continues the author just quoted, "we are persuaded it is not impossible that a plain representation of the truth should be sufficient to dissipate error."

From this point the Apologists advanced a step farther, and proceeded to show that there is *another* religion which omits all the absurdities, supplies all the deficiencies, and far surpasses all the excellences of Paganism. The benevolence of Christianity did not propose to take away what it could not replace, or wound where it could not heal. It was an infinitely blessed exchange! A contrast, they thought, would deduce and illustrate this." †

I have endeavored, but in vain, to arrange the matter of this chapter under minor heads, without doing injustice to the continual comparison, or connection of ideas in each author's mind. It is a consolation, therefore, to think that though less condensed than it might be,‡ the method of a simple chronological succession which I shall give, is more characteristic, and will perhaps be, under the circumstances, more interesting. At the same time it may assist the reader to have an idea of the plan usually adopted by the Fathers, in arguing upon doctrine.

They commonly began with the *heathen* side of the question. This they separated into several views of theology, as

* The author of the Epistle to Diognetus, tells his Pagan friend, that "he must not expect to be taught the mystery of true religion by any man but by God only." And so other Fathers.

† Palmer, c. 1, *Of Development and Consc.* includes the contrast between Christianity and false Religion, as one of the Apologetic evidences, p. 10.

‡ As it is, these chapters are the essence of many volumes.

taken by different classes of men. There were the gods of the poets: these they proved to be human and wicked; human, by their births, their sexes, their relationships, their numbers, their various adaptations to localities and times, which are mere earthly distinctions, their passions, their calamities, and their deaths;* and wicked, by their adulteries, their cruelties, discords, and the bad effect of their example upon the minds of their devotees. "But these were feigned pictures of the poets," said some, "invented only to please the populace." The gods of the philosophers were therefore next discussed. Under this division, were investigated the different materialist and physico-theological theories of the ancients, which honored the works of God with a worship and glory due only to the Creator. Thus the heavenly bodies, fruits, animals, the world's elements, the world itself, animated nature, mind, were each and all exalted into the place of God. These opinions are proved vain, by their want of spirituality and dignity, and by the great contrariety of views they engendered. Then came the images or gods of the people. The poets might be jealous of another art beside their own, the philosophers might despise all the arts together; but the people wanted something visible and tangible. Here they found it. The Apologists attacked idolatry, on the score of images being mere matter, fabricated by men, subject to purchase, liable to insult, damage, and decay, and utterly unable to help themselves, much less others. Once more, the gods of the magicians, whether demons, or auspices, or oracles, were condemned alike for their impurities, their extravagances, their fallacies, and their general worthlessness.

Many of these false and idle notions of Deity were attributed by the Fathers, to the deceptions of the evil spirit,

* The Apologists make good use of Cicero's candor, in his volume *De Nat. Deor.*

ever bent on turning men's minds from the contemplation of the true God, and inserting himself or his ministers in his place.

Having exposed the fabulous origin and the degrading profligacy of the heathen mythology, the Apologists turned to the *true religion,* and with all these vanities, contrasted the God, the Teacher, the prophets, and the writings of Christianity: the one God, holy, just, invisible, and incomprehensible to finite reason, without passions, parts, or variableness; the one Word and Saviour, active, wise, powerful, pure, gentle, beneficial; and the harmonious, because filled with the one Spirit, calm yet energetic, eloquent yet simple, poor yet useful prophets, and their books. Thus the day was made to succeed the night, and to gain additional lustre by contrast with the shades it had chased away. This matter of precedence* was often intentional on the part of our authors, and the reason for it is given. For instance, Athanasius takes care "first to rebut the ignorance of unbelievers, in order that the truth may shine of itself;"† and Lactantius holds that "the first step towards the temple of truth, is to understand the false religion; the second, to know the true God; the third, to follow his messenger Jesus."‡

It might also be expected that the *preponderance,* as well as the precedence of matter, would belong to the heathen side. The one system was something of the heathen's acquaintance: they could undertake its discussion. The other was altogether strange and hard of carnal comprehension. The one was intricate and multiform, as error always is, and could not be exposed in a volume; the other was simple and quietly operative, almost expressible in a sentence.

* Eusebius however reverses this order, upon the ground of our theology being the most ancient and popular *now.* But the truth was, the tables had just been turned. Hellenism was almost out of fashion.

† *Con. Gent.* c. 1.

‡ *De Ira Dei,* c. 2.

Moreover, there were the Scriptures themselves at hand, (to the consultation of which the Fathers ever pressed their opponents,) and the constant contemporaneous expositions of the ministers of the Church.

Such appears to have been the train of thought by which this argument was approached, and the mode of its application, though its course varies more or less (within these limits,) according to the nature of each particular treatise. Taken as a mass, it forms one of the most striking kinds of proof* in favor of Christianity, and none the less perhaps, because its edges are somewhat indefinite.

THE AUTHOR OF THE EPISTLE TO DIOGNETUS† asks his heathen friend to consider the substance and forms of the gods; "whether one is not made of the stone you tread upon, and another of the same brass that is used for vases; one of wood, worthless because it decays, another of silver, so precious as to require protection from thieves; this of rusting iron, that of fragile pottery, out of which at the same time the commonest utensils are manufactured? And are they not all liable to corruption, the end of all material things? Might they not have been as well made into anything else, and could they not even now be converted to other uses? Yet these are the gods you worship and invoke, until almost as senseless as they are you become! Wherefore Christians are hateful to you, becouse they do not account them gods, but ridicule and despise them."

He likewise‡ denounces the Jews for adhering to their superstitions.

With these "vain ceremonies" he contrasts the marvellous wisdom displayed in the Incarnation and Atonement of

* Compare Grotius *On the Truth of Christianity*, Book IV. with the substance of this chapter.

† *Ep. ad Diog.* c. 2. ‡ *Ib.* 3-4. § *Ib.* c. 7.

Christ. "It is no human system," he says,* "that we so carefully follow. God himself has placed his heavenly truth, his holy word with men, that it may become firmly established in their hearts. He sent it not by a man, nor yet by an angel, but by his Son, even the Creator of all things; not in terror, but in love and mercy; to call them, not to condemn them. Though the son of a King, yea, though God himself, he became a servant. Surely such a transaction as this is not after the manner of men; it is the power of God, the sign of his presence. How vain† and trifling, compared with ours, were the ideas of the philosophers respecting God! Some thought he was fire, because fire benefited them, or water, or the other elements ordained by him. All such notions are lies and impostures, for we cannot see God except by faith." Finally he shakes the Jewish dependence upon sacrifices, by a beautiful eulogium on the Atonement. "God himself," he exclaims, "bare our sins; He gave his only Son as the price of our redemption. He gave him in whom was no sin, for the sinful; the just for the unjust; the incorruptible for the corruptible; the immortal for the mortal. Oh! sweet exchange! oh! inscrutable device! oh! mercy beyond hope! that the iniquity of many should be put away by the righteousness of one."

JUSTIN MARTYR.‡ "We do not imagine," he says to the emperor, "that God has a bodily shape, as some pretend. Why should I repeat to you who know so well, in what way the fabricators of images treat their materials, cutting, polishing, melting, hammering them, frequently out of the meanest utensils, merely changing their form, fashioning them anew, and giving them the names of gods? In our opinion this is not only unreasonable, but offers great dishonor to God, when He who possesses a glory and form which

* *Ep. ad Diog.* c. 7. † *Ib.* c. 8. ‡ *Apol.* I. c. 9.

cannot be expressed, is thus named after corruptible things, and such as need care for their preservation." He then* hints at the confused and melancholy contrast in which Jupiter and his sons stand to Jesus. "How many sons your approved writers attribute to Jove! such as Mercury, teacher of men; Æsculapius the physician, struck by lightning; Bacchus, torn in pieces; Hercules, who burned himself to escape torments; Castor and Pollux, children of Leda; Perseus, the son of Danäe; and Bellerophon, carried off by Pegasus; to say nothing of Ariadne and her company, whom, with your emperors, you exalt to the stars of heaven. But I need not relate their various actions, you know them all by heart; but this much I will say, that the documents relating to them, tend to corrupt and pervert the mind of any reader or hearer. We, on the other hand, have been taught that they only are worthy of immortality and a place in heaven, who have lived holy and virtuous lives here.

"Some of the nations," he continues,† "worship trees, and rivers, mice, cats and crocodiles, or other brute beasts, according to the country they inhabit; and, what is still more astonishing, they account every foreigner impious, who will not worship what in his own land are not regarded as gods, but as animals or victims. Others again, offer libations and the fat of beasts to the dead. How absurd is this! and yet they reproach us for not doing the same, and for not presenting senseless images with garlands and sacrifices. But‡ we out of every nation, who formerly adored Bacchus the son of Semele, and Apollo the son of Latona (whose infamous abominations it is a shame even to mention,) together with Proserpine and Venus (inflamed with passion for Adonis,) do now, for the sake of Jesus Christ, despise all these mysteries, and though threatened with death, dedicate ourselves to the true God who is unbegotten and without

* *Apol.* I. c. 29. † *Ib.* c. 32. ‡ *Ib.* c. 33.

passions, of whom we believe not as you do of Jupiter, that under the influence of base desire he followed Antiope or Ganymede, and was released from bonds by Briareus. Nay, we sincerely pity those who can credit such fables, and feel persuaded that evil spirits must be the authors of them."

The *Oratio ad Græcos* opens* with a protest against idolatrous worship. "Think not, oh Greeks," says Justin, "that I have withdrawn from your ceremonies without reason or reflection. The truth is, I found nothing in them that is holy or worthy of God. The works of your poets are monuments of frenzy and lust." Instances of heroes are then cited to show that they did not deserve their honorable titles. The great Agamemnon is found sacrificing his own daughter, and disturbing all Greece to recover Helen, while he himself is led captive by Chryseis. Achilles slays Hector, and yet is compelled to serve Polyxena, and is overcome by a dead Amazon. "I contend not," exclaims our author, "for such virtue as this. Homer is nothing more than a rhapsodist, and the beginning and end of the Iliad is a woman." Referring† to the trifling and immoral theogony of Hesiod, he says: "Read to Jove, ye Greeks, your laws against such as strike a parent, and the punishment inflicted for adultery. Teach Minerva and Diana the duties of wives, and Bacchus those of husbands. How unfeminine is it for a goddess to appear in arms; how unseemly for a hero to wear female attire, and with cymbals and flowers, to celebrate the orgies among a troop of women!" The bad examples which the gods set the young are next noticed. "How," he expostulates,‡ "can you, a father, be angry with your son for plotting against your life, or defiling your marriage-bed? He only imitates Jove! How can you punish him, and yet reverence your God for the same thing? Can you, a husband, blame your wife because she lives an abandoned life, while you yourself

* *Orat. ad Græc.* c. 1. † *Ib.* c. 2. ‡ *Ib.* c. 4.

frequent the temple of Venus? These specimens are taken from your own literature; they are not invented charges of ours. . . . .Come then, rather, and be partakers of incomparable wisdom, be instructed by a virtuous king. He and his heroes* (the apostles) did not slaughter people; our chief is the divine Word, who rules us, delighting not in strength of body, but in purity of mind only, and in good actions."

Addressing the Jew,† he argues: "Those who were under the law, were under the curse, because they could not or did not perform all things contained therein; and is it not still more evident that all the Gentiles who worshipped idols, corrupted youths, and committed every kind of wickedness, were under a curse? If therefore it pleased the Creator of all things that his Christ should take upon him the curse of all mankind, and you reject and despise him, will not his blood be justly required at your hands, who have put him to death, for no vicarious reason, but in the murderous malice of your hearts?"

The author of the *Admonition to the Greeks* proposes‡ to discuss the subject of true religion, by "inquiring about the masters of the respective systems, taking into account both who and what they were, and when they flourished, in order that those who formerly indulged a false faith, may be freed from their error, and that we for our parts, may clearly prove ourselves to be followers of our ancestors, according to godliness." Who then,§ he demands, were the masters of the Grecian religion, and what did they teach? He first draws attention to the poetical theogonies, and finds that "Homer, called the prince of poets, deduces the Deity from water." He then hints at the quarrels, the unbridled lusts, the perjuries of the gods; at the indignities which some of them suffer at the hands of mortals (as Venus and Mars wounded by Diomede;) all of which is confirmed by Hesiod: "so that

* *Orat. ad Græc.* c. 5.
† *Dial. cum Tryph.*
‡ *Cohort. ad Græc.* c. 1.
§ *Ib.* c. 2.

if you are to believe your own famous writers who have furnished divine genealogies and histories, you must either admit your gods to have really been such characters, or deny that they were gods at all. But* if you refuse to abide by your poets, because they have invented fictions, then, I ask again, who were the masters of your religion? Tell us from whom did your poets obtain the ideas they have thus embellished; for they must have learned them from some one? Do you say the philosophers? Yes, to these, as to a fortified wall, you are wont to fly, when any objection is made to the descriptions of the poets." He then commences "with the elder philosophers," and endeavors to show that their notions "are equally ridiculous." Thales the Milesian, the head of the physical school, asserted that all things were made from water, and into water are resolved. Anaximander considered space to be the principle of all things; but Anaximenes (also of Miletus) found it in air; whilst Anaxagoras, the Clazomenian, placed it in the symmetry of homogeneous elements. Again, Archelaus of Athens supposed it to reside in boundless air, and its variations of temperature. Such was the sect of Thales. Another branch† of philosophy sprang from Pythagoras. It indulged more in abstractions, and called number the principle of things, or its proportions and harmonies. But Epicurus, not content with anything so indefinite and intangible, sought it in corporeal matter, perceived by reason; while Empedocles fancied that it was better explained as the four elements, with the double ruling force of attraction and repulsion. Thus you see in what an unsettled state of opinion were the very doctors of your religion. How then can it be safe for those who would be saved, to sit at the feet of men who cannot agree among themselves? "But perchance you will yet say, you have not received your instruction from the ancient, but from the

* *Cohort. ad Græc.* c. 3.

† *Ib.* c. 4.

more modern philosophers, as Plato and Aristotle, men celebrated both for wisdom and virtue. Well, but we shall find upon examination, that neither do these agree together. Plato* affirms the three principles of the universe to be God, matter, and form; Aristotle, only God and matter. Again, whereas Plato teaches that the supreme God and ideas live in the first sphere of the highest heaven, Aristotle ranges, not ideas, but other deities after the supreme God. Moreover, it is plain to any one studying the writings of these men, that they are not consistent with themselves. Plato at one time talks of three principles, at another of four, having added the soul of the universe, which is supposed to personate all things. Now he speaks of matter as created; then as uncreated: now, of form as self-originating and self-subsistent; and presently as the motion of the mind. So that your sages do not appear to harmonize either with one another or with themselves; and if this be the case with regard to mundane matters and objects so apparent, how much more must it be when the subjects are spiritual and invisible?" In proof of this diversity of opinion, various hypotheses on the nature of the soul are produced, which would make it fire, air, wind, an exhalation, a stellar influence, a numeral endowed with the power of motion, or generative water. "Wherefore,"† he infers, "since you find so little truth is to be learned from your teachers, nay that, on the contrary, they display their ignorance by mutual disagreements, it seems to me that we should all turn together to our ancestors, our masters, who were both older and wiser than yours; who have taught nothing according to their own fancies, and who have never disagreed or attempted to overthrow one another's statements, but have without prejudice handed down what they learned from God himself. The fact is, that neither by nature nor art, can the human mind

* *Cohort. ad Græc.* c. 6.

† *Ib.* c. 8.

attain to the knowledge of divine things. For such lofty flights of thought it was needful that the gift of God should descend into the breasts of holy men, not exciting in them a care for the artifices of language, or sentiments of strife and envy; but purifying and using them, being just men, like some instruments of music, to reveal to others the certainty of heavenly doctrines. In this way alone can we account for the constant harmony and consistency of our prophets, although they delivered their doctrine in various places and at different periods of time."

TATIAN.* "We (Christians) distinguish God from what he has created, and only admire his works as they are proofs of his skill and power. I cannot bring myself to adore an object like the sun or moon made by him on purpose to serve us. It would be like worshipping my own slave: still less can I dare to deify wood and stone, mere substances, pervaded by an inferior kind of spirit, if by any at all."

Speaking† of the Grecian gods, he calls them "demons, who first tempted men to believe in fate, and suggested the collocation of animals in the Zodiac, the origin of brute worship." "Consider," he continues,‡ addressing the Greeks, "that these demons, who you say determine your destinies, can be transformed at your own pleasure. Rhea becomes a tree; Jupiter a dragon, for the sake of Proserpine; and a bull is translated to the skies, whilst you are slaying its fellow on the earth." How§ can we approve of an administration which boasts of such governors? How could we be so self-deceived as to believe in fate? It was our own choice that ruined us. We made ourselves servants, who were free; we are sold under sin. No evil is of God; we have

* *Orat. ad Graec.* c. 4.
† *Ib.* c. 9.
‡ *Ib.* c. 10.
§ *Ib.* c. 11.

brought it upon ourselves. This is our doctrine.* We have thoroughly investigated the stratagems of your furious demons: they are degrading, and easily seen through; but the doctrines of Christianity are too sublime for a wicked world to understand." He beseeches† them "to give up the dogmas of fatality, and the worship of demons, which only pretend to heal the ills of men, while they seduce them by means of the arts of life. Whence Justin has truly called them robbers."

Again,‡ he says: "We are not so foolish as you who publish fables concerning God incarnate. Compare your fictions with our narrations before you reproach us. You relate that Apollo fed the curved-footed oxen of Thessaly out of gratitude to Admetus; that Prometheus was chained to Caucasus for having benefited mankind; and that Jupiter, being jealous, withdrew sleep from men, in hopes that they would perish. Surely if you admit such tales as these, you cannot but approve of ours, especially when you find them to be in no respect foolish or trifling. Do you not see also that in such accounts you admit the humanity of your gods? Nor does any allegorical interpretation help your cause. One of two things is true: either these gods and their shameful conduct go together; or else, with their names transferred to natural objects, they are no gods at all; for the worship of the elements is too idle to think of."

ATHENAGORAS,§ in meeting a charge of Atheism, reminds the Athenians that formerly, with some color of justice, they condemned Diagoras for this crime, because he not only divulged the Orphæan and Eleusinian mysteries, but took the statue of Hercules, and burned it to boil his rapeseed; yea, he utterly denied the existence of a Divine Being.

* *Orat. ad Græc.* c. 12. † *Ib.* c. 18. ‡ *Ib.* c. 21.
§ *Legat.* c. 4.

"But *we* only distinguish God from everything material, and believe him to be self-existent and eternal. Far be from us then the great impiety of Atheism. The poets* and philosophers vainly endeavored to search out to perfection, that God who is inaccessible to all the attempts of natural reason. They deservedly failed, because they sought not from God himself, but from their own imaginations, the knowledge of spirit and matter, form, and the world. But we have the prophets for vouchers of our faith; men who spake as they were moved by the Holy Ghost, concerning God and the things of God. They teach† us that there is one invisible Being, not subject to passions, not circumscribed by space, incapable of divisibility, only to be comprehended by the mind; as one endued with inconceivable glory, beauty, power, and majesty; by whom all things were made through his Word, were disposed into harmony, and are so continually maintained. We believe too in the Son of God, though we hold not the same views concerning his generation as your absurd mythologists have, who make their gods as wicked and insane as themselves. We hold that the Son of God is the Wisdom and Word of God, to whom all matter was subject by formation. We believe likewise in that Holy Spirit who speaks by the Prophets, proceeds from God, and returns to God, as a beam of light passes from the sun, and is reflected back again. Who then cannot wonder to hear us charged with Atheism, though we declare there is God the Father, and God the Son, and the Holy Ghost, and acknowledge their power in unity and distinction?‡ But§ with respect to your gods, they are allowed not to have been from eternity, but were every one of them born as we are. Orpheus, who first invented names for them, and gave us their genealogies and lives, is

* *Legat.* c. 7. † *Ib.* c. 10.

‡ Dr. Waterland quotes this confession. *Serm.* 8, Camb. 1720.

§ *Legat.* c. 18.

supposed to have delivered the most correct accounts, and from him Homer drew largely. He makes ocean or water the fountain from whence all the gods sprang. How then* can these gods live forever, seeing they are no way self-existent, but originated? Or wherein can they be thought superior to matter, who derive their nature from the first material, called water? There are other theories as to the origin of the gods, quite as unstable, and which indeed are only worth a thought as they prove the disagreements of your theology." He then † passes to "the forms and figures so monstrously and unwarrantably bestowed upon the Deity. Heracles is a writhing serpent: the Titans have a hundred hands: Jupiter's daughter by Rhea or Ceres, has four eyes, a bird's beak, and horns on her head," &c. Again he calls attention to the crimes of these divinities. "Saturn mutilates his father, and hurls him headlong from his chariot; he in his turn is put in chains by his sons, and driven out of heaven. This worthy son then makes war with the Titans for his empire, tries to ravish his mother Rhea, and has a son Dionysius by his own daughter, Persephone. Who can conceive that forms and crimes like these are compatible with the idea of gods? Moreover‡ we find Juno in a rage, Jupiter in sorrow, and unable to save his son Sarpedon; Venus wounded in her body and in her heart; Vulcan lame; Mars pierced and baffled, though the god of war, and finally caught in the act of adultery! These are your gods! § But it may be said, 'this is a dress the poets have given to theology. There is a philosophical explanation of these matters.' Well, then, let us view the subject in the best light that can be put upon it; and as Empedocles says, 'let Jupiter be fire, Juno the air, Pluto the earth, and Neptune the sea.' But these are the elements of the world, and not gods. They are all material, which God is not; they are all variable, but God is

* *Legat.* c. 19. † *Ib.* c. 20. ‡ *Ib.* c. 21. § *Ib.* c. 22.

unchangeable:* the worship offered to them is strangely cruel, whilst the true God is beneficent." Our author† therefore will not accept of the physical theory of the gods, but proceeds to identify them with departed heroes by means of their names. He finds, "Herodotus, in the epistle of Alexander to his mother, assuring us that the priests of Heliopolis, Memphis, and Thebes, knew and confessed their gods to be but men. Orus, son of Osiris, (by the Greeks called Apollo,) they acknowledged to have been the last king that reigned after he had destroyed Typho. By Osiris is meant Bacchus in the Greek. Thus the last, and therefore all the preceding kings of Egypt, were men, from whom are derived the names of the gods among the Greeks. Their queens also were deified. Hermes Trismegistus and many others agree that the gods have not been from eternity, but had reigned on the earth; and the Egyptians themselves confirm this, by informing us that the temples are their tombs. Apollodorus says thus much in his book concerning the gods; and Herodotus adds that their passions or deaths were mysteries, which for decency's sake, he declines to explain. Indeed not only is the place where Osiris was buried, exhibited, but also his mummy. It was on this account, doubtless, that the Greek poets never scrupled to impute anything human to the gods. Pindar and Hesiod are quoted in attestation. But," he continues, "the Divine nature must be above the want or desire of anything, nor can it die."

Moreover these deities of the Pagans were not only human, they were wicked, illiterate, covetous, &c.: "Castor and Pollux and crazy Ino with her son Palæmon, for example; also Semiramis, a blood-thirsty and lustful woman, who is worshipped in Syria." Some have been adored for strength of body, as Hercules and Perseus; some for their actions, as Æsculapius; and many princes through love or fear, have

* *Legat.* c. 26. † *Ib.* c. 28.

been treated with divine honors. So Antinous not long ago by favoring one of the emperors, obtained among his subjects the esteem of a god. And observe this extract from Callimachus:

"The Cretes are always liars;* they presume to show the tomb of Jove; but great Jove lives."

Dost thou, Callimachus, believe his birth and doubt his death? Dost thou think to conceal the truth by talking thus to the ignorant? Canst thou look on the cave, and acknowledge him to be born of Rhea, and view his urn, and yet question his decease? Art thou ignorant that the only God without beginning of existence, is the Eternal One? Either then all the accounts of the poets and philosophers are false, and therefore the worship of the gods vain; or if the narrations of their births, amours, murders, robberies, mutilations, and judicial deaths are true, then are they evidently deceased, they must have died, because they were born, &c. I have thus proved at least, that we (Christians) are not Atheists, but believe the Creator of all things, and the Word, to be God.

* Warburton, in his *Divine Legation* (p. 182, Vol. I.), gives "the Cretans on the authority of Diodorus Siculus, as an exception to the general rule observed by other nations, of keeping their mysteries secret. The great secret of the earth-born nature of the gods, they proclaimed to all the world by showing and boasting of the tomb of Jove himself, the Father of gods and men." It was this that so exasperated the other Grecians against them, and gave birth to the proverb, "The Cretans are always liars." This opinion seems to have been commonly held by the Fathers. They quote two heathen poets in affirmation. (1.) Epimenides the Cretan prophet, (alluded to by St. Paul in his epistle to Titus) who lived circ. B. C. 650. His work (probably upon oracles) is lost. It is quoted by Clemens Alex. *Strom.* Lib. I. Art. 3. (2.) Callimachus, a later poet, said to have filled the post of librarian to Ptolemy. His versus (the one before us) occurs in a hymn of Jove still extant. (Vid. Schol. on these lines, and "proverbium in Chiliad." Erasm.) Other references to Callimachus, by the Apologists, will be found in Tatian, c. 27; Clem. Alex. *Hortat.* c. 2; Theoph. *ad Autol.* c. 10; Origen, *Contr. Cels.* Lib. III. s. 43.

THEOPHILUS* being asked to exhibit his God, replies that he has no form, nor beginning, because he is unbegotten; and that he is immutable as he is immortal. He† moreover refers the inquirer to the works of Nature. "And‡ thus," says he, "I show you my God, the Lord of all, who alone stretched forth the heavens, and established the earth; who opened the deeps of the sea, and set a bound to its waves; whose spirit enlivens all things, without which the universe would cease to exist. Your faculty of speech, your very breath is from Him, of whom you are ignorant, because of the darkness and hardness of your heart. But there is a remedy for this disease: the Word, the Wisdom of God, heals and revives: if you understand this truth, my friend, and live purely and justly, you can see God—having faith coupled with fear in your heart, you will perceive him here, and being made immortal in heaven, you will see him who is immortal, hereafter.

"But§ as to *your* gods, who and what were they? Their names are but those of dead men! Their characters yet more despicable! Was not Saturn the devourer of his children? Are not Jupiter's adulteries described by Homer? Did not one of his sons, Hercules, burn himself to death? Was not another, Bacchus, a drunkard and a madman? Behold! Apollo a fugitive for fear of Achilles; and though a god, ignorant of the death of his beloved Hyacinthus! Venus wounded! Mars, the destroyer of men! We even meet with traces of blood flowing from the gods! I do not assert these things myself, but on the authority of your own historians and poets. And why‖ should I enumerate the variety of creatures worshipped by the Egyptians, reptiles, birds, cattle, wild beasts, fish, besides washing vessels, and even obscene sounds; and though the Greeks may not have debased

* *Ad Autol.* Lib. I. c. 3, 4. † *Ib.* c. 6. ‡ *Ib.* c. 7.
§ *Ib.* c. 9. ‖ *Ib.* c. 10.

themselves quite so low, yet we see them adoring stones and blocks, and other material things, images, as we have just said, of dead men." He farther observes of these images, that they are mere human productions, ascribing the Olympian Jove at Pisa, and the Minerva in Arce at Athens, to the well known sculptor Phidias. Passing on, he reckons at least eight Jupiters belonging to different countries, and having different origins; and reminds Autolychus that "he who is called the son of Saturn was once a king of Crete, where his sepulchre is pointed out to this day." He thinks* that he would rather worship the emperor than the images of dead men, but concludes that "God is the only true object of adoration," as is found confirmed by a careful investigation of the prophetic Scriptures; † a safe way of avoiding eternal punishment, and of obtaining eternal blessings.

Having thus‡ dispelled these illusions of the arts, and asked ironically how it is that Mount Ida is so deserted now, and whither Jupiter Olympus can be gone, our author§ next turns to the philosophers. He quotes "the Stoics denying a God altogether, or at least his providence, and the followers of Epicurus and Chrysippus, of the same opinion: others asserting that the world was made by chance, or not created at all, but self-existent; or, that God is merely another name for the consciousness of every individual, or the spirit pervading all things. Plato, however, and his disciples confess that God is not produced, but is the Creator himself; yet, at the same time, they inconsistently hold that matter is also unproduced." He then exposes‖ the discordances and follies of the heathen writers generally. He points out the differences between Homer's explanation of the origin of the gods and of the world, and the theories of the philosophers; also between both of these and Hesiod; and¶ concludes therefore that "all

* *Ad Autol.* Lib. I. c. 11. † *Ib.* c. 14. ‡ *Ib.* II. c. 1–3.
§ *Ib.* c. 4. ‖ *Ib.* c. 5. ¶ *Ib.* c. 8.

the historians, poets, and philosophers of the Greeks, only sport with those who give them credit, whether they exhibit the gods in their true characters, as drunken, lascivious, murderous men, or endeavor to explain them away by psychological and physical theories." He attributes much of the dreadful delusions of the poets, to their having sought their inspiration, and attributed their gifts to the profane Muses.

With such false prophets* he now compares the *true* prophets, and begs his hearers to consider the variety, the beauty, and the force to be found in their writings. "As rivers and fountains nourish the sea," says he, "so has the law of God and the prophets preserved the world by a continual supply of gentleness, pity, justice and obedience, that else had failed long since on account of the great wickedness in it; and as there are fruitful and salubrious isles in the sea, and many ports affording a shelter to the tempest-tossed or shipwrecked mariner, so God has set his churches in a world ebbing and flowing with sin, in order that those who desire salvation, may fly thither and learn to avoid his anger and just judgment."

In contrasting† Plato's story of Deucalion's‡ flood, with the Mosaic account of the deluge, our author shrewdly observes, that the latter "explains *how* such a dreadful visitation came to befall the earth, with all its particulars."

HERMIAS.§ "Some of the philosophers assert that the soul is fire, as Democritus; some, air, as the Stoics; some, motion, as Heraclitus: an exhalation or emission from the stars furnished with motion, as Pythagoras; some, generative water, as Hippon; or harmony, as Dimarchus; or blood, as Critias; or breath, or unity, &c. Behold the variety of

* *Ad Autol.* Lib. II. c. 14. † *Ib.* Lib. III. c. 18.

‡ Theophilus fancifully derives the name "Deucalion" from Noah's mission of "calling" man "to God."

§ *Irrisio.* c. 1.

opinion entertained by the sophists, each of them pretending to the truth. Again,* one calls pleasure the chief good; another calls it an evil; and a third places it between the two extremes. Some assert the immortality, some the mortality of the soul. Some reduce it to a bestial level, or dissolve it into separate bodies, or give it a migratory circuit of three thousand years. What else is this but fiction or madness, or both together? And† being at such a loss with regard to their own nature, is it any marvel that they should fall short when they begin to investigate the nature of God? Nevertheless they have had the boldness, not to say stupidity, to attempt it. They who know nothing about themselves, freely discuss God. They who are ignorant of the construction of their own bodies, undertake the fruitless task of explaining that of the world. But‡ at the very outset they oppose one another. Anaxagoras differs from Melissus; Parmenides and Anaximenes from Empedocles; § Protagoras from Thales and Anaximander; and|| Archelaus from Plato and Aristotle. Even those who are more ancient yet, as Pherecydes (who said that the gods were only natural principles,) and others, exhibited the like rivalry. Leucippus, Democritus, and Heraclitus,¶ all think differently from Epicurus and his followers, whilst** Pythagoras concludes that the beginning of all things is unity, from whose figures and numbers the elements were made, thus dissenting from all. These things†† I have related, that the contrariety of philosophical opinions may be made manifest, and the endlessness and inutility of their theories exposed."

CLEMENS ALEXANDRINUS‡‡ examines the origin of the Pagan orgies, and discovers that "they are founded on profane and dangerous fables, the inventions of atheistical

* *Irrisio.* c. 2. † *Ib.* c. 3. ‡ *Ib.* c. 4. § *Ib.* c. 5. || *Ib.* c. 6. ¶ *Ib.* c. 7. ** *Ib.* c. 8. †† *Ib.* c. 10. ‡‡ *Hort. ad Gent.* c. 1, 2.

men; for by right," it is added, "are *they* called ungodly who venerate a little boy torn from the Titans, a wailing woman, and even parts of the human frame! They know not God, whosoever worship that which is not God, but commit a double crime. Atheism and superstition are the extremes of ignorance. Originally," he continues, "there was free intercourse between earth and heaven, which has been interrupted by man's seeking his present happiness in the earth alone, and prostrating himself according to *seven* species of idolatry. He has deified (1) the heavenly bodies, as the Phrygians and Indians, who adore the moon; (2) the fruits of the earth which the Athenians honor in the person of Ceres, and the Thebans in Bacchus; (3) or, urged by a consciousness of guilt, they ascribe divinity to punishments and calamities, whence the furies of the dramatists; (4) or, to the passions and affections; so the philosophers treat hope, fear, love, joy, &c., even as Eumenides of old built an altar to impudence; (5) or, to the incidents of life; thus fate, justice, &c., came to be esteemed goddesses by the Athenians; (6) or, they have accepted the twelve gods of Hesiod; (7) or, the common benefactors of the race, who, (in place of that God from whom all good comes,) were feigned to be his servants, like Bacchus, Hercules, and Æsculapius." Our author, taking the last explanation as the most satisfatory, now goes on to show that the common gods of Greece were men by their actions, their numbers, and their names. He reminds the Pagans that their own writers mention three Jupiters, five Minervas, as many Apollos, and Mercuries and Vulcans *ad libitum.* He then glances at the native countries of the deities, their occupations, their sepulchres, each attesting their earth-born and mortal nature. Mars is confessed by some to have been a Spartan, by others a Thracian chief, and the poet himself makes him change sides in war, and presently puts him in chains for thirteen months. Vulcan is hurled out of heaven by Jupiter, falls on Lemnos, and being lamed in his feet, works a forge with his hands. But besides a smith, the gods have a doctor among them, a certain Æsculapius, whose humanity, however, is betrayed by his avariciousness. Hercules was accounted a mortal man by Homer, and the Muses are styled by Alcander, the daughters of Jove and Mnemosyne. Then follows a review of the vices and misfortunes of the deities. Their marriages, their childbirths, their adulteries, their intemperance, their wounds and servitude, their laughter and quarrels over the festive cup, are all brought into requisition as witnesses against their divine essence. Nor can the minister of God here refrain himself from a practical remonstrance. "These are the gods whom your wives, your children, worship; obnoxious to all the passions and sufferings of men; goddesses revealing their charms to a shepherd judge; wounded; in tears: gods struck in the stomach, losing blood, feeding on human flesh, not knowing the while that it was their own children. Behold your gods, and they that worship them will be like them. Better would it be, like the Egyptians to follow dumb animals from city to city and street to street, than to have such immoral gods as these."

He next comments* upon another class of gods, the demons, who are described as impure, gluttonous, and cruel, deceiving men by means of oracles and statues, and delighting in and abetting the bloody contests of the world.

This† leads him to consider the subject of images or symbols of idolatry. He shows that first of all, men began by worhipping senseless things; the Scythians, a scimitar; the Persians, a river. The first figure of Diana was a mere block of wood, and that of Juno, a hewn trunk. Afterwards statues began to be shaped into human figures. It is well known that the statue of Juno at Athens was cut by the chisel of

* *Hort. ad Gent.* c. 3. † *Ib.* c. 4.

Euclides. Philochorus says that Telesius executed the sculpture of Neptune and Amphitrites, nine cubits high, which the inhabitants of Tenos adore. Demetrius in the second of the Argolics states that the figure of Juno Tirynthia was made of a pear-tree, by an Argive: the statue of Morychus Bacchus was cut out of Phellensian stone by Simon the son of Eupalamus, as we gather from a letter of Polemon: and to conclude, who does not know that the great demon of the Egyptians, Serapis, whom all countries honor with a peculiar reverence, was constructed by men's hands? The history of this statue is supplied, as well as of the temple containing it; our author observing upon the dishonor cast by Cambyses and Darius upon this and other Egyptian gods, that though not done from any proper motive, it certainly proves their inherent weakness. A like inference is drawn from their having "suffered from fire and earthquakes, which seem to regard an image no more than a pebble on the seashore." Another fact going to prove the worthlessness of statues, appears on the authority of Posidippus, who tells us that Praxiteles carved the Venus of Cnidus, as like as possible to Cratina his own mistress; so that in reality the mistress of Praxiteles is worshipped: and also that at one time all the painters expressed the form of Phryne, the Thespian courtesan, in their pictures of Venus; whilst the sculptors were copying Alcibiades in their Mercuries. "Judge ye," he exclaims, "whether it is right to adore base harlots, and effeminate men; but, being dead yourselves, you worship the dead! Truly these things are called images or shadows with some propriety! Yonder figure is fair Parian marble, and not Neptune; beautiful ivory, and not Olympian Jove! Matter requires art to turn it to account; the true God needs nothing. Will you then be more senseless than apes, and worship representations of wood, or gold, or ivory, a mighty medley introduced into the world by sculptors and painters?"

Lastly,* he detects the philosophers "making a god out of nature and the elements of the world; or, if it be allowed that any of them saw the truth at all, it was only as in a dream." Each of the philosophical systems, with their principal opinions, is then reviewed, and the conclusion arrived at, that "though the philosophers have not worshipped stocks and stones like the Greeks, nor the ibis and ichneumon like the Egyptians, yet they have fallen into other errors, equally grievous and fatal." Elemental worship is traced back to the Persians, on the authority of Berosus.

"And thus,"† reflects our author, "amidst all this crowd of demons and deities, images and fables, man lies like one in a nightmare. It is the Christian alone who looks above material things, to God. How different‡ are the sacred books from which *he* derives instruction! They stand as the foundation of all true worship. They will be found upon examination, free from obscurity and mere outward ornament; evidently intended to withdraw us from vice, to teach men to despise the various misfortunes of this life, to subdue their passions, and to seek salvation." He therefore exhorts every one§ to be "both a participator and a follower of the one God, 'crying, Abba, Father.'" "If you truly desire‖ to seek God, you may become a partaker of the atonement, which pleases him, and be encircled not with garlands, but with leaves of temperance. Jesus saith, 'I am the door:' this is the reasonable gate which is opened by the key of faith. Explore then no longer the impious adyta of your temples, nor the mouths of deep and wondrous caves, the Thresprotian cauldron or the Cirrhean tripod, or the knotted tree among the sands of the desert. By the side of the decaying trunk, leave also these worn-out fables: the Castalian fountain is silent; the wave of Colophon is dried up:

* *Hort. ad Gent.* c. 5. † *Ib.* c. 6. ‡ *Ib.* c. 8.
§ *Ib.* c. 9. ‖ *Ib.* c. 2.

the oracles are deserted, (greedy ventriloquists that they were, performing their divinations for wheat and barley;) the palmistry of the Etruscans, and the secret arts of Egyptian jugglers deceive no more."

TERTULIAN* is led, in his defence of the Christians, to prove that the gods of the Gentiles are no gods. On this point he refers his opponents to their own works of antiquity, from which alone they derive any knowledge of their deities. "These," he says, "are found to bear testimony to the humanity of the gods, by naming the cities where they were born or died, and the countries in which they had left traces of their achievements." Owing to the great number of the gods, he is obliged to make a compendious summary.† He gives us an account of Saturn, Bacchus, Ceres, Minerva; and wonders why the Pagans did not deify Socrates and some other *really* worthy characters. He observes‡ that "Seneca has severely inveighed against these divinities; and § that the heathen themselves continually treat them with irreverence, by neglecting some out of such numbers; by buying and selling the Lares; by converting them to the basest purposes, when battered and worn; by letting out the revenues of the temples to the highest bidder, so that the more popular the divinity, the higher it is taxed; and by admitting the lowest and vilest characters into the circle of gods."

He next ‖ glances at the weaknesses and calamities of the heathen deities; how they fought in pairs like gladiators, for Trojans or Greeks; how they were wounded, imprisoned, released, in sorrow, in disgrace. "Which of the poets," he asks, "does not calumniate them? One sets Apollo to keep sheep; another hires out Neptune to build a wall; Pindar declares Æsculapius was deservedly scathed for his

* *Apol.* c. 10. † *Ib.* c. 11. ‡ *Ib.* c. 12.
§ *Ib.* c. 13. ‖ *Ib.* c. 14.

avarice in exercising the art of medicine to a bad purpose; whilst the writers of tragedy and comedy alike, take for their subjects the crimes or the miseries of the deities. Nor are the philosophers behindhand in this respect. Out of pure contempt, they would swear by an oak, a goat, a dog; Diogenes turned Hercules into ridicule; and the Roman Cynic Varro introduces three hundred Joves without heads."

From the stage abuses,* our author selects those of Diana being flogged, the reading of Jupiter's will after his decease, and the three half-starved Herculeses! Of some of these things he mournfully reverts to his having been an eye-witness: "We have joined in the laugh at the cruel entertainments with which you beguiled the mid-day, when Mercury went about with a red-hot caduceus to ascertain whether the bodies were really dead! We have seen also Pluto dragging off the corpses of the gladiators, with a hammer in his hand."

In passing,† he rebuts the charge made against the Christians, of worshipping an ass's head, which he attributes to "Tacitus (his loquacity and falsehood ill agreeing with his name") by stating that neither among Jews nor Christians, have any images been allowed; and makes it return upon his accusers, by showing that they worship the beast entire. Again, he‡ illustrates the inability of the gods to help their worshippers. He observes that, "even while M. Aurelius lay dead, the high priest of Cybele was offering vows and drinking impure blood for his safety, and that too for seven days after his decease; that Jupiter allowed his own kingdom of Crete to be subdued by the Romans; and Juno, her beloved Carthage, to be desolated." As to their dates, he finds that "Rome reigned before the circuit of her Capitol with all its gods, was erected; and to look further back yet, the ancient monarchies of Babylon, Media, Egypt, and

* *Apol.* c. 15. † *Ib.* c. 16. ‡ *Ib.* c. 25.

Assyria were established, long before the Pagan priests and virgins, and even gods were heard of."

In contrast* with all this, a simple sketch of Christian doctrine is set forth, to show that the object of our worship is one God, the Creator; Christ† is introduced as God, and his nature, incarnation, and death dwelt upon; and the written word referred to, as "indited by holy men, who have lived at various intervals from the beginning,‡ under the inspiration of the Holy Spirit."

MINUTIUS FELIX,§ with the intention of exposing the vulgar belief concerning the Divine Nature, remarks: "Our forefathers credited every monster and prodigy, Scylla with all her bodies, and Chimæra with all her shapes, the many-headed monster hydra reviving from its fruitful wounds, and centaurs, half man and half horse; in short, fame could not be better at lying than they were at believing. What do you think of the metamorphoses of men into beasts, and trees, and flowers? And this credulity extended to the very gods they worshipped. From venerating their kings and desiring their effigies after death, they grew to treat these memorials with adoration, and now every country has its founder, or hero, or queen, or inventor, for a god. This‖ the Stoics confess. Euhemerus explains how men were deified for their courage or wit. He furnishes us with their nativities and their tombs, in every province. Proditus mentions that travellers who imported useful products, were esteemed gods by their countrymen; and Perseus the philosopher adds, that fruits often went by the names of their discoverers." "The vain and wicked mysteries" are next handled. "It is deplorable to see how the Egyptian Ceres, with a serpent for a girdle and lighted torches in her hands, searches pensively for her ravished Proserpine; or how, in the rites of Jove, a

* *Apol.* c. 17. † *Ib.* c. 21. ‡ *Ib.* c. 18.
§ *Octav.* c. 20. ‖ *Ib.* c. 21.

goat is introduced for a nurse, and to drown thé cries of the boy (stolen from his father, lest he should be devoured,) the Corybantes play on cymbals; while those of Dindymene Cybele, practised among the Gauls, are too shameful to rehearse. Besides, what figures do you make of your gods? There is Apollo, though so old, without a beard; and yet smooth Apollo's son, Æsculapius, with a very respectable one; there is green-eyed Neptune, blue-eyed Minerva, goggle-eyed Juno; Mercury with wings to his feet; Pan hoofed; Saturn in fetters; and Janus with two faces as if he walked backwards. There is Diana the huntress, under the title of Trivia, branching out into three heads, and hands innumerable; Jove, with or without a beard, horned as Ammon, armed with thunder as Capitolinus, or as Latialis, smeared with gore; Erigone, who died by a halter to live a virgin in the skies; Castor and Pollux, who live and die by turns; Æsculapius, who was struck by lightning to rise up a god; and Hercules, who was scoured from his human dross in the Ætean flame, and turned into a divinity. These strange stories* the poets have embellished, still more to prejudice the truth; on which account Plato, to his eternal honor, banished Homer with all his laurels from his imaginary commonwealth. For *he* is the first poet that introduces the gods to men, with jest and raillery. He sets them quarrelling, wounds Venus, enchains Mars; he sings of Jove's escape by the help of Briareus, and how, when the mighty god could not deliver his son Sarpedon, he wept showers of blood. He tells likewise of Venus' enchanted girdle to draw the god from his mistresses, and make him a kinder husband to Juno. Sometimes Hercules is a hostler, Apollo a cow-herd, and Neptune, Laomedon's mason, cheated of his wages. There we have the thunder of Jove, and the arms of Æneas forged on the same anvil (as if the heavens and the thunder and lightning were not in

* *Octav.* c. 22.

being, before Jove was born in Crete;) the adultery of Mars and Venus; the lewdness of Jupiter with Ganymede, all of which were invented for the gods, to authorize men in their wickedness." The history of Saturn, and his flight from Crete to Italy, by which he is proved to be a man, completes the research; and "having thus," says our author,* "proved the fathers to be mortal, it must needs be that none can doubt the humanity of the children."

Of the practice of turning men and emperors into gods, the folly is plainly seen, "inasmuch as none of them wish to die and be deified, but would rather by far remain here."

Images† are yet more absurd. "Man makes and dedicates his gods of wood, stone, and brass! Why, the very mice, the swallows, the kites, know better than that; they tread on them, and sit on them; the spiders crawl over their faces, and use the sacred heads for blocks on which to spin their webs. You yourselves wipe, and scrape, and clean them, and yet fear what you make and are compelled to protect. Moreover, the temples in which they are erected, become the resorts of wickedness. In some processions, the most noted adulteress is dressed up, and the high priest sacrifices with his own blood, or practises the greatest obscenities. Where‡ are there more sins contracted for, more assignations made, more adulteries concerted, than by the priests in the temples, and at the very altars?"

Lastly,§ the deceptions of the auguries must be exposed. "Regulus was taken prisoner notwithstanding all his observation of the auspices; while Caius Cæsar sailed to Africa, in spite of them, and gained an easy victory. Amphiaraus pretended to prognosticate his own fate, but did not know that his own wife would betray him for a necklace; blind Tiresias could foresee things to come, but nothing present; in the case of Pyrrhus, the poet Ennius helped out the Pythia

* *Octav.* c. 23. † *Ib.* c. 24. ‡ *Ib.* c. 25. § *Ib.* c. 26.

with an answer; and, to conclude, how wise it was in the oracles to leave off riddling, just as men began to be incredulous!"

ORIGEN* asks Celsus, why it is he can discover the profoundest mysteries "in those strange and senseless accidents, which, according to the most admired poets and historians have befallen his gods and goddesses, making them out to be polluted with crimes, contending with their parents, and doing many shameful things of a like nature; whilst Moses, who says nothing derogatory to the character of God, angel, or man, is treated as an impostor." He continues,† "I would openly challenge any one to set author against author. I would say, Pray sir, produce the poems of Linus, Musæus, and Orpheus, and the history of Pherecydes, and compare them with the laws that Moses gave to the Hebrews. Examine which have had the greatest and best influence over the minds of men. Impartially consider how few of your writers have had any effect upon the common people; whereas the works of Moses are fit for all classes, both learned and illiterate. I do not see what public service your books render; but the books we boast of, have persuaded Jews as well as other nations, to believe that the laws they contain were given by God himself." He applies this argument to Christianity, by showing that Moses was as far inferior to our Lord, as he was superior to the wisest of the philosophers or poets.

"St. John tells us‡ in his Gospel, of the majesty with which the Saviour uttered the divine and important truths that formed the subject-matter of his teaching, and of the authority with which he engaged the affections and attention of his audiences."

* *Cont. Cels.* Lib. I. s. 17. † *Ib.* s. 18. ‡ *Ib.* Lib. II. s. 73.

"Only show me* what Bacchus and Hercules have done. Whom have they made better by their discourses and examples, that they deserve to be called gods? Let us unfold the many histories written about them, and see whether they themselves were free from intemperance, injustice, folly and cowardice. If none of these vices are discovered in them, then may Celsus compare them with Jesus. Jesus† was never charged with any sin, even by his enemies; every one‡ acknowledged the wisdom of his doctrine."

Our author § also alludes to the brutal nature of the Egyptian deities; to the dissolute lives ‖ of those of the Greeks, as well as to the vain stories¶ of their heroes; to the temple of Antinous,** a minion of the emperor Hadrian; and to the tomb†† of Jove in Crete; as proofs of the essential carnality and absence of divine marks in the heathen systems.

He then‡‡ proceeds to illustrate out of the holy Scriptures, the Christian doctrine of the immutability of God, quoting the texts, "but thou art the same," and "I change not." With these he compares the Epicurean rationale, which deduces the gods out of atoms, and dissolves them again at pleasure; likewise the god of the Stoics, who is corporeal, or at best mental, evidently a vain endeavor to form a natural notion of Deity, as of something incorruptible, uncreated, and indivisible.

The genealogies §§ of the Pagan Divinities, as furnished by Hesiod, are contrasted with those of the Jews; also ‖‖ the respective accounts of the creation, upon which the observation is repeated¶¶ that "the simplicity of the Scriptures and their accommodation to the multitude (qualities quite overlooked by the philosophers) speak much in favor of Christianity. On the other hand, what can be more suspicious than

* *Cont. Cels.* Lib. III. s. 42. † *Ib.* s. 23. ‡ *Ib.* s. 33.
§ *Ib.* s. 17. ‖ *Ib.* s. 22. ¶ *Ib.* s. 31–33. ** *Ib.* s. 36.
†† *Ib.* s. 43. ‡‡ *Ib.* Lib. IV. s. 14. §§ *Ib.* s. 36.
‖‖ *Ib.* s. 38. ¶¶ *Ib.* s. 50.

the fact that, on account of their obscurity,* as well as their licentiousness, Plato felt compelled to banish Homer,† and the authors of poems like his, from his Republic?"

Origen,‡ continuing his contrast, points out, that while the heathen have used birds' entrails, &c. to obtain an imaginary insight into futurity, the true God uses not animals for such a solemn purpose, nor even common men, but selects the holiest and purest souls, whom he fills with his own Spirit, and renders prophetic. Wherefore Moses commands, "There shall be neither augur nor soothsayer among you; but a prophet will the Lord your God raise up unto you from your brethren, like unto me."

Again, he asserts § that "not only are the works of the prophets more ancient than those of Homer and Plato, but also more worthy of God who inspired them. They are greatly to be admired for loftiness of thought; and those persons are not wise who through idleness read them not; or, for a better understanding of them, never ask, as Jesus commanded, that God would give them wisdom, and open the closed door of their minds." As instances of the superior sublimity of the Scriptures, to the epistles and sentences of Plato, he quotes Psalm xvii. 12; Exodus xx. 21; xxiv. 2; Psalm ciii. 6; Isaiah's description of the seraphim, Is. vi. 12; and Ezekiel's vision of the cherubim, Ezek. i. 5.

The respective claims to the prophetical spirit are next ‖ considered. "If the Delphic oracle was truly divine, he ought to use his knowledge of the future in attracting men to a change of life, to the cure of the soul, and to the improvement of morals. But nothing of this sort is recorded of him in history. He prefers what contributes to his own advantage, rather than to the furtherance of honor and truth. The like may be said of the other oracles.¶ On the contrary,**

* *Cont. Cels.* Lib. IV. s. 36. † *Ib.* s. 50. ‡ *Ib.* s. 95.

§ *Ib.* Lib. VI. s. 7. ‖ *Ib.* Lib. VII. s. 5.

¶ In Lib. VII. s. 46, an instance is furnished of the Pythia being bribed.

** *Cont. Cels.* Lib. VII. s. 7.

the Jewish prophets, whether wise before, or enlightened by the reception of the gift of God, all followed a life rarely imitated, a life of constant exposure to danger and death. They were not in favor with the men of their day. It was to such persons the divine oracles were committed; and even our reason teaches us that their dispositions were such as became true prophets; by the side of which, the character of a Crates, or a Diogenes, is mere child's play." He particularly alludes to "their reprehension of sinners, to Isaiah's austerities, to Daniel's abstinence; these are they who had the honor of prophesying concerning Jesus, and it is no wonder that we, possessing them, make nothing of the heathen oracles, falsely called prophetic. We cannot help admiring the constancy and upright lives, so worthy of the Divine Spirit, which these Jewish teachers displayed, and who, for every reason except that which moved the predictions of demons, foretold future events."

Finally,* our author contends that the Christian system is to be preferred to that of the poets, for the clearness of its doctrines, and to the Jewish superstitions, for the catholicity of its spirit. "It is agreeable to reason," he says, "that God should leave none ignorant or unacquainted with his will, from any want of capacity. The Gospel therefore which instructs unlettered men, women, and even slaves in doctrines they can understand, and in morals which elevate them, must be divine. The Greek philosophers† may have said, and their priests have done some good things (though often only to gain esteem for apparent sanctity), but here is something much more influential, a perfect system of virtue. How can the precepts of Æsculapius, Orpheus, Anaxagoras or Epictetus be compared with those of Jesus, whose words are accompanied with a divine power, and though so simple, convert the world?"

* *Cont. Cels.* Lib. VII. s. 41. † *Ib.* s. 49.

CYPRIAN* grieves that "vice should come recommended to the heathen with such an appearance of authority as the example of the gods. Venus is represented as a harlot, Mars as an adulterer, and the famous Jupiter descends upon the stage and enters upon his amours with all the insignia of Godhead about him. At one time his divinity is cloaked in the feathers of a swan; again he is pleased to let himself down in a golden shower, or his eagles are employed to pander to his lusts. Now let me put the question whether any man is likely to be a spectator of such scenes, and yet preserve the purity of his thoughts, and the chastity of his life, untainted? People are ever found imitators of the gods they worship; and thus the most enormous sins are consecrated into acts of devotion."

"There is evidence† enough that they were really no gods, whom the vulgar honored. They were but ancient kings or persons of eminence, to whom after death religious honors were paid in memory of their greatness. Temples were raised over their ashes, and statues were made to represent their living bodies, while sacrifices and holidays were appointed to comfort the survivors, and to immortalize the dead in the minds of posterity." He gives particular cases of this transition from the natural to the superstitious, in which he closely follows Minutius Felix, only adding that "the Moors avowedly and openly adore their kings, nor attempt to cover the practice." He then ‡ points out how the heathen religions vary with soil, climate, and language, all disagreeing in their objects and modes of worship. He questions whether according to the popular separation of the deities into sexes, the progeny by this time ought not to be innumerable; and wonders why none are born in his own day. "But, perhaps, some are being born now, which would account for certain late Roman divinities, as the goddess Cloaca, the gods assigned

* *Ad Donat.* c. 5. † *De Idol. Van.* c. 1. ‡ *Ib.* c. 2.

to various passions, fear, pallor, the goddess of fever, also Acca and Flora, infamous women; while even doors, hinges, thresholds, and all ascents, as well as orphans, have now each their proper patron."

He comments upon the folly of Æneas in caring about those domestic gods, which could not preserve him from exile; and upon the indecency of modern times, "wherein Venus is more exposed than she was even by Homer, when he represented her as wounded by a mortal arm."

He gives* Scripture proofs, first that idols are nothing, and that the maker must be worthier than his manufacture; and secondly, that the Lord God is the only fit object of adoration.

ARNOBIUS,† in reply to a charge of atheism, asks if it is atheism to worship the Maker of all things, to call upon him, and in the midst of every trouble to embrace him with the affections of the heart! "Is this why your gods are so severe against us, and why you yourselves strip us of our goods, banish us from our country, torture us, burn us, cast us to the wild beasts? are men who will do these things, and gods who are supposed to encourage them, worthy of the names they bear? and who or what are we to be thus treated? Nothing more nor less than Christians, under the teaching of Christ. This is the gravamen of the charge, and this is the proposed end of our duties. Before him we all bow according to custom, and present him with our prayers. But‡ do you affirm, 'you have also a supreme god, Jupiter?' It is true, but he has a father, a mother, brothers, and cousins. He was himself but lately borne in the womb; how then can he be God? At any rate, you see that our religions so far harmonize, that it must be unjust in you to persecute *us*, and it is manifest by this inconsistency of yours, that you know not God."

* *Tract. ad Fortun.* † *Adv. Gent.* c. 7. ‡ *Ib.* c. 11.

"We acknowledge* that Christ was one of us, as to his human condition and physical infirmities; indeed it is this great condescension of his, and the benefits accruing from it, that make him worthy to be accounted a God. You honor Bacchus because he discovered the use of wine; Ceres, of bread; Æsculapius, of medical herbs; Minerva, of oil; Triptolemus, of the plough; and Hercules, for his subjugation of robbers and wild beasts. With what additional honor then should He be treated who drew us from fatal errors to the light of truth! who raised us from serving figures of vile clay even to heaven itself, and introduced our prayers to the Lord of all! Ought we not to account this Christ a God? A short time since, and I myself (alas! what blindness!) was venerating images fresh from the anvil and furnace; gods wrought out of iron, or carved in ivory; logs of wood, crowned with flowers. But now I see no virtue in anointed stones, but only in my anointed Teacher: I pray no more to senseless trunks, but only to the true God: I treat such things with the utmost contempt, while I adore and magnify the Divine name."

He therefore implores† the heathen, "no longer to keep themselves from Christ, who when on earth healed all that came to him; for he was the sublime God sent to be a Deliverer."

"What can induce you," he‡ further complains, "to reproach and hate Him who was never charged with any crime? Your tyrants and kings may desecrate the temples of the gods, lay waste entire states, and slaughter the inhabitants; yet you admire and applaud them, you raise them to the skies, and preserve their deeds in your libraries. Oh! unreasonable, ungrateful age! If a physician had come from some regions unknown, bringing such a medicine as would heal your bodies of every disease and sickness, would you not all run to him

* *Adv. Gent.* c. 13. † *Ib.* Lib. I. c. 19. ‡ *Ib.* c. 25.

and honor him? Well, Christ has appeared the announcer of the greatest good, pertaining to the salvation of the soul! Adopt his doctrines, rather than the hallucinations of your poets."

Pursuing* the contrast, he begs the Gentiles to consider "whether Christ has overrun the world with hostile legions, claiming his royal authority. Has he avariciously collected all the wealth of nations? Has he indulged himself in pleasure, idleness, or arrogance? Rather,† did he not introduce a religion than which there can be nothing more true, more practical, more just, more salutary? It is to know the great God, and to supplicate him, the fountain of all power and goodness."

Some excellent chapters occur here, showing that the philosophers were vain and presumptuous, in trying to explain the nature of God, the origin of evil, moral and physical, &c.; and that ignorance on such subjects as these is no crime, but only makes it more evidently the duty of man to submit his reason to the word of God.

To expose‡ the absurdity of idolatry, allusion is made to the number of gods inhabiting Olympus. He tells§ the Pagan that out of a thousand, or rather five thousand, he *must* neglect some; that the supposition of deities having sex is an unworthy notion, as indeed the furnishing them with a corporeal nature at all; and that‖ if it be said, these forms, whether human or animal, are but the assumptions of poetry, the insult to divinity seems only the greater.

He refers¶ to the usual disagreements of the oracles and theologians respecting the gods, asking, "how any one is to tell which is the right god, amidst such a confusion;" and then** to the sad example they set to the people; where he observes that all the miseries of men have arisen from the

* *Adv. Gent.* Lib. II. c. 1. † *Ib.* c. 2. ‡ *Ib.* Lib. III. c. 3. § *Ib.* c. 5. ‖ *Ib.* c. 8. ¶ *Ib.* Lib. IV. c. 8. ** *Ib.* c. 11-16.

indulgence of their private gratifications, in which the gods have set them the example. They are therefore the more hurtful on account of their exaltation; and the first duty,* both of the government and all who have any respect for Deity at all, is to destroy the books and pull down the theatres which encourage such licentious fables regarding it. This, he submits, would be doing something better than giving Christian writings to the flames, and razing churches to the ground; churches in which the great God is worshipped, and we pray for peace and pardon for magistrates, for armies, for kings, for slaves, for enemies; wherein nothing is heard but what tends to make men gentle, chaste, affable, and united in the closest brotherhood.

Touching upon† image-worship, he thus addresses idolaters: "You laugh at the Persians for adoring a river, and at the Scythians with their scimitar for a god; but it is equally ridiculous to mould and then supplicate little figures of men. How absurd to worship the work of your own hands! Look inside of your images, and observe the hollow spaces; can you conceive that the gods abide within such plaster and pottery? Consider moreover how these figures have to be kept under lock and key, lest they should suffer detriment." He gives,‡ for an illustration of their helplessness, the story of Antiochus (Cyricenus) carrying off a golden Jove, fifteen cubits high, and substituting one of wood in its place. "Now," says he, "if the gods are really so nigh as to inhabit these statues, in what business or care was Jupiter entangled that he could not avenge this personal insult? Their weakness and their misfortunes make them objects of contempt."

"Come then,§ to sum up, let us compare notes, and see whether *you* or *we* think most worthily concerning heavenly things. First, you profess that the gods whom you believe

* *Adv. Gent.* Lib. IV. c. 17, 18.

† *Ib.* Lib. VI. c. 5.

‡ *Ib.* c. 11.

§ *Ib.* Lib. VII. c. 18.

to exist in the nature of things, and whose images you place in every temple, were born and produced after the manner of men. We, on the contrary, even allowing that they exist and have their right names, assert that as gods they cannot be produced; it would be impious to suppose such a thing. Secondly, you give them sex; but we deny that the celestial powers are distinguished in this way, since it is a mark of an earthly nature, for the continuation of the species. Thirdly, you conceive of your gods after the likeness of men; we reckon that God has no corporeal form or feature, that we can understand. Fourthly, you furnish them with symbols, like any workman; we laugh at such an idea, holding that arts, which are merely means of subsistence, are not necessary in heaven. Fifthly, you relate their discords, and wars, their thirst for blood, their indulgence in the basest passions, their performance of all the functions of mortality; we esteem these things opposed to the nature of God. You* think to honor heaven with offerings of wine and frankincense; we think it monstrous to suppose that God can be dignified by smoke, or appeased by drops of wine, holding rather that opinions worthy of his name, are the best gifts, the truest sacrifices. Again, you are wont to charm your gods with the tinkling of brass and the sound of pipes; with horse-races, and other spectacles; we consider it wicked even to imagine that God takes delight in what a wise man ridicules and despises, as sports invented to humor the people.

"When, therefore, there is such a diversity of sentiment between us, you ought not to claim the monopoly of piety, or undertake to punish us, until the whole matter has been weighed in the scales of reason and conscience."

LACTANTIUS,† after stating the Christian doctrine concerning the eternity, the immortality, and the impassiveness

* *Adv. Gent.* Lib. VII. c. 60.

† *Epitom.* c. 7.

of the divine nature, begins an examination of the heathen notions of deity, and shows that the actions of the gods, according to the poets and historians, plainly prove their humanity. Thus Hercules* basely born, and addicted to the vices of his father, is conquered by a woman; murders his wife and his own children; is afflicted with ulcers; and, impatient of grief, constructs a funeral pile for himself. Other fables† are cited of Apollo, Mars, Castor and Pollux, Bacchus, &c.; after which the attention is directed to their crimes. He insists that Jove's lusts, even though feigned by poets, must mean *something*. The story of Danaë may stand for the effect of gold on virtue; the iron shower, for darts and weapons of war; the eagle, for a legion; and Europa's bull, for a ship. But these metaphors do not get rid of the wickedness, nor do they explain the generations and connections of the deities.

Jupiter‡ is next proved to have been a mortal man, on the authority of Euhemerus; also his father Saturn (called Chronos because he was full of years, as Cicero says,) and his grandfather Cœlus (Ops according to the Stoics,) to have been some wealthy and powerful chiefs. He gives§ it as Cicero's opinion, that men were deified for their virtues, or for the benefits they did to their fellow-creatures. This appears in a volume written to console himself on the occasion of his daughter's death; which testimony should be the more respected, in that the author was not only an augural priest, but a reverer of the gods, notwithstanding this persuasion.

Lactantius‖ then shows that divinity cannot be distinguished by sex, or misfortune; "for which reason," says he, "the Stoics endeavored to explain away the names and offices of the gods, by references to natural things. Do you not see,¶ asks Cicero, that reason falsifies the old women's

* *Epitom.* c. 8. † *Ib.* c. 10. ‡ *Ib.* c. 13.
§ *Ib.* c. 15. ‖ *Ib.* c. 16. ¶ *Ib.* c. 17.

fables of the gods, their shapes, their ages, their vestures, their ornaments, their generations, their alliances, all traced after the manner of human infirmity?"

Image-worship our author traces to Prometheus (called the son of Japeth, uncle of Jupiter) and to the sculptors generally.

Elemental worship,* and superstitions connected with magic† and oracles, are then discussed; and lead to a consideration of the origin of evil, which he ascribes to a wicked power created by God, abusing his free-will, and deceiving mankind in Paradise.‡

Calling his hearers now from the false to the true doctrine,§ our author introduces them to Christ as the divine Logos, explaining out of the prophets, his double nature of God and man. He observes‖ that one reason why the sacred Scriptures have obtained such credit is, because the prophets have spoken in simple and natural language.

EUSEBIUS.¶ "They who follow many gods are like children, and commit a grievous mistake, when they deify the constituent parts of the universe, and virtually divide the world into many;** as if we should say the eyes of a man, or

* *Epitom.* c. 26. † *Ib.* c. 27.

‡ I omit here, as elsewhere, an allusion to the strange theory of a second fall of the angels, so commonly held in the early church, and to be traced through the Jews to a misinterpretation of Genesis vi. 2. It is not true, however, as has been asserted, that all the Fathers give credit to this legend. Many of them never mention it, whilst Augustine (*De Civit. Dei*, Lib. xv. c. 23. s. 2.) distinctly says on the above passage, "Men they were, without doubt; the sons of Seth, who married the daughters of Cain." He shows, in support of this exposition, that "the sons of God were called 'angels,' and John the Baptist also;" and that "Aquila, the best Jewish expositor, calls the persons in question the Sons of God, and not angels."

§ *Epitom.* c. 42. ‖ *Div. Instit.* Lib. v. c. 1.

¶ *Theoph.* Lib. I. c. 26. ** See *Demonst. Evan.* Lib. IV. c. 5.

his ears, or his hands, were the man. Still worse* is it to imagine that this entire world is God, not considering† that the divine nature cannot consist of parts, or of the qualities of matter."

Pursuing his exposure of the philosophers, our author shows how "the evil demons blinded men and turned them to the worship of the heavenly bodies; of the elements under the names of Neptune, Vulcan, Jupiter, Juno, and the like; or of fruits of the earth, under the titles of Ceres, Proserpine, Bacchus; even the faculty of thought in man, they called Minerva, and of speech Mercury; while the memory and the muses‡ were not neglected. Descending yet lower, men made themselves gods out of their very passions, and the grosser members of their bodies. They had their Cupid, Priapus, their Venus, &c.; and when *men* were once transformed into gods, every species of irrational animal soon followed, with noxious reptiles. Trees were cut down, rocks hewn, metals run into the shapes of men, women and brutes. To these figures the appellations of gods were given, and to them and to the devils inhabiting them, sacrifices were offered. Thus§ the Egyptians, the Phœnicians, and the Greeks obtained their gods from the elements, fruits, their own passions, mortal men, and demons to complete the list. And then,‖ as the natural result of all irreligion, they fell under the error of fatalism, neglecting virtue as well as God.

"And¶ while the masses of the people were thus bewildered and corrupted, the philosophers, with all their pride of learning, were equally at a loss. Some accounted indivisible atoms the origin of all things; some** found rest to be the supreme good; these limited Providence within the moon's orbit; those banished it from the world altogether. Aristotle

* *Theoph.* Lib. I. c. 27. † *Ib.* Lib. II. c. 3.
‡ Theodoret more at length, *Gr. Aff. Cur. Serm.*
§ *Theoph.* Lib. I. c. 13. ‖ *Ib.* c. 16. ¶ *Ib.* c. 19. ** *Ib.* c. 20.

determined the extreme good to be neither virtue nor philosophy, unless attended by wealth and rank. Some affirmed the soul was immortal or only a quality, like color to the body; others taught that God was a body, or fire, or sensible earth; infamous doctrines! Plato* alone of all the Greeks, came nearer to the truth, and held what was right concerning the First Cause and the Logos. Yet† even he, though he knew God, honored him not as God; he dared not confess him before men, but, with the inhabitants of Athens, conducted himself as no philosopher at all, going down to the Piræus, to pray to the goddess, and to complete the feast of Bendis. How inconsistent‡ this, in one who had driven Homer and Hesiod out of his republic!§ The Peripatetics and the Stoics,‖ whatever may have been their private views, also submitted through fear to the law which commanded the worship of the gods. But¶ why should I exhibit sages, arranging themselves in ranks, separating one from another, and all contending together with their rival opinions, until, as one of the poets sings,

> 'Behold the abundance of the uproar thickened,
> Of the destroying, and of the destroyed;' **

or with Plato himself, it might be said, 'The conflict between them might be assimilated to that of the giants, because of the contention they had one with another about matter?' Aristotle opposed Plato,†† others opposed Aristotle. The sceptics put forward Pyrrho, and ridiculed everybody; the only thing in which they all agreed, was that which they all ought to have opposed, the multiplicity of gods." This is attributed to their dependence upon human teaching.

"The oracles‡‡ were equally fallacious; nor could those of Delphos, Lebadia, Colophon, or Miletus, lead men to the

* *Theoph.* Lib. I. c. 24. † *Ib.* c. 26. ‡ *Ib.* c. 41.
§ Theodoret. *Gr. Affect. Curat. Serm.* II. p. 486, seq. Tom. IV.
‖ *Theoph.* Lib. I. c. 43. ¶ *Ib.* c. 47. ** *Iliad*, Lib. IV. l. 451.
†† *Theoph.* Lib. I. c. 49. ‡‡ *Ib.* c. 50.

truth. The philosophers, together with the very refuse of society, attended the oracular rites. But what did they consult these diviners about? About things advantageous to philosophy? No one can say this. But with respect to the common commodities of life, the discovery of a slave or a missing ship, the purchase of an estate, or the choice of a wife. Thus philosophers, kings, and people, had themselves, through an estrangement of the intellect, learned to place the divine essence in material bodies and crafty demons; and to these they sacrificed their own children, which is against nature,* and strangers,† which is against the rights of hospitality." He introduces other cases of cruelty in the Pagan services, arguing that the "tree is known by its fruits."

In contrast‡ with all this, Eusebius has occasionally dropped a reflection, to show "how needful then was a Divine Saviour, to turn men back to the original simplicity of worship handed down through the Hebrews,§ who were considered worthy to receive the revelation of the Word of God, of prophecy, and of the doctrines of righteousness;" and he now‖ draws attention more directly to the character of Christ, indicating how completely he realizes all that could be required in a Saviour. "He excels men and gods too. Let any existing philosopher come forward and say what god or hero has at any period delivered the doctrine of eternal life, and of the kingdom of heaven to mankind, as our Saviour has done. Who has caused innumerable multitudes to be instructed in his own doctrines and wisdom, and has persuaded them to follow after the life which is heavenly, and to despise that which is temporal, and to hope for mansions in the skies reserved for the souls that love God?"

* *Præp. Evan.* Lib. I. c. 4. † *Theoph.* Lib. I. c. 53, 54.
‡ *Ib.* c. 19. § *Ib.* Lib. II. c. 42. ‖ *Ib.* Lib. III. c. 33.

He farther* asks, in answer to the charge of Jesus being a deceiver: "Was there ever a man heard of, who as a magician† and deceiver, was also a teacher of meekness, chastity, and every other virtue? He would not allow that men should indulge even an impure desire. He taught his disciples to give rather than to receive, to follow peace and retirement, and commanded men to honor truth above all things. Surely every one must confess that he was the Word of God in truth, and the teacher of righteousness. He raised our minds to God and denounced idolatry, taught the worthlessness of sacrifices, and admonished men of the day of judgment.‡ Such then being the instructions contained in the doctrinal ordinances of our Saviour, there is no room for imagining him to have been a deceiver. He was§ a doer and preacher of righteousness, and was himself an example to his hearers."

ATHANASIUS‖ opens his discourse with tracing the origin of idolatry to the temptation of the serpent in Eden, who turned men off from the contemplation of God, to a desire after earthly things. The Greeks, he says,¶ affirmed that evil was self-existent; they erred indeed in one of two ways, by robbing the Creator of one of his peculiar attributes, or by making him the author of evil. He himself** prefers with the Scriptures, to lay the blame on man,†† "who having once departed from God, fell lower and lower, and having commenced with the deification of the heavenly bodies, at length descended to crawl on the earth like a worm, and worship the very brutes. Others ventured to number their chiefs among the gods, either on account of the benefits done by them, or through fear of their tyranny. This‡‡ ancient practice is often mentioned in history."

* *Theoph.* Lib. v. c. 2. † *Dem. Evan.* Lib. III. c. 3.
‡ *Theoph.* Lib. v. c. 7. § *Ib.* c. 19. ‖ *Con. Gent.* c. 1.
¶ *Ib.* c. 6. ** *Ib.* c. 8. †† *Ib.* c. 9. ‡‡ *Ib.* c. 10.

From the humanity he passes to the immorality of the gods, which appears to have been "such as even men are not allowed to commit with impunity, by the common law of Rome."

He then glances* at their infirmities, their contentions, and, above all, their attempts to stir up the evil passions of men's minds.

Images are the next theme. He is astonished at any one's adoring wood and stone, that he has just purchased of the artificer, with money and thanks. Still more surprise is manifested, that the artist himself can supplicate the work of his own hands, and salute as a god, what he has lately been hammering and cutting. "The people ought rather to esteem the sculptor the worthier, of the two, of divine honor. For the material does not cause the art, but the art adorns and immortalizes the material. And this† indeed is the way, some say, the gods were made out of men, because of their merit, or the benefits they conferred on their fellow-creatures. Jove, it has been supposed, was the inventor of the plastic art, Neptune of navigation, Vulcan of the forge, Minerva of the loom, Apollo of music, Diana of hunting, and Juno of dress. By this confession,‡ the idolatrous gods were but men, whilst their crimes prove them to have been not only men, but base men."

He perceives § an additional proof of the vanity of idols, in the care and protection they require; in their need of renovation through age, or of repair after a storm, or the act of some mischievous animal. If cast down, they must be set up again by hands not their own, and at all times have to be enclosed in shrines and temples.

And again,‖ in their variety, and the differences of national sentiment with regard to them. The Phœnicians know not

* *Con. Gent.* c. 12. † *Ib.* c. 18. ‡ *Ib.* c. 16.
§ *Ib.* c. 21. ‖ *Ib.* c. 23.

the gods of the Egyptians, nor the Scythians those of the Persians; in short, there are as many gods as there are countries, states, villages. The Crocodile is adored here, and dreaded there. The Lion is worshipped in one place, and hunted in another. A fish that is honored in some parts, is eaten in others. All this difference of opinion arises from the contempt of the one God. "Since* then," he argues, "neither the heavenly bodies, nor any other part of created Nature; nor images of stone or gold or any material; nor the gods of the poets, nor the heroes of antiquity are to be accounted gods; and since the worship of such is the greatest impiety, and tends to evil and not to good; come, let us, having refuted the error, enter upon the way of truth, and contemplate the Creator of the World, the Word of the Father, that we Gentiles may know the Father also, for the way of truth leads to him."

Our author concludes† by pointing out that the superiority of man over the beasts, lies chiefly in reason and the immortality of the soul; in his capacity for meditating on eternal things, and looking forward to the future; all which is alone duly recognized in the Christian system of doctrines.

MATERNUS‡ shows that the worship of the elements is founded upon a notion of their beneficial effects. "Thus the Egyptians pretend to explain their absurd mysteries by making out Osiris to be the seed of fruit, Isis the earth, and Typhon generating heat; but then why need they have added the story of the incest, so that men, naturally sinful, should be tempted yet more, by an evil example?"

He asks § also, "how it has come to pass that obsequies and funeral rites are usually connected with the mysteries of the heathen. Surely this is a mixture of earthly and celes-

* *Con. Gent.* c. 29.
† *Ib.* c. 31, 32.
‡ *De Err. Prof. Relig.* c. 1.
§ *Ib.* c. 7.

tial things; of darkness and light; of the regrets of men, with the honors of Divinity."

After reckoning* the Persians and other Orientals as worshippers of the Sun, he imagines that luminary addressing an assemblage of its idolaters and reproving them for their folly. He suggests by the way, that if fire is worthy of regard for its usefulness, it should have had cooks instead of Vestal virgins for its attendants.

The idolatrous ceremonies† of Adonis, Venus, Jupiter and the Corybantes, are lastly brought under review. By the latter it seems that parricide was taught. "In truth," he adds, "the bad example which these stories offer to the public, is one of the worst features about them. A palliation is thus set up for giving and receiving the wages of lewdness; the gold of Jove is seen in the bosoms of corrupt women; wicked traitors are allowed to betray a father and a kingdom to an ungrateful son; and all the laws of hospitality, friendship, and religion are publicly abused."

GREGORY NAZIANZEN‡ asserts that the fables of the Gentiles are not to be compared to the mysteries of the Christians.

PAULINUS§ says antithetically, in his poem, "When God had formed man, man dared to form God. The Platonists‖ have sought in vain to define the nature of the soul. The Cynics¶ act ridiculously and ungraciously towards God, in refusing the gifts his hand bestows upon them. But what shall I say of the different religions, the temples, the gods and goddesses? In the Capitol you may see a god, or his wife, or his sister, which ever you please." This leads him** to notice the immoralities of the gods, and finally†† to point out the light and peace that have dawned in the person of

* *De Err. Prof. Relig.* c. 8. † *Ib.* c. 9–13. ‡ *Orat. ad Jul.* l. 30. § *Ib.* l. 29. ‖ *Ib.* l. 35. ¶ *Ib.* l. 44. ** *Ib.* l. 62. †† *Ib.* l. 137.

Christ, who has "regained what Adam lost. Christ the Word creates and arranges all things, becomes incarnate, and offers pardon to all."

AUGUSTINE* proves the inherent weakness of the heathen deities by historical facts. "Æneas saw Priam slain before the altar he fled to, and the gods of the Romans have not been able to save them in the late sack of the city (by the Goths.")

He affirms† that "the gods never troubled themselves about the lives or manners of those states that worshipped them, but contrariwise, led the way to all kinds of abominable deeds. Let any one who denies this, show us where any worthy lessons of the gods were ever rehearsed, and whether their worshippers were ever wont to hear of such matters as we discourse of continually in our churches, erected for this purpose in all places where the religion of Christ is diffused. The truth is,‡ the instructions of the philosophers were weak and useless for want of authority, and because § of the bad examples of the gods, which are enough to vitiate anything. How could the gods be justly offended with the adultery of Paris, since they did the same thing so frequently and freely? How hate in Paris what they saw in Venus? It was Varro's opinion that it was politic for some men to feign themselves begotten of the gods. By this at least he acknowledges that they *may* be false; and what a broad road is here opened for chicanery!"

In the ninth chapter of his fourth book, our author has shown that according to the Pagan theologians, all the universe is full of Jove. "But now Juno is added in the air, Neptune in the sea, Pluto in the earth, and that there may be no lack of them, Neptune must have Salacia, and Pluto, Proserpine, for wives! But the world and its elements being

* *De Civit. Dei*, Lib. I. c. 2. † *Ib.* Lib. II. c. 6.
‡ *Ib.* c. 7. § *Ib.* Lib. III. c. 3.

thus more than complete, where is Minerva's share? 'She is related by the poets to have issued from Jove's brain.' Why then was she not made mistress of heaven, seeing she sits above Jove? 'Because it is not proper to exalt the child above the parent.' Wherefore then was not this principle observed between Saturn and Jupiter? 'Because Saturn was conquered.' Did they fight then? 'Oh! this is only a fable: Saturn, meaning length of time, the king of all gods, is said to be born of time, that is, in time.' But how is this? Terra is also called the mother of the gods, though Juno is Jove's wife, sister, and mother also; and the same earth is styled both Ceres and Vesta; and then Vesta is called Venus, though the one was a virgin and the other an adulteress! Do you grieve to hear these things from our lips? then why do you applaud them on the stage? But* let us suppose there is only one Jupiter (to omit the odious catalogue of his transmutations), as Virgil says in the 4th Georgic; let him be Jupiter in the sky, Juno in the air, Neptune in the sea, &c. . . . Numeria for teaching children to count 20, Camœna for singing, and Fortuna barbata for our chin's sake, let him be all these and more; or, as those hold who make him the soul of the world, let all these be but his parts and virtues: I ask, why not take a shorter course, and adore but one God? Thus only can he be completely worshipped. For if the stars are parts of him, some must be neglected; and will they not be incensed, that while they shine above disregarded, filthy Priapus stands below in great request and credit?"

He next† calls attention to the impious consequence of the theory that the world is the body of God, "since in that case a man treads a part of God under his feet, and every creature he kills is a portion of Deity. Or,‡ if only animated life is of the divine essence, then when a child is beaten, can it be supposed that a portion of God's essence is beaten?

* *De Civit. Dei,* Lib. IV. c. 11. † *Ib.* c. 12. ‡ *Ib.* c. 13.

and will God be angry with man (a part of himself) for not worshipping him?"

He remarks,* casually, that the Romans, quite in character with their turbulent disposition, would not allow the temple of the goddess Rest, within the city walls, nor any public honors to be paid to her. "How differently does our Jesus speak to us, saying: 'Come unto me, all ye that labor and are heavy laden, and I will give you rest.'" And presently again,† our author is found gladly "turning from the midst of all this confusion in which the city of this world seems to lie, to the city of God, alone kept unmoved." "Just so long," says he, "as the Jews worshipped the true God, so long were they happy and prosperous. They never called on the heathen gods to help them; yet they grew and flourished, and that too, notwithstanding the opposition of their enemies. They prayed to no nymphs when the rock was cleft in the wilderness, and the water flowed out; to no Mars when they fought and conquered; they had corn and oxen, honey and apples, without Legetia, Babona, Melona, or Pomona. In fine, whatever the Romans begged from so many false gods, they received of the one true God, in a far happier measure."

He now‡ returns to the heathen deities and casts doubts upon their existence, by quoting the acknowledgments of Varro,§ and the criticisms of Seneca. The more abstruse physiological doctrine,‖ which attempts to cover the falsehoods of Polytheism by natural expositions (commended by Varro,) our author thinks an equally unfortunate theory; for the obscenities and cruel sacrifices cannot be thus resolved, while it is plain that¶ all the honor the naturalists refer to the world's parts and qualities, ought to be rather referred to God. Christianity,** he observes, is the only power that was ever able to explain and chase away the abominable

* *De Civit. Dei*, Lib. IV. c. 16. † *Ib.* c. 34. ‡ *Ib.* Lib. VI. c. 4. § *Ib.* c. 10. ‖ *Ib.* Lib. VII. c. 5. ¶ *Ib.* c. 29. ** *Ib.* Lib. VIII.

tyranny of the gods over men. It was Christ who routed the gods."*

He next considers the philosophers more particularly, and though he allows that some of their later doctrines were worthy of praise, he proves by the general diversity of opinion they manifest as to the nature of God and the origin of things, that their authors knew nothing of the truth, but were, at the best, and Socrates included, mere idolaters.

But whilst† among this world's philosophers, there was such a diversity in trying to attain the one point, happiness, "our canonical authors do not either contradict one another or themselves; whence it is, that so many nations believe that God spoke in them and by them. Our prophets are not numerous, but their concord is wonderful. In the multitude of philosophical writings, scarcely two can be found to agree. The Epicureans in the gardens, opposed the Peripatetics in the schools, and they in their turn the Stoics in the porch.‡ The philosophers could never teach the people aught else but confusion. Their city might well be called Babel. How different the city and king of the true Israel!"

He thinks§ that one of the principal marks of falsity about Paganism, is the insincerity of its wise men, who, while they held their own sceptical opinions concerning the nature of the gods, nevertheless frequented the public sacrifices and the temples of the gods, with the rest of the people. This‖ is even true of Socrates; and those who succeeded him, were too much alarmed at his fate, to be so bold as he, in mocking superstition.

To conclude,¶ he warns his brethren against pleasure, ambition, and curiosity, against the Manichæans (or rational-

* Reminding us of Milton's fine hymn on *the Nativity.*

† *De Civit. Dei,* Lib. XVIII. c. 41.

‡ It is observed elsewhere that Varro allows 288 sects to the single subject of the perfection of goodness.

§ *De Vera Relig.* c. 1. ‖ *Ib.* c. 2. ¶ *Ib.* c. 55.

ists,) against the wickedness of the Pagans in adoring demons, the elements of the world, the stars and planets, or spirit, whether it be of men, however excellent, or of angels. To draw us from all these delusive hopes Christ came, was incarnate, and has taught us that men ought to adore only that which all intellectual and rational beings adore. We are to honor angels by loving, not by serving them. He refers to the case of the angel in the Revelation, xix. 10, forbidding St. John to worship him, and saying, that he himself adores the only Sovereign Lord, of whom both are equally subjects. We are also taught to respect men,* says Augustine, but only according to the command, "Render unto Cæsar the things that are Cæsar's." He acknowledges the holy Trinity to be the object of *his* adoration.

*In allusion to the practice of swearing by the genius of the emperors; the primitive Christians accounting all genii, demons.

CHAPTER VI.

THE ARGUMENT FROM SUPERIOR MORALITY.

"Talk they of morals? O thou bleeding Love!
Thou maker of new morals to mankind!
The grand morality is love of thee."

YOUNG.

THE subject of this chapter is intimately connected with the one which we have just been considering. Here we see the legitimate result — the good fruit of the good tree. It is the glory of Christianity to have done what all other religions have failed to do, viz., to make people better and happier. Not that the heathen systems overlooked morals, or did not consider them as necessary in religion, and to be highly recommended. Far otherwise: there are indications enough amidst the thousand inconsistencies of men, to prove that they have ever had an excusing or else an accusing conscience, which has compelled them, at least outwardly, to recognize the propriety of moral maxims and virtuous conduct. But the authority, "the power" was wanting. Their theory, like that of Archimedes by which he could poise the world, was good enough, but where was a fulcrum to be found? The Religion of Christ came to effect what the sign of Nature, the voice of Philosophy, the law of Moses were too weak to do. The mission of God's own Son was doubly executive; to save men from sin, both as regards its penalty and pollution; "to bear our sins in his own body on the tree," and "to redeem unto himself a peculiar people, zealous of good works." He did not come to *introduce* morality, the world had never been without a sense of it; nor altogether, as Paley remarks, to teach it, *that* also had been more or less conscientiously done in every age; but to cause it to be carried out; to change a faded notion into a lively practice; to supply sufficient motives and sanctions; in fine, to exert a power *from above*, without which the dead could not live, or the blind see. Hence Christianity is as much distinguished by its actual morals, as by its peculiar doctrines. It furnishes the only example of a Religion, giving all the glory to God, and producing a hearty and complete morality in man.

It must therefore redound to the credit of the early Christians, that they exemplified this holy end of religion in their lives, and insisted upon it in their writings. Indeed, it may be asked, how could they have succeeded in overcoming, as they did, the prejudices of a sinful world, had not this been the case? Dr. Hey supposes that, "even miracles could never have gained the assent of mankind, if the internal evidence of the Gospel plainly contradicted the external, or if the precepts it promulgated were evidently unworthy the Deity, and productive of the misery of human nature:" while Origen affirms much the same thing of prophecy, which he thinks is not necessarily to be accounted a divine gift, unless accompanied by morality. And again, without morals how could we account for the unmitigated persecutions endured by the early Church? It was, as some of our authors observe, as if all other religions were bent upon destroying this. To what can such a unanimity of opposition be attributed so reasonably, as to its demanding a purity of life, which the rest most certainly neglected?

But the best proof of the morality of the early Christians, and of the immense importance they attached to it, lies principally in the writings before us; and it is truly delightful to find that no argument was so much and so feelingly urged by the Apologists. Lactantius is but an echo of the rest when he says, "Nulla alia religio est vera, nisi quæ virtute ac justitia constat." Hereby do they prove their connection with patriarchs, and prophets, and apostles in the clearest manner; hereby they prove their acquaintance in a practical way with that Holy Word, whose province it is to "enlighten the eyes," and "cleanse the heart;" hereby they prove their religion to be from Heaven; for behold the heavenly graces in their heart and on their tongues, and throughout their lives!*

It will scarcely be thought strange, if in some of these arbitrary divisions of so united a subject as the Christian Religion, the proofs occasionally run one into another. Such an excuse is particularly needed with regard to the contents of this and the preceding chapter. I have said that the two classes of subjects are intimately connected; the consequence is, that some of our materials might be said to belong to both of them. It has been my aim, however, to distinguish them as much as possible, into ideas intended to include the relations of God to man, or (strictly speaking) *theology;* and the relations of man to God and to his fellow-man, or *morals:* the one being an appeal to reason or judgment, looking objectively; the other an appeal to conscience, looking subjectively: *that* regarding opinions more; *this*, actions. Where the object of an Apologist seems to have been the combined one, it can matter little into which of these divisions it falls. Whether, for instance, the Philosophers and Evangelists are exhibited as *teachers*, and so associated with doctrine; or as

* Palmer sums up the evidences of the Apostles and Christian Fathers as derived, first, from prophecies; second, from miracles; and third, from the *purity* and excellence of the Christian doctrines, as compared with those of other religions.—*On Develop. and Consc.* c. 2, p. 21.

exemplars, and so ranked with the rules of life they professed. But the reader must judge for himself.

With regard to any summary of the method adopted by the Fathers in pressing this argument home, I have only to repeat, that it generally consists of a *comparison* between the systems of ethics under discussion, a knowledge of the difference between right and wrong being taken for granted.* The unity and definiteness of the subject of morality seem to leave room for no further explanation.†

AUTHOR OF EPISTLE TO DIOGNETUS,‡ while he charges the heathen with having become as wicked as their gods, says of the Christians: "They may not perhaps be distinguished from other men by earthly abode, by language, or by custom; their home is any region, however barbarous or remote; for they are but strangers and foreigners here: but, with this conformity to the various usages of the countries they inhabit, as to dress, food, and external matters, they exhibit a peculiar morality, wonderful and striking to all. They obey the existing laws, and triumph over them by their conduct."

Exhorting§ his correspondent, he says: "If you really desire this faith, and accept it, then first will you know God, and with what joy will you be filled! How will you love him, who so long before loved you! And if you love him, you will then be an imitator of his goodness; for‖ neither is life without knowledge, nor knowledge safe without a true life. They must be planted near together, like the trees of Paradise."

* The epistle to the Romans opens much in the same way.

† Not a little of the substance of Paley's main argument, drawn from the voluntary sufferings of the original witnesses, will be found under this head.

‡ *Ep. ad Diog.* c. 2. § *Ib.* c. 10. ‖ *Ib.* c. 12.

JUSTIN MARTYR.* "Many assume the name and garb of philosophers, who act not at all in conformity with their profession. You [the emperors] well know that men holding dissentient opinions and doctrines among the ancients, are styled by the common name of philosophers. But some of these taught atheism, and some immorality, without your prohibition. Nay, you propose prizes and honors to such as shall eloquently illustrate the disgraceful lives of your gods.† Now we confess indeed that we are unbelievers in these pretended gods, but not in the most true God, the Father of righteousness and temperance and all other virtues, in whom is no mixture of evil: Him we worship and adore, with the Son and the Prophetic Spirit, knowing them in reason and in truth; and to every one who wishes to learn, we freely deliver our opinions, even as we have been taught."

"When questioned‡ as to our profession of Christianity, how easy would it be for us to deny it, and escape; but we choose not to live by falsehood, desiring to attain a purer and eternal life, where no evil can assault us."

"Neither§ do we honor with numerous sacrifices and garlands those whom men have invested with a bodily shape, and placed in temples, and denominated gods. You well know that these images are senseless and dead; and also the impure lives of the artisans who make them, so that they even corrupt the women assisting them in their works. Oh! astonishing blindness that men thus impure, should be said to form and change the fashion of gods for the purpose of worship; and that such men should be placed as guards of the temples where they are erected, not considering that it is impious to imagine or say that men are the keepers of gods."

"We‖ are firmly persuaded that God requires not from men material offerings, seeing he hath given us all things;

* *Apol.* I. c. 4. † *Ib.* c. 6. ‡ *Ib.* c. 8.
§ *Ib.* c. 9. ‖ *Ib.* c. 10.

those persons only are accepted of him who imitate the perfections of his holy nature, chastity, justice, humanity, and whatever virtues belong to God, to whom no name can be ascribed. To exist at the beginning was not in our power, but to obey what is conformable to his will, making our choice by means of the rational faculties with which he has endowed us; thus he persuades us and leads us to faith."

"We confess* that we are Christians, though we know that the punishment of death awaits us."

He argues† that truth is to be honored before established practices, and that "as all avoid the inheritance of poverty or disease or disgrace from their parents, so will every wise person reject that which right reason commands him to refuse."

"We have learned,"‡ he says in answer to a charge of impiety for not sacrificing, "that the only honor which is worthy of God, is not to consume with fire what he has given us for our nourishment, but to use it ourselves, and to distribute among those who have need; and that our thankfulness to him is best expressed by the solemn offering of prayers and hymns."

"We who§ once delighted in fornication, now embrace chastity only; we who once used magical arts, have consecrated ourselves to the good and unbegotten God; we who loved above all things the gain of money and possessions, now bring all that we have into one common stock, and give a part to those in need; we who hated and killed one another, and permitted not the people of other nations, on account of their different customs, to live with us under the same roof, now, since the appearing of Christ, live at the same table, and pray for our enemies, and endeavor to persuade those who unjustly hate us, that they also living after the excellent institutions of Christ, may have good hope with us, to obtain the same blessings from God the Lord of all."

* *Apol.* I. c. 11. † *Ib.* c. 13. ‡ *Ib.* c. 16. § *Ib.* c. 17.

He then* expatiates upon the purity of mind, and the universal kindness† that Jesus himself inculcated, reminding his royal judges, how "Christians avoid swearing, are careful to pay tribute,‡ and custom, and keep the peace§ above all men; which things‖ Jesus Christ has taught for the reformation of manners, and the improvement of the human race."

With this conduct,¶ he compares "the injustice and impiety of the heathen nations in exposing their infants, in the corruption of the youth of both sexes, in the prostitution of wives, and in the shocking offerings made to her who is called the mother of the gods."

In replying** to the allegation that Christians voluntarily sought death, he says: "First, it is false, for they account suicide contrary to the plain will of God; and secondly, the reason why they do not fear death is, that they are guilty of no evil, and consider it better to die, than to live by denying the truth."

The effect produced†† on a heathen mind by the constancy of Christians under the severest trials, is well described by Justin, from his own experience before conversion. "I saw," says he, "it could not be that they lived in pleasure."

"Our circumcision,"‡‡ he proceeds, addressing the Jew, "is not made with iron like yours, but with sharp stones (that is, the preaching of the apostles of Him who was the chief corner-stone, cut out without hands) from the worshipping of idols, and from all iniquity; our hearts are circumcised from sin." "I affirm§§ that the prayers and thanksgivings which are offered up by worthy persons are the only offerings perfect and acceptable to God."

The author of the *Corhortatio ad Græcos*‖‖ condemns the public festivals and games, "where every indulgence in vice

* *Apol.* I. c. 18. † *Ib.* c. 20. ‡ *Ib.* c. 23. § *Ib.* c. 12.
‖ *Ib.* c. 31. ¶ *Ib.* c. 36. ** *Ib.* II. c. 4. †† *Ib.* c. 12.
‡‡ *Dial. cum Tryph.* c. 14. §§ *Ib.* c. 17. ‖‖ *Cohort. ad Græc.* c. 4.

is allowed; flutes excite you in the frenzied dance, and unguents and flowers cover your heads. Thus you banish modesty, temperance and peace." These accompaniments* of an idolatrous system, he contrasts with the power of the Word of God, penetrating the soul. "Oh! soothing music to the troubled heart; Oh! refuge from woe; Oh! doctrine that quenches the passions of the mind; which does not, perhaps, make men poets, or philosophers, or orators; but in truth renders mortals immortal, makes gods of men, and translates them to heights above Olympus! Come then, be instructed; be what I am, since I was what you are. These things have captivated me, both by the divinity of the teaching, and the efficacy of the word. Just as the skilful charmer draws from its hole, and then puts to flight the dreaded serpent, so the divine Word expels from the depths of the soul the most fearful passions, and above all, lust, by which every evil is generated, hatred, envy, strife, emulations, anger, and such like; when these are expelled, the soul becomes calm and serene; and being freed from the pollutions that surround it, returns to its native place, to him who made it."

TATIAN.† "What sort of character have your most preëminent men borne? Diogenes, who boasted of his abstemiousness, out of a tub, died of intemperately devouring shell-fish; Aristippus was a thankless spendthrift; and Aristotle taught that none could be happy unless they were wealthy, comely, strong, and of noble birth. Then there was Heraclitus,‡ who arrogantly said, "I have investigated myself;" and Zeno, with his absurd cycles; and the rash Empedocles, whom the fire of Ætna confuted. Wherefore let not a solemn conclave of philosophers, who are not true philosophers, carry you away against your better judgment; for

* *Cohort. ad Græc.* c. 5. † *Orat. ad Græc.* c. 2. ‡ *Ib.* c. 3.

they dispute among themselves, and say whatever comes uppermost. But they have other faults of a worse complexion. They hate one another; they contend fiercely together with their rival dogmas; and choose the chief places under the influence of the most insufferable pride, not serving others, but being themselves waited upon."

"We,* on the other hand, are peaceable and orderly. The king demands tribute, we pay it; the governor orders us to obey him, we acknowledge our obligations. Man is to be respected as man, God as God. It is only when required to deny God, that we disobey and would rather die, than prove false or ungrateful to him. We desire† neither power, nor wealth; lewdness we abhor. We trade not for gain, to gratify avarice; we fight not for a crown, to gratify ambition; we despise death, we are above disease and sorrow; if I am a slave, I endure servitude; if free, I glory not in my birth; I see the same sun shining upon all; the same end happening to all, whatever their station in life may be; nay, I perceive that the rich have many temptations which the poor and the moderate know not of. Ah! why do you watch for fate, to satisfy your avarice? Why, so often seeking, are you as often befooled? Befool the world in return, by rejecting its mad schemes; live to God by knowing him, and casting aside these ancient and inveterate errors."

"The soul‡ dies not if it be instructed in the knowledge of God. The Holy Spirit is not in all men. He only resides in those that live justly; who by embracing him entirely, have even thereby been enabled to announce future events; and all those who obey wisdom atttract to them this cognate Spirit, while they who are disobedient, seem rather to fight with God than to worship him. And such§ are you, ye Greeks, polished indeed in language, but in thought foolish. You have served many lords instead of one, and honored

* *Orat. ad Græc.* c. 4. † *Ib.* c. 10. ‡ *Ib.* c. 13. § *Ib.* c. 14.

devils as if they were all-powerful, being thereby deceived into the greatest wickedness."

He next* notices the divination of presaging trees, and the flights of birds, which he tells the heathen, "are mere slaves to their desires. Whosoever makes you eager after anything takes care to prophesy accordingly, and he that excites seditions or wars, the same also predicts a sure victory."

"And† what is your discipline and your worship? Who must not condemn your solemn rites, your public sports, performed at the public cost, and only tending to spur men on to shameful deeds?"

"I have often seen, and as often marvelled at and despised the actor in his different characters, now melting away in luxurious effeminacy, now rolling his eyes like a madman; one moment a Venus, the next an Apollo, and in a third an accuser of all the gods, criticising their actions, their murders, their adulteries; a very master and teacher of wantonness. Yet this man will be applauded by the multitude; but by me, he is rejected for his impiety and his lasciviousness. How is it that such things captivate you, and that you insult those who think differently from them? Is it anything very wonderful or worthy that such men do? They utter base things through their nose; they throw themselves into indecent postures; and though your sons and your daughters are among the spectators, exhibit the whole art of adultery, and publish deeds of wickedness which should be left at least under cover of the night. I have seen the gladiators‡ encouraged by the presidents and umpires of the games, not to any illustrious action, but to contention and blows. He who was the best striker was to be crowned; and what is the result of such popular spectacles? The idle and the poor sell themselves to be butchered. The rich man can purchase

* *Orat. ad Græc.* c. 19. † *Ib.* c. 22. ‡ *Ib.* c. 23.

as many assassins as he pleases; some support whole bands; and when these ruffians go forth to mortal combat, you act as judges, and are only grieved when they do not slay one another. You kill animals, that you may feast upon their bodies; but you buy men, that you may feast your eyes and your mind with human flesh and gore. A robber commits a murder for gain, but you for pleasure."

"How* can I admire the fury-stricken Alcmæon of your poet Euripides? Does he not slay his mother? How spend my time like another Aristoxenus upon a Theban Antigenides? We yield to you such worthless themes."

"And observe† the conduct of your sages; they bare one shoulder, they cut off their hair, they cultivate beards, they neglect their nails, and declare they need no one's assistance or sympathy; and yet whilst they are speaking, Proteus-like, they show their need of a mistress for their wallet, of a tailor for their robe, of a carpenter for their staff, of a cook for their belly; and then, as if to establish their independence beyond all dispute, abuse you roundly if you do not give them a penny. Their philosophy is only an art of getting money: they care nothing about wisdom or God."

"Whilst‡ you think you know God, you perceive not what he does in you; gaping at the clouds, you fall into the ditch. Your books are like labyrinths, and as treacherous as the daughters of Danaus: your actions are specious, but irrational: you are one thing in public, another in private. How inconsistent§ you are! You charge those who follow the word of God with eating human flesh, forgetting that you yourselves serve up Pelops as a banquet for the gods, in spite of Neptune's love for him; and make Saturn devour his own sons, and Jupiter his pregnant Metys. You punished Diagoras for revealing your mysteries, and yet you cite his book against us. You preserve the opinions of Apion con-

* *Orat. ad Græc.* c. 22. † *Ib.* c. 25. ‡ *Ib.* c. 26. § *Ib.* c. 27.

cerning the Egyptian gods, while you would exterminate us for saying the same things, as if we were the most impious of mankind. The sepulchre of Olympian Jove is shown to you; though some of you say that the Cretans lie. Your writings are a war of words, not an illustration of the truth. Nor are your rules of life any better: there are as many codes of morals, as there are kingdoms in the world. Among the Persians, a man may marry his mother; while the Greeks do not permit such incest: but on the other hand the corruption of youths is condemned by the barbarians, and yet allowed by the Romans."

"For myself,"* says Tatian, "when I had gone the round of these things, and had been moreover initiated into the mysteries of every religion, and perceived the wickedness of the worship of all the gods, I wondered where I could find the truth; and after much research I fell in with some foreign writings, more ancient, when compared with the age of any Grecian works, and more divine when compared with their errors. In the perusal of these Scriptures, I could not help giving credence to them, on account of their style, which is as devoid of arrogance as it is of artifice, although the subjects treated are of vast importance. The whole creation is explained in language simple and easy to be understood. They are full of knowledge of the future, and of most excellent precepts, and above all, distinctly teach the unity of the Creator. These† I found to be divine doctrines, able to liberate me from the thraldom of many gods: and now being instructed, and initiated anew, how different is the result! I would now fain be like a child, despoiled of all my pride and folly!"

Touching upon‡ the Christian discipline, he says: "The poor as well as the rich may learn at our schools, and that gratuitously; for whatever proceeds from God is too valuable

* *Orat. ad Græc.* c. 29. † *Ib.* c. 30. ‡ *Ib.* c. 32.

to be purchased with money. All who are willing to hear, we admit; young and old, women as well as men: we respect age and sex; but lasciviousness is far from us: in this we lie not, God being our witness. We do not select our catechumens by their countenances or address; all we want is fortitude of mind, which we believe can exist in weak and infirm bodies: but in your schools of philosophy you are either invidious in making distinctions, or careless about character." Wherefore* "I think it is manifest that our institutions tend to promote temperance and chastity; yours, sin and madness. For while you blame us for trifling among a set of women and children, see what trifles are most popular with you. Your fine arts are a mockery, and the images of your gods are in higher estimation than the gods they represent. Praxilla who uttered nothing of any value in her songs, and Sappho, that shameless woman, who immortalized her own passions, are honored in brass by Lysippus. On the contrary, among us all are pure, and we can boast of virgins more chaste than your Delphian prophetess."

Having further exposed the loose characters of their heroines, he urges the heathen† to "forsake everything of this kind, and seek that which is more honorable and wise, and instead of hating Christian institutions, to hate the infamous inventions of a Philænis or an Elephantis."‡

ATHENAGORAS,§ after an exposition of divine doctrine, calls attention to morals, and quoting the injunction of Christ, "love your enemies," thus proceeds: "seeing I make my apology before emperors who are philosophers, let me charge any of the sophists who pretend to instruct and reform their readers, to show such a mild disposition of soul, a heart so

* *Orat. ad Græc.* c. 33. † *Ib.* c. 34.

‡ Philænis was a courtesan; Elephantis a poetess who wrote immodest verses. *Vid.* Martial, 12 *Ep.* 43.

§ *Legat.* c. 11.

free from rancor and malice, as to return even to their enemies love for hatred, blessing for cursing, and prayer for persecution. Do they not ever act the contrary part? Do not they persecute in a revengeful manner those that injure them? Do they not teach the art of logic, rather than a rule of life? But among us you meet with unlettered men, common mechanics and even women, who though in words they may not be able to defend or serve our religion, yet adorn it by a bright example. They study not the refinements of language, but the practice of virtue: in short, they love their neighbors, that is, all men, as themselves."

"These* are a few arguments by which you may judge betwixt us and our adversaries. But the truth is that most of them are persons of the greatest stupidity, being neither philosophers nor theologians: they know not themselves the difference between a God and a cloud; and yet they accuse us, only because we do not believe those to be gods whom the generality of states and cities fondly trust in."

"Be pleased,† great sirs, to weigh well each branch of the charges brought against us. And first as to our not offering sacrifices. Surely the great Father and Creator of the universe needs neither blood nor sweet incense, seeing that he is perfection itself. The best sacrifice we can give him, must be to study to know him. This is our 'reasonable service,' and this he requires. Again,‡ as to our not praying to statues, or not honoring such gods as the cities and countries about us do, it were wiser for those who charge us with Atheism, to agree among themselves which gods are to be worshipped; for the day would end ere I had reckoned all the variety of their deities. Look only at the Egyptians: how absurd is it to see them in their temples, beating their breasts, and lamenting their idols as deceased, and then immediately worshipping them as alive and as gods. But really nothing can be thought

* *Legat.* c. 12. † *Ib.* c. 13. ‡ *Ib.* c. 14.

strange of a people that deify brute beasts, and when they die, bury them in sacred ground, shave themselves for them, and order public fasts. If then we are atheistical, because we differ from the Egyptians, so is the whole world, for no other nations adore such gods as these. But* suppose our opponents were agreed in a uniformity of worship; shall we fall down and worship dead images and statues? If God and matter were the same thing, then indeed were we impious in not worshipping wood and stone, gold and silver; but we have learned to distinguish between what is uncreated and what is created."

"Our accusers† further charge us with feasting on human flesh, and with incest. This is not the first time vice has vilified virtue. Pythagoras with 300 more was burned; Democritus was starved out of Ephesus; Heraclitus, the Abderite, accused of madness; and Socrates put to death by the Athenians. But as the virtues of these men were not lessened by the false opinions of the vulgar, so neither is the integrity of our lives blemished by the slanders of our enemies; before God we are still innocent. And ‡ how unlikely it is that we who consider ourselves responsible, not only for our actions, but for our thoughts to an Omnipresent and Omniscient God, should be guilty of such crimes? Had we no hopes beyond the present life, it might be; but we look for a happy eternal life hereafter; a life with God, which truth we affirm even at the stake and in the flames. But is it any wonder our accusers should charge us with such crimes when they do not hesitate to impute them to their own gods, and to call their lusts mysteries? If they were in good earnest, and really vexed at incest and concubinage, what would they not say of Jove, or (if this is a lie of Orpheus) how would they not abominate his historian?"

* *Legat.* c. 15. † *Ib.* c. 31. ‡ *Ib.* c. 32.

"But our Lord and Master gave us an exact and heart-searching divine law; so that* having a good hope of eternal life, we despise all present sensual enjoyments."

Lastly,† he defends the Christians against the imputation of eating human flesh, by an indirect argument (since the heathen would not investigate for themselves), observing that, "not even a slave had ever witnessed or confessed under torture, such a thing of their feasts. Besides," he adds, "consider our general character for humanity: the spectacles,‡ the theatres, the games, the gladiatorial combats, the fights with wild beasts are hateful to us. We consider them steps to murder. And who that is persuaded of the future resurrection of the body, would make himself a sepulchre of other bodies, which are to be raised? Those who do not believe in this great doctrine may commit such a crime with impunity, and may eat the flesh of animals gloated with human victims, but not so Christians. Thus § I have shown to your majesties that we are religious towards God, inoffensive towards men, and pure in our own souls. Moreover, who can put in a fairer claim to your royal favor than they who continually pray for your life and prosperity?"

THEOPHILUS,‖ speaking of the knowledge of the true God, remarks that as a mirror must be bright, so must the soul of man be pure. "Tell me then, whether you are an

* *Legat.* c. 33. † *Ib.* c. 35.

‡ The subject of amphitheatrical shows, in which either men or animals are destroyed for the public amusement, often occupied the pen and tongue of the Apologists. They were viewed as essentially cruel and demoralizing spectacles. What a reflection does this fact cast upon the silent encouragement given to such exhibitions in Spain, by those who profess to belong to a church, once, and essentially humane. "On the 4th of July last (being Sunday) the Catholic monarch, Queen Isabella, with her family and whole court, attended a bull-fight at Madrid." *Vid.* "Times," of that date, 1852.

§ *Legat.* c. 37. ‖ *Ad Aut.* Lib. I. c. 2.

adulterer, a fornicator, a thief, contumelious, an evil-speaker, passionate, envious, proud, a striker, covetous, disobedient to parents, a vendor of your own children? God does not appear to such as do these things, nor will he until they have cleansed themselves from every defilement."

"By the command* of God we are taught to abstain from the wicked worship of images, and of the elements; from adultery, murder, and the like; in short, from doing to another what we should not wish another to do to us."

"It is worthy of observation,† that all the prophets have spoken consistently with themselves, and harmoniously with one another; a strong proof that they were inspired by one and the same spirit. They also were all vexed in their inmost hearts, and bewailed the sins of the human race." These assertions are maintained by numerous references.

He says,‡ "it is the duty of a historian to affirm only what he has seen with his own eyes, or accurately learned from the testimony of others." By this rule he judges the profane writers, and finds that whilst the poets have done nothing but seek their own glory, the tragedians and comedians, the historians and philosophers, have only uttered wicked and useless sentiments. "None§ of them either perceived the truth themselves, or excited others to it; their works prove that their glory was but folly and ignorance. Moreover, to say nothing of their disputes and mistakes in doctrines and physics, did not your moralists actually recommend all sorts of uncleanness to be practised, and introduce crimes that are to be abhorred? And ‖ these precepts, together with the inveterate traditions and evil examples of your gods, have so reacted upon you, that you charge us Christians with the very crimes your writers have invented and feigned." He instances Plato's sanction¶ of a community of wives in his Republic, and to the permission of incest by Solon and Epicurus.

* *Ad Aut.* Lib. II. c. 34. † *Ib.* c. 35. ‡ *Ib.* Lib. III. c. 2.
§ *Ib.* c. 3. ‖ *Ib.* c. 4. ¶ *Ib.* c. 6.

CLEMENS ALEXANDRINUS,* addressing the Gentiles, contrasts their domestic lasciviousness with the holiness of Christians in private life. He says, in reference to the indecency of heathen pictures, "We are compelled to prohibit altogether the exercise of this deceitful art." Instead of bending to images, he calls upon his hearers to "remember what the philosophers themselves have said, viz., that 'man was made erect, for the better contemplation of the heavens.' Not indeed to adore the sun, but the Maker of the sun; he who thus truly worships God will be led where no temptation of devils can deceive him."

In answer† to the question how far it is reasonable in men to overturn the customs of their ancestors, our author urges upon the heathen to give up at least their old habits of intemperance, and other vices; that as they have followed death, they should now seek life. "No shame," he adds, "nor loss shall deter us from serving you. Openly, like moral gladiators, we strip ourselves for the sake of truth, and lawfully contend, the holy Word being our judge, the Lord of hosts our helper, and immortality our reward. The best praise that can be offered to God is an immortal man instructed in righteousness, and who has the oracles of truth engraven on his heart."

On the saying‡ of Zeno that the sight of one Indian martyr burning in the flames, would be conclusive proof of his sincerity, Clemens remarks that "Christianity could furnish numerous instances of men who have been not only burned, but tortured and beheaded, and even of women who have shed their blood for Christ."§

* *Hortat. ad Gent.* c. 4. † *Ib.* c. 10. ‡ *Strom.*

§ Cumulative evidence of this kind is greatly in favor of Christianity. There are some inferences which thus become important, though still comparative, arguments.

TERTULLIAN.* "It is said that the numbers who are persuaded to embrace Christianity is no proof that the religion is good in itself; for how many are prone to evil! Doubtless; yet not even they dare to defend evil as good. Evil doers are anxious for concealment, and when detected, tremble; when accused, deny; when condemned, grieve; and attribute the sins arising from an evil heart, either to fate, or to the stars. For they would not have that which they acknowledge to be evil, to belong to themselves. But how different is the conduct of a Christian. No one is ashamed, no one is sorry, except that he was not a Christian long before. If he is pointed out, he glories in the charge; if accused, he makes his defence; if questioned, he confesses even of his own accord; and when condemned returns thanks. What kind of evil then is this, which has none of the natural attributes of evil, fear, shame, subterfuge, repentance, sorrow? What kind of evil is this, in which the culprit delights; in which accusation is the completion of his wishes; and punishment, his happiness?"

"In describing † persons, whom before their professions of Christianity they had known to be given up to licentiousness and immorality, our enemies use terms which are those really of approbation; and thus in the blindness of their hatred bear testimony to the excellence of what they condemn. They say of a female for instance, 'How wanton, how gay she used to be!' of a man, 'What a libertine, what a profligate he was;' 'now they are both become Christians;' thus‡ our name is coupled with reformation."

Again, he argues that "the very fact of Christians being persecuted by such monsters as Nero and Domitian, is a part-proof that our principles are eminently good."

He then proceeds to rebut the charges usually brought forward to the disparagement of Christian morality, very

* *Apol.* c. 1. † *Ib.* c. 3. ‡ *Ib.* c. 5.

much after Athenagoras' manner, but with a freer use of irony and retort, adding, that "the claim of Christ's divinity is founded upon this, that by knowledge of him a man is formed anew to everything."

He next* proposes to state the real mode of worship among Christians. "We look up," says he, "with hands extended because they are innocent; with head uncovered, because we have nothing to be ashamed of; and pray without a prompter, because we pray from the heart. We pray for blessings on the emperor and people, in faith. Thus we offer to God the rich and more excellent sacrifice, which he himself has ordained, prayer out of a clean heart, and an innocent mind, and a sanctified spirit. I offer not a grain of frankincense, which is sold for a farthing; nor the tears of an Arabian tree; nor a few drops of wine; nor the blood of a cast-away ox, that would be glad to die; nor after all other abominations, a defiled conscience, so that it is a wonder when the most reprobate priests are appointed to examine your victims, why the inquiry is made into the heart of the sacrifices, rather than into the hearts of the sacrificers."

After† showing that Christians are bound to love their enemies, and to be loyal to those in authority, and that their service to God is seated in the heart, he condemns the public festivals of the heathen as scenes of excess. His testimony is that "they are only an excuse for licentiousness, and occasions of luxury; tables and couches are placed in the streets; the whole city is turned into one tavern; and the troops are permitted to perpetrate any act of violence and outrage; while even the senate and the court take advantage of the general license."

He reminds the heathen‡ that it is only a God-like sense of duty which keeps Christians in submission to the government. "If we wished to avenge ourselves of our persecutors," says he, "think you that we should lack numbers or

* *Apol*. c. 30. † *Ib*. c. 35. ‡ *Ib*. c. 37.

forces? If such a multitude as we are should suddenly remove to some remote extremity of the earth, the loss of so many of your citizens would overwhelm the empire with shame; you would be dismayed at the solitude in which you found yourselves, and all things would wear the awful stillness of a dead world. But* Christians do not leave their field of duty; nor are they idle in it, as their enemies allege. They are no dwellers in woods, or exiles from ordinary life; and though temperate, they reject none of the gifts of God; they unite with their fellow citizens in navigation, in war, in husbandry, and in trade; and give the benefits of their arts and labor to the state, with the rest of mankind."

He† acknowledges, however, that "some parties among the heathen may have reason to complain of the little support they receive from Christians; such as the vile panderers to every kind of lust, murderers, poisoners, fortune-tellers, soothsayers, and astrologers. But to be fruitless to such as these is surely a great gain! And even if you really did sustain any loss by us, it is counterbalanced by our prayers, aud by your having nothing to fear from us."

He concludes‡ by explaining the principle of Christian morality. "It is a religion which governs the thoughts as well as the actions, and presents to its followers the rewards of eternal happiness or misery. Epicurus taught men to despise pain and torture, because it was of short duration; whereas we who are to give an account to an omniscient God, and who know that he will inflict eternal punishment, are justly considered the only persons who uphold innocency of conduct, as well on the ground of the extent of God's knowledge, as of the difficulty of escape, and the greatness of the punishment, which will be not only of long but of eternal duration."

* *Apol.* c. 42. † *Ib.* c. 43. ‡ *Ib.* c. 45.

MINUTIUS FELIX.* "We were once as you are now; we were equally confident with you that the Christians worshipped monsters, devoured infants, and committed incest, without ever considering that these charges were never proved, and that no man, however tempted or tried, was ever found to reveal such atrocities. We ourselves heretofore, when engaged at the bar in defence of the really sacrilegious and incestuous, and even of parricides, were prejudiced enough to think it just for Christians not to be heard upon their indictment; nay, sometimes we have shown ourselves more savage in our pity than in our rage, by torturing confessors in order to save them, hoping that they would be induced to deny their religion. What an abuse of torture was this! And if the pain proved too great for some infirm Christian, and he renounced his faith, we immediately acquitted him; as if by renouncing his Christian name, he cleared himself of every charge.

"The calumnies† you cast upon a chaste and modest people are such that we should think them incredible, did not you convince us to the contrary by your practice." These remarks lead to a description of heathen vices, which, as usual, are attributed in a great measure to the licentious example of the gods.

"It is *our* endeavor, on the other hand," he says,† concluding this part of his subject, "to be as modest in our minds as in our countenances. Our meals are always decent and sober; and we are equally quiet and inoffensive in the more public assemblies. Christians are faithful adherents to their holy profession, and call themselves brethren because they are children of the same God, and partakers of the same grace and hope. But as for you, you have no such lovely characteristics to discern one another by. Mutual

* *Octav.* c. 28. † *Ib.* c 29. ‡ *Ib.* c. 31.

hatred is the most distinguishing mark about you, nor do you ever call a man brother, but when you design to assassinate him."

He admits* and defends the absence of temples, statues, &c. among Christians, asking: "What image can represent God? what building contain him? Is it not more becoming to dedicate the mind for a temple, and to consecrate our hearts into altars? Shall I bring such sacrifices and oblations to my God, as he has made for my use, and thus turn his bounteous presents back upon his own hands? He who studies innocence, is at his devotions; he who does justly, offers sacrifice; to abstain from injuring another, is to please God; and to save a man, is to slay the noblest victim. Behold the Christian sacrifices! the Christian rites! Among us the best worshipper is the most upright man!"

He instances the case of the Jews,† as furnished either by the sacred penmen, or by Josephus, to show that "purity and innocency of life are well pleasing to God, and that sin and obstinacy are the ruin of any people."

Expostulating ‡ yet again with the heathen, he tells them, "You prohibit adultery by law, and practise it in secret; you punish wickedness only in the overt act; we look upon it as criminal even in thought. You dread the inspection of others; we stand in awe of nothing but our own consciences, as becomes Christians. And lastly your prisons are overflowing with criminals; but they are all heathens; not a Christian is there, unless he be an apostate."

"How§ fair a spectacle in the sight of God is a Christian entering the lists with affliction, and with noble firmness combating menaces and tortures, or with a disdainful smile marching to death through the clamors of the people, and the insults of the executioners; when he bravely maintains his liberty against kings and princes, and submits to God

* *Octav.* c. 32. † *Ib.* c. 33. ‡ *Ib.* c. 34. § *Ib.* c. 36.

alone, whose servant he is; when like a conqueror he triumphs over the judge that condemns him! for he certainly is victorious, who obtains what he fights for. He fights under the eye of God, and is crowned with length of days. You have exalted some of your Stoical sufferers to the skies; such as Scævola, who having missed his aim in an attempt to kill the king, voluntarily burned the mistaking hand. Yet how many among us have suffered not only the hand, but the whole body to be consumed without a complaint, when their deliverance was in their own power! But why should I compare our elders with your Mutius, or Aquilius, or Regulus, when our very children, our sons and daughters, inspired with patience, despise your racks and wild beasts, and all other instruments of cruelty? Surely nothing but the strongest reasons could persuade people to suffer at this rate; and nothing else but Almighty power could support them under their sufferings."

Once* more, respecting various ethical questions of the day: "We touch not your food, not because it is essentially worse than any other; but lest you should conclude that we serve those demons to whom it has been offered in sacrifice; or that we are ashamed of our religion. We are not afraid of flowers: we gather the lily and rose in spring-time; we strow them upon our couches, and wear them on our bosoms; but pardon us for not placing them as chaplets on our heads, for it is our way to take in the scent of an agreeable flower with our noses, and not with our hair. Nor do we crown the dead with garlands; for if they are happy, they feel no want; and if miserable, they are beyond the refreshment of flowers."

Finally, he says, "Let Socrates, the Athenian scoffer, shut himself up in his avowed ignorance; let Archelaus and Carneades, and Pyrrho, and all the race of Sceptics doubt on;

* *Octav.* c. 37.

let Simonides procrastinate forever; we despise all the haughty tribe of philosophers, whom we know to be mere dogmatizers, and corrupters of the truth, and always eloquent against the vices they practise; we wear not our wisdom in our beards, but in our minds; we talk not great things, but live them."

ORIGEN.* "When false witness was brought against our blessed Saviour, he held his peace, and when he was accused returned no answer, being fully persuaded that the tenor of his life and conversation among the Jews was the best apology that could possibly be made in his behalf. He knew, both by experience and of his infinite wisdom, that he could not repel their charges by any verbal defence. The spotless Jesus† was scarcely ever free from unjust accusations, so long as the perverse dispositions of men whose minds were corrupt, and lives vicious, remained the same as they have been in all ages of the world. And even now he preserves the same silence, and makes no other answer than the unblemished lives of his sincere followers; they are his most cheerful and successful advocates, and have so loud a voice that they drown the clamors of the most zealous and bigoted adversaries."

"I think ‡ I may safely say that a physician cannot recover his patients without the blessing of Almighty God upon the methods he prescribes; and if any one can cure the more fatal distempers of the soul; can suddenly and in a great degree dispossess those rooted and dangerous vices, which have long maintained dominion there; can deliver it from its former natural intemperance, injustice, irreverence, and as a proof of skill can instance hundreds of persons whose morals he has been happily instrumental in forming, — I presume you will not say that this can be done without some unusual

* *Cont. Cels.* Lib. I. Præf. Sect. 1. † *Ib.* sect. 2.
‡ *Ib.* s. 26.

interposition of Providence." In further application of this argument to Christianity, it is shown, "how just and eminent the commendation of the Saviour appears, if we compare the course of life which his followers once ignorantly led, with the nature of their subsequent conduct, wherein they became illustrious examples of the contrary virtues. Thus it will be seen," he proceeds, "that Jesus attempted what was vastly beyond the sphere of mere human ability, and that the event also remarkably answered his design. And * it is a matter of surprise, that if our Lord's disciples had not been eye-witnesses of the truth of his resurrection, and had seen nothing but what was common or contemptible in his person, they should not be afraid to follow him in his sufferings, to encounter the greatest hardships and dangers, and to leave their native land in order to publish the doctrines which their crucified and blessed Lord had taught them. For I believe that no unprejudiced person who examines these matters will say that they would ever have undergone the fatigues of itinerant preaching, if they had not been fully persuaded of the obligation that lay upon them, both from reason and gratitude, not only to conform their own manners to the holy precepts of the Christian religion, but also to do what they could to bring others under the same holy and happy bonds; when as things were at the time, they were sure to incur the displeasure of a heathen world, zealous for its ancient laws and customs, and for the pompous ceremonial of its religious worship." Our author† supports his assertion of the change of character which the apostles underwent, by quoting from Clement, to the effect that the apostles had been wicked to the last degree; also from Luke v. 8; and 1 Tim. v. 15; likewise the case of St. Paul, which Celsus had skipped, and adds,‡ "Christ chose these men for the sake of the contrast of their former and after lives. So Socrates

* *Cont. Cels.* Lib. I. s. 27. † *Ib.* s. 63. ‡ *Ib.* s. 64.

took Phædon ; and so Polemon, the successor of Xenocrates, had once led an extravagant life. But these are the only cases I know of among the Greeks, of a change of morals ; whilst in the schools of Christ, besides the apostles, we see daily a great number of persons who become virtuous and pious, and join in a blessed chorus, acknowledging with the deepest shame the many false and almost fatal steps which they took." And again,* he remarks, "there might have been some ground for the comparison that Celsus makes between Jesus and certain wandering magicians, if there had appeared in the latter the slightest tendency to beget in persons a true fear of God, and so to regulate their actions in prospect of a day of judgment. But they attempt nothing of the sort. Yea, they themselves are guilty of the most grievous crimes ; whereas the Saviour would have his hearers to be convinced by the native beauty of religion, and the holy lives of its teachers, rather than by even the miracles they wrought."

Speaking† of the expressions made use of by the apostles, he says incidentally, "I might challenge my adversary to cite any words of our blessed Saviour that were vain, or indicate the least pride or ostentation. How can *He* be accused of pride who was so meek and lowly of heart, and who deigned to wash his disciples' feet, becoming a servant? Let Celsus' Jew‡ make it appear, if he can, that Jesus was ever guilty of the least impiety ; and let him name any one who ever gave such useful precepts to the world, or so thoroughly reformed the morals of mankind."

"The integrity§ of the evangelists is made clear from a consideration of the dreadful calamities, to which they knew their religion would expose them ; for we cannot conceive that the followers of our blessed Redeemer would embrace the most painful deaths with undaunted courage and constancy,

* *Cont. Cels.* Lib. I. s. 68.

† *Ib.* Lib. II. s. 7.

‡ *Ib.* s. 8.

§ *Ib.* s. 10.

had they been the scandalous inventors of the history they transmitted to posterity. But on the other hand, we must suppose them to have been men fully persuaded in their own minds, of the truth and importance of what they published to the world; since their observation and experience taught them, that scorn and infamy were the attendants, and persecution and death the almost certain results of professing the name of Jesus."

Moreover* it is observed, that if the disciples had not been men of the greatest candor, but had designed to impose upon our credulity by false narratives, they would certainly have seen the policy of omitting Peter's denial of his Lord, whose cause he had so resolutely promised to maintain; nor would they have mentioned the offence which some of the disciples took at the mean condition our Saviour thought fit to assume. Indeed, had not these things, which seem to represent the followers of our blessed Lord to a disadvantage, been set down by the evangelists in the Scriptures, how could any infidel have taken occasion to reproach Christians with them? In a like strain,† he continues, "how easily might the evangelists have omitted that expression of Jesus in his agony, 'If it be possible, let this cup pass from me;' upon which Celsus had raised the charge of weakness against our Lord! It is plain that either they were men of integrity, and uttered nothing but what they believed to be true; or else, their Gospels are full of trifling fictions of their own, and consequently they could not be persuaded that our Saviour was God." The latter supposition our author has already shown to be groundless, by adducing their voluntary sufferings. He now‡ calls on us again to admire the integrity of the evangelists, in noting all the insults our Lord received at his trial; and at the same time to be filled with sacred awe at the amazing condescension of Jesus in sealing his doctrine

* *Cont. Cels.* Lib. II. s. 15. † *Ib.* s. 27. ‡ *Ib.* s. 34.

with his blood; adding, as a proof of divine patience, that "his conduct after the sentence of condemnation was passed upon him, in not uttering the least complaint or word, seems worthy of the greatest hero in the world."

He then* defies the Epicurean to "name a vice that ever stained the life or obscured the fair character of Jesus, remarking,† that had he not assumed our nature, we should want the brightest example of submission to the will of God which mortal man ever gave."

Of the Apostles he says‡ once more; "their unparalleled sufferings bore testimony to the truth of Christ's doctrines, for they were the only persons whose bare religion ever brought them into trouble."

Celsus§ having reproached the disciples with leaving their Master, when exposed to danger, Origen observes, that "his opponent only notices the failings, but not the repentance and subsequent zeal of the Apostles, wherein they surpassed all that is related in ancient history concerning the constancy of any of the Grecian heroes."

"We‖ shall continue," he presently observes, "our endeavors to convince the ignorant heathen; for I am sure if we lead persons aside, it is a very happy seducement, since the eternal welfare of their better part is honestly aimed at, and effectually consulted by us, who are honored sometimes with being instruments in the hands of Almighty God to reclaim them. By the grace of God they are prevailed upon to leave their former intemperance, or at least to make some slow and imperfect advances towards virtue. They give up their unjust dealings; they renounce their superstition and folly, and are at least conducted into the highway of justice, wisdom, and courage; as appears, when they resign their cowardly and sordid tempers and offer up their lives for their most holy religion."

* *Cont. Cels.* Lib. II. s. 41. † *Ib.* s. 42. ‡ *Ib.* s. 45. § *Ib.* s. 46. ‖ *Ib.* s. 79.

A charge* of sedition is met by showing that Christians keep the gentle laws of Christ, whereby they are taught not to avenge themselves, even when it lies in their power. "We are taught," he says,† "neither in peace to live carelessly, nor to despond in adversity."

He asks‡ Celsus how he can believe Herodotus and Pindar to be infallible, and yet not give the least credit to men who are ready to die for their religion: or again, how he can prefer those useless prodigies which are related of Aristæus, to those things related of Jesus, and which are so conducive to good morals and true piety towards God. We,§ on the contrary, give credit to the writers of the Gospels, because of the piety and candor which shine forth in them, allowing of no suspicion of collusion or deceit. Add to this the simplicity of their style, which renders the power of God more manifest than it would have been in the use of a studied eloquence, and all the apparatus of Grecian rhetoric.

"I am sure‖ that if Celsus had read the epistles of St. Paul with attention, he would have admired them as containing great thoughts in common terms;¶ not to mention all that is so well written in the Gospels, and parables of Christ."

Our author** concedes for the sake of argument that Æsculapius cured men, and that the oracle of Apollo prophesied, but he contends that "neither the art of curing nor the prophetical gift is, essentially and alone, a proof of divine power." He affirms that the good and bad alike may heal and predict. "Some physicians and some patients are altogether *immoral*, and some of the Delphic responses have been quite inconsistent with reason." Examples follow; whence it is inferred that "since the gifts above-named exhibit nothing inherently divine, why should their patrons be venerated as gods, however skilled they might have been?" He is arguing here for the obligation of morality.

* *Cont. Cels.* Lib. III. s. 8. † *Ib.* s. 15. ‡ *Ib.* s. 27.
§ *Ib.* s. 39. ‖ *Ib.* s. 20. ¶ *Ib.* s. 21. ** *Ib.* s. 25.

"But* God who sent Jesus to destroy the works of the devil, caused the Gospel to have most extensive influence in changing and correcting the morals of men, so that the Churches of his people, being governed by new laws, should be very different from the assemblies of the heathen. The conduct of the masses in crowded cities is notorious for injustice and intemperance; but if the people of God, as taught by Christ, are compared with those among whom they dwell, they will appear like lights in the world; yea, the very weakest in our Churches shall excel all those who frequent the Pagan temples." He instances the Church of Athens, "in which love and good order reign, whilst the political assemblies in that city are always involved in trouble and confusion." A like remark is extended to the Church at Corinth; and upon the whole he suggests, that if a contrast were instituted between the officers of state, and those of our religion, it would decidedly turn out in favor of the latter. This† happy condition of things is attributed to the divine teaching of Christ.

Of the more reasonable worship of believers, and their not having temples or statues, he says,‡ "these things are the appliances of demons; and Jesus has called us away from whatsoever merely affects the senses, to a true worship of God, even by pure morals and prayers."

Celsus§ has likened the meetings of Christians to those for the public amusement of the citizens; Origen explains that they are very different in their occupations and objects. "We kindle a spirit of piety towards God, and of imitation of his virtues, by reading and expounding: we ‖ especially inform the minds of those who desire to hear about Christ; and when these persons seem sufficiently determined to live uprightly, we admit them into our congregations; but if any

* *Cont. Cels.* Lib. III. s. 29. † *Ib.* s. 31. ‡ *Ib.* s. 34.
§ *Ib.* s. 50. ‖ *Ib.* s. 51.

cannot renounce the pleasures of the world, they are prohibited."

Celsus* objecting that Christians acknowledge themselves sinners, our author admits the charge, and quotes Rom. vii. 9, to prove that we are born of a sinful nature; but adds, "far be it from us to teach that the unjust will be received by God, however guilty they may feel themselves to be, unless they condemn their past lives, and walk circumspectly for the future."

He calls† attention to the fact that "even Plato did nothing to advance his hearers in sincere piety, whilst on the other hand those who study the sacred Scriptures in good earnest, and in whom the light burns, fed by that good oil with which the wise virgins are said to have filled their lamps, are replete with a certain divine ardor, by the very simplicity of their style. Jesus‡ himself taught us humility; he came not to be ministered unto, but to minister. Plato only described this virtue; and the Cynics' vows of poverty were a mere pretence: such men were not happy.§ But Christians,‖ according to the command of Jesus, spend their whole lives in the study of the Scriptures."

"The Chaldeans introduced¶ the wicked art of magic; the Egyptians worshipped animals; the Persians permitted incest; the Indians devour each other; but the Jews never committed any of these crimes."

He enlarges** with much force upon the utility of our prophetic communications; and contrasts†† this quality with the impurity of position and imputation, and with the extravagant wildness of manner and matter attributed to the Pythia.

He observes once more: "The sweetness of temper and the firmness which Jesus manifested under his sufferings are

* *Cont. Cels.* Lib. III. s. 62. † *Ib.* Lib. VI. s. 5. ‡ *Ib.* s. 15.
§ *Ib.* s. 28. ‖ *Ib.* s. 36. ¶ *Ib.* s. 80.
** *Ib.* Lib. VII. s. 55. †† *Ib.* s. 4.

without a parallel;" and* also "that his words are of more vital power than Plato's."

Insisting† upon true morality, he recommends us, "for the comprehension of what idolatrous objects truly are, to consider the characters and actions of those who worship them; and how constantly they are invoked for purposes of revenge and lust."

Lastly,‡ reverting to the charge of having no external ceremonies like the Pagans, Origen replies: "Celsus does not reflect that with us the mind of every just man is an altar, from which truly and spiritually sweet incense ascends, even prayers offered from a pure conscience." In place of statues, Origen would substitute virtue, justice, temperance, fortitude, wisdom, and examples of piety; and as to temples, "we are unwilling," says he, "to build mere inanimate walls; our bodies are the temples of God." Speaking§ of the Festa of the heathen, he remarks: "A true feast," as was said by one of the wise Greeks,‖ "is nothing more than to do your duty;" adding, in reference to the Sabbath, the days of Preparation, and the Pentecost, "to a pure Christian every day is a Sabbath; he is always preparing himself to live justly and chastely; *he* celebrates the Pascha who believes that Christ was slain for us; and whoever can say, 'We are risen with Christ,' keeps the Pentecost. Consider,¶ then, whether if our Christian feasts were compared with those of the heathen, they would not prove to be more holy, being free from everything like intemperance and uncleanness."

CYPRIAN** inveighs against the enormities and sensuality practised by the heathen in private, and against the venality, perjury and injustice†† of their courts of law. "The

* *Cont. Cels.* Lib. VII. s. 61. † *Ib.* s. 69. ‡ *Ib.* Lib. VIII. s. 17.
§ *Ib.* s. 21. ‖ *Thucydides.* ¶ *Cont. Cels.* s. 23.
** *Ad Donat.* c. 8. †† *Ib.* c. 9.

excesses* of ambition, the vanity of worldly wealth, and power," he says, "are pursuits which yield both pain and pleasure." It is inferred,† therefore, that "piety is the only way to happiness. A man who has raised himself above the world, will not eagerly expect nor importunately seek anything from it. Oh! what a blessed state of repose and safety! How solid is the security derived from Heaven! What a felicity it is to be disengaged from the entanglements of this perplexing scene; to be purified from the dross of this sinful world; and to be fitted for immortality, notwithstanding all the attempts of our great adversary to seduce and corrupt us! Nor is there need of cost or labor to attain this highest dignity and happiness of human nature. It is the free gift of God, and is easily obtained. His heavenly grace flows into the soul, as the sun of its own accord enlightens the dark places of the earth; as an overflowing fountain offers its waters to any who will use them; as the refreshing dews descend unasked upon the thirsty meadows." In conclusion, our author recommends to his friend, diligence in prayer, and in the perusal of God's word. "Sometimes," he reminds him, "you must speak to God, and sometimes he must speak to you. Let him instruct you by his precepts and inform you by his counsel. Let humility and righteousness adorn you, who are the temple of the Holy Ghost, as becomes the dignity of such a guest. This is a portion no one can impoverish: these are ornaments which neither time nor accident can injure."

"He observes,‡ that gibbets, racks, &c., are tests of sincerity, and such sure witnesses of the truth, that no man will go through them in support of a falsehood." Applying this rule, he shows how "Christ the Son of God, whom we believe to have been sent to give life to the world, has not only the acknowledgment of our lips, but the testimony of our suffer-

* *Ad Donat.* c. 10. † *Ib.* c. 13. ‡ *De Idol. Van.* c. 7.

ings for the sake of his truth; for this is the sum of the Christian's hope, that if he is a follower of Christ here, he shall be a partaker with him in his kingdom and glory."

He touches in his bold expostulation with Demetrian,* upon the wicked lives of the heathen, and their malice in trying to hinder Christians from worshipping the true God, as a more probable cause of the famine and plague of the year A. D. 253, than the spread of Christianity which had been alleged.

ARNOBIUS† allows that "if Christians were really the cause of the earth wandering from its laws, of the gods being driven away, and such a host of evils being introduced into the earth, as is laid to their charge, they deserve to be hated." But he casts back the accusation upon the heathen themselves, telling them that those are rather guilty of this crime, who while they profess to be worshippers of Deity, are given up to deep-rooted superstitions.

Alluding‡ to the exercises of Christian worship, he argues "not that Christ needs our prayers; the benefit is ours; and this is agreeable to reason. They help us by heavenly contemplations, to purge ourselves from all crime. And § yet for this reasonable service we are accounted foolish and brutish. But, I pray you, are your Lares or Fauns, your Fates, your Genii, your Pausi or Bellones, worshipped for a better reason? Are these not, to say the least of them, mere servants of our God? and do you then hold that he is to be rewarded with honors who serves the slave, but he with a cross who serves the master?"

Again,‖ he acknowledges that the philosophers were wise and erudite, but declares that they knew nothing of religion, and never agreed together.

* *Ad Demetr.* c. 5, 6, 7. ‡ *Adv. Gent.* c. 1. ‡ *Ib.* c. 7.
§ *Ib.* c. 8. ‖ *Ib.* Lib. II. c. 5.

He contends* that "God neither needs nor requires sacrifices. Is no honor to be paid to the gods then?† some one is ready to exclaim. Not in this way, I reply, with meats and drinks which they care not for, or wine, or incense, flowers, or music. All these things‡ imply a depraved taste, and arise from forgetting what God really is, and what truly pleases him."

LACTANTIUS,§ in showing that the prophets announced one God, confirms their testimony by appealing to their harmony, their candor, their active correction of human depravity, and their sufferings.

Passing‖ on to the subject of images, he asserts that "true religion is inconsistent with representative figures, on the ground that they are of an earthly nature, and can have nothing heavenly in them, as their name indicates."

He turns now¶ to the consideration of "false wisdom (false religion having been discussed) which the philosophers professed as a rule of life. Aristippus** thought it lay in bodily pleasure; but he was condemned by both philosophers and people, inasmuch as he seemed thus to lower men to the condition of sheep. The chief good of Hieronymus, was not to be in pain; of Diodorus, to abstain from grief; and of Zeno, to live consistently with nature. Epicurus affirmed that it was ease; Dinomachus and Callipho approved only of honorable enjoyment; the Peripatetics made it up of a good state of mind, body, and fortune; the Stoics more rationally rested it in virtue; and Eryllus, the disciple of Pyrrho, in knowledge. But we†† think the highest wisdom is to know God, not nature; not to follow science or honor, riches or poverty, pain or pleasure; but to do justly, as our sacred writings teach. We abjure‡‡ the opinions of Epicurus

* *Adv. Gent.* Lib. VII. c. 1. † *Ib.* c. 7. ‡ *Ib.* c. 17.
§ *Divin. Instit.* Lib. II. c. 4. ‖ *Ib.* c. 19. ¶ *Epitom.* c. 30.
** *Ib.* c. 33. †† *Ib.* c. 34. ‡‡ *Ib.* c. 37.

and Pythagoras; that there is no Providence, and that our souls migrate into the bodies of animals; as also* those of Socrates, who though accounted the wisest of men, confessed that he knew nothing, and fully to establish his ignorance swore by a goose, and devoted a cock to Æsculapius;† together with even the more refined sentiments of Plato (called by Tully, the god of philosophers;) for he erred in holding all things in common, even wives and children; or those of Zeno, the head of the Stoics, who accounted pity but a disease of the mind. Many‡ other strange things might be said of these sages to illustrate their folly; but it is enough to know that they were teachers of a justice which they did not understand, and of a virtue which they did not practise. Since then there appears to be no human wisdom, let us follow that which is divine, and return thanks to God who has given it to us; and congratulate ourselves upon receiving from a heavenly benefactor what the greatest minds sought for so many ages, but were unable to discover."

On the other side, in illustration of the moral effect of Christianity, he exclaims,§ "Produce me a man addicted to anger, to evil-speaking, to any unruly and disorderly behavior; I will only apply to him a few words out of the book of God; and by the charm of them, he shall become as meek and tame as a lamb. Give me an avaricious, covetous person; I will restore him to you open-handed, and open-hearted. Let me see a man impatient of pain, and afraid of death, and I will presently make him perfectly fearless of dangers and torture. Show me an adulterer, or a lascivious person, and he shall return to you continent, chaste, and sober. Let a man much given to cruelty and bloodshed adopt the Christian faith, and all his rage will be turned to clemency and mildness; in short, let the most unjust, the most thoughtless and grievous sinner fall under the influences

* *Epitom.* c. 37. † *Ib.* c. 38. ‡ *Ib.* c. 40. § *Div. Instit.* Lib. III. c. 26.

of the Gospel, and you shall soon observe him a lover of equity, innocent, and prudent in his whole behavior. For all his wickedness shall be washed away in a single laver. Such is the force of divine wisdom, that when it is poured into a man, it can drive out folly, the origin of every crime, at once by one impulse; and to effect this, there is no need of money, or books, or study. None need be afraid of coming to us; we do not sell our water, we do not bestow our sun at a price. The overflowing fountain of God is open to all, and this celestial light rises upon every one who has eyes. Which of your philosophers was ever willing or able to make such an offer as this? Though they spent their lives in the study of philosophy, they could never make either themselves or any one else better. Their wisdom, at the most, only served to hide, not to destroy vice. But a few precepts of our God so change and entirely renew a man, that you would not know him to be the same person."

Of such a faith "the most excruciating tortures* have never done more than draw a recantation from a few Christians, and even they have returned to us with prayers and tears."

In a word, "Justice† is what God desires, and this is the true sacrifice, this is the true worship. To keep the law of God is more pleasing to him than victims; he is better served by piety than with the blood of beasts."‡

"Your spectacles§ tend to corrupt the mind, and are to be avoided by all those who respect their own peace and happiness. We renounce all noxious pleasures, lest we should be seduced by their fatal fascination, and so fall into the snares of death."

EUSEBIUS.‖ "The heathen have assimilated themselves to their deities, and become worse and worse; in-

* *Epitome*, c. 54. † *Ib.* c. 58. ‡ *Ib.* c. 65.
§ *Ib.* c. 63. ‖ *Theoph.* Lib. II. c. 14.

dulging in every excess of crime, and even in crimes against nature.* They who placed their minds under irrational fate, neglected God and virtue."

He urges† "that no religion ever appointed laws so pure and just for the whole world, as are promulgated by the Christians. So merciful‡ are they that they have already induced the Scythians and Persians and other people to give up their brutal sins, caused the abolition of human sacrifices,§ and persuaded men everywhere to become holy.‖ Whoever," he asks,¶ "before induced women and children as well as men, voluntarily to suffer want, to sleep on the ground, to be obedient and chaste, and to prefer the food of the soul to that of the body? Whoever** taught barbarous men, women, and children, with a multitude of slaves, to despise death, to be persuaded of the immortality of their souls, and of their responsibility to God; so that they must be just and temperate, having suffered,†† though they knew it beforehand, arming their souls with righteousness as with adamant? How does this surpass all description of miracles; especially when we consider that the enthusiasm was continued from generation to generation!"

Again‡‡ he observes, "I need not proceed with the sacred history; those who saw the occurrences of the Gospel, will be the witnesses best qualified for the purpose of setting forth the truth; those, I mean, who from having seen the acts themselves, did, both by their blood and persons, attest their faith in him, and by his aid filled the whole creation with the righteousness which they preached."

Defending Christians against the imputation of using magic, he contends,§§ "no one has ever been found, during all this time, a magician and at the same time a disciple of

* Cicero allows as much, *De Nat. Deor.* I. 16. Lee's note, *Theophania.*
† *Theoph.* Lib. III. c. 6. ‡ *Ib.* c. 7. § *Ib.* c. 16. ‖ *Ib.* c. 21.
¶ *Ib.* c. 22. ** *Ib.* c. 23. †† *Ib.* c. 30.
‡‡ *Ib.* c. 63. §§ *Ib.* Lib. V. c. 9.

the Saviour; although princes and governors have made the most careful inquiries by means of torture into these matters. Look also at the Acts of the Apostles, where the burning of the magical books is described."

"And such," he argues,* "were the disciples; so pure, so noble, so abundant in love; they allowed nothing impure to be concealed near them; but, on the contrary, boasted of their change from vice to virtue. Since then the disciples were so, must not the master have first been much more excellent?"

"The Greeks† may have a Democritus,‡ who left his place for the sake of philosophy, or a Crates,§ who distributed his possessions amongst his fellow-citizens; but we have our tens of thousands of such, as any can testify. How many barbarians and Greeks have been raised by the doctrines of the Saviour above all the errors of Polytheism; and, unlike Plato, who was afraid to speak of God before men, have formed themselves into assemblies among all nations, men and women, children and slaves, townsmen and villagers!"

He notices‖ the extraordinary unanimity of the evangelists; and their sincerity, as shown by their suffering bonds, torments, and death in attestation of the fact that they saw Christ give sight to a blind man; a thing which no one had ever heard of before. He refers to¶ the candor of St. Matthew in stating his former disreputable manner of life, which the other evangelists have not mentioned; and also** his humility in including himself among the sinners, and reckoning himself†† second to his fellow-apostle, whilst the rest of the evangelists reverse the order of the names. Of St. John‡‡

* *Theoph.* Lib. v. c. 13.
† *Ib.* c. 14.
‡ Cicero *Tusc. Quest.* Lib. v. c. 39.
§ Diog. *Laert.* Lib. vi. Serm. 85.
‖ *Theoph.* Lib. v. c. 27, 28.
¶ *Ib.* c. 37.
** *Ib.* c. 38.
†† Estius and Dr. Hammond have noticed this instance of Peter's humility; see Prof. Lee's note. *Theophania.*
‡‡ *Ib.* c. 39.

he observes, that he does not so much as name himself, or call himself an apostle; and on St. Mark's Gospel,* that "Peter who employed this evangelist to note down his declarations concerning the life of our Saviour, omits to mention any testimony in favor of himself;† such as the word of Christ, 'Thou art Peter, on this rock will I build my church.' St. Mark, he supposes, did not record this, because Peter did not notice it in his teaching; but his denial of Christ he preached to all men, and caused it to be recorded against himself. Must we not then confess that these men were distinguished by an evident love of truth? and if so, how could they be deceivers? Their characters were guileless, as their words indicate; and‡ if their self-abasing accounts are credited by infidels, why must not also their glorious testimonies in other respects be credited also?"

After § describing the cruelties connected with idol-worship, and the fallacies of oracles, our author sums up true religion by defining it to be "the reception of God through the dispensation of our Saviour into a soul free from passion, and a life agreeable to his will."

"We declare‖ further, that the honors and worship paid to these (heathen) deities, are accompanied by acts of wantonness and profligacy."

"Christians,¶ like noble martyrs in the cause of true godliness, have resolved to welcome death in preference to life. They have mocked at fire, the sword, the cross; at exposure to wild beasts; at drowning in the sea; at the cutting off and searing of their limbs; at the digging out of their eyes; at mutilations of the body; at famine; at labor in the mines; at captivity: nay, all these sufferings they counted better than

* *Theop.* Lib. v. c. 40.

† Estius and Dr. Hammond have noticed this instance of Peter's humility; see Prof. Lee's note. *Theophania.*

‡ *Theoph.* Lib. v. c. 43.

§ *Præp. Evan.* Lib. I. c. 4.

‖ *Const. Orat.* c. 4.

¶ *Euseb. Orat.* c. 7.

any earthly good or pleasure, for the love they bore to their Heavenly King. Even women evinced a constancy of spirit not inferior to men, and boldly sustained every variety of suffering."

ATHANASIUS,* having noticed the diversity of opinions among the Pagans, and the cruelty of their worship, turns to their immoralities, and mentions that the Phœnician women formerly prostituted themselves in the temples, consecrating their gains to the gods. He quotes Romans i. 26, as illustrated by this circumstance.

MATERNUS† condemns the heathen rites, on account of the licentious conduct they engender. He says, "the mysteries of the Gallic priests consist of base and impious acts; and the Assyrians and Africans in their worshp of Venus, confess and publish their evil deeds, denying that they are men, and decorating themselves in female dress. But we know that it is only by faith and penitence, we can ever hope to regain that which was lost through the vile persuasion of the devil."

And again;‡ "the crowd of wicked heathen have collected all the seeds of impiety from their own gods, and thus confirmed their innate depravity, by a show of authority and of divine example."

EPHRAIM.§ "The glorious One humbled himself to all similitudes. He taught and *did* all that he taught, that he might be a mirror to his hearers. He exemplified his own teaching; he made the path of duty as clear as his doctrines; he lowered himself‖ to our comprehension, so great was his humility.

* *Cont. Gent.* c. 26. † *De Err. Prof. Relig.* c. 3. ‡ *Ib.* c. 13.
§ *Ad Scrut. Serm.* 30. ‖ *Ib.* 31.

"The truth is set as a mirror;* he whose eye is clear, sees the image of truth therein.

"The Scriptures are agreed; men are divided. This strife has originated in an abuse of free-will. The Scripture† has sealed to us, that 'the just in faith, findeth life.' God has fixed the truth like a glorious root, and works, like fruit, he has hung upon faith."

GREGORY NAZIANZEN‡ affirms that "the sentiments of the philosophers were various and discordant; having followed human theories and left the guidance of God, they erred and drew other men into error."

He observes§ that "Christians are holier in a time of persecution than in a time of peace;" and "Julian," he exclaims,|| "may insanely forbid them to study letters; they care not; they despise outward eloquence; as they sacrifice their bodies with its pleasures, so they yield up their mind with its amenities."

Our author¶ charges the generals whom Julian admires, with "serving their own ambition; and the philosophers,** with various weaknesses and follies. Nor does he find that the poetical fables†† have induced good morals, chiefly‡‡ because of the bad example set by the gods. On the other hand,§§ the Christian religion teaches charity; forbids covetousness and perjury; commands|||| us to bless our enemies, to overcome insolence with kindness, and only to be anxious after virtue."

AUGUSTINE,¶¶ speaking of the vices of the Romans, alludes to suicide as being prevalent and approved. In his judgment it evinces no magnanimity of soul. Cato*[a] killed himself because he was unable to bear Cæsar's victory;

* *Ad Scrut. Serm.* 67. † *Ib.* 68, 80. ‡ *Orat. adv. Jul.* 4, c. 44.
§ *Ib.* c. 32. || *Orat.* 5. ¶ *Ib.* c. 71. ** *Ib.* c. 72. †† *Ib.* c. 117.
‡‡ *Ib.* c. 120. §§ *Ib.* c. 123. |||| *Ib.* c. 124.
¶¶ *De Civit. Dei*, Lib. I. c. 21. *[a] *Ib.* c. 22.

wherefore Job far excelled him in patient endurance; and Christians in general surpass Regulus, in that very virtue by which he excelled most. He did not destroy himself: Christians follow his example, but from a better motive; they aim only at eternal mansions.

Our author * next reproaches those who complain of Christianity, with desiring nothing but to live in sensual pleasure. He reminds them that Scipio Nasica foretold the calamities that would naturally result from ambition and corruption; and how, when the Senate proposed to build a theatre in Rome, he endeavored to persuade his countrymen not to let the luxury of the Greeks creep into their cities.

Augustine† farther reminds the Romans, that it was at the command of the gods that stage-plays were introduced, in order to assuage a pestilence; adding that they are only scenes of licentiousness and vanity.

He remarks‡ that the worshippers of the Pagan gods never received any moral instructions from them; but practised all manner of uncleanness in their services. "We ourselves," says he, "in our youth, once went to view these spectacles, these religious mockeries; there we saw the devotees raging violently; we heard the pipers, and took delight in the vulgar sports they acted before the gods and goddesses, even before Berecynthia the celestial virgin, mother of all the gods; and that too in the sight and hearing of a multitude of both sexes. But § in *our* assemblies there is nothing of this sort; the precepts of the true God are taught, his miracles related, his gifts acknowledged, and his blessing invoked."

He shows‖ that "the ambition allowed and recommended by profane philosophy, is only for a temporal reward. How much better that which has heaven in prospect, the eternal city. The citizens of this world prefer for their gods wicked

* *De Civit. Dei*, Lib. I. c. 29. † *Ib.* c. 31. ‡ *Ib.* Lib. II. c. 4.
§ *Ib.* c. 28. ‖ *Ib.* Lib. V. 13--20.

and proud spirits, but the godly and holy submit themselves to the God of gods, and love rather to worship, than to be worshipped.

Two sorts of affection* have given rise to the earthly and heavenly states: self-love in contempt of God, to the one; love of God and contempt of self, to the other: that seeks the glory of men, this the glory of God; that boasts of ambitious conquerors led by the lust of power, this of serving one another in charity. The philosophers of the earthly city follow the desires of the body or mind, living according to the flesh, and with the people serving the creature more than Creator: but in the heavenly city, there is no wisdom of man, but only the piety that serves the true God, and anticipates the society of saints and angels.

After† declining to discuss with the Epicurean, who despises all morality, our author says: "True religion cannot be found amidst the confusion of Pagan philosophers, the impurity of heretics, or the blindness of Jews; rather‡ and only, are its foundations laid in that sacred history and prophecy which reveal the method of God's providence in the course of time for the salvation of men; and by believing which, and also having the heart purified, we recognize the offices of the Holy Trinity. Therefore§ it is that we put away far from us the wicked folly of plays and poets, and employ ourselves in the study of the Sacred Volume, nourishing with its celestial viands our souls, fainting from hunger and tormented by the thirst of a vain curiosity. The beauty and the order of the world is to us the most magnificent theatre."

* *De Civit. Dei,* Lib. XIV. c. 28.
† *De Vera Relig.* c. 5.
‡ *Ib.* c. 7.
§ *Ib.* c. 51.

CHAPTER VII.

THE ARGUMENT FROM THE SUCCESS OF THE GOSPEL.

"Come then, and added to thy many crowns,
Receive yet one as radiant as the rest,
Due to thy last and most effectual work,
Thy word fulfilled, the conquest of a world!"

COWPER, *Task*, B. vi.

THE last specific kind of argument to be noticed as advanced by the Apologists, is that of *success*. The attainment of its object seems, in truth, to be only the natural consequence of any divine operation. It must needs go on overcoming evil, and perfecting good: but in this case there were two considerations tending to make success eminently satisfactory; first, that it had been foretold, and secondly, that it was unprecedented.

In the one view, the Gospel was seen leaguing itself with the entire system of venerable and venerated prophecies; and in the other, with the series of Mosaic and Christian miracles, itself as great as any: a continuous miracle, offering the advantage of personal evidence, and like the angel of Manoah "doing wondrously" in the very presence of the humblest Christian. Such success was found to be unprecedented under *any* circumstances. The religions of different countries, including even the Jewish, had scarcely extended beyond their native and original boundaries; and if so, they had either laid no claim to universality, or existed either by compromise or by crime. Still less had any approach been made to such success, under the actual circumstances of the case. Here was a criterion by which to judge of the superiority of Christianity not only over every other religion, but over any philosophical, political, or ambitious excursion that the world might have witnessed.

The circumstances of the case especially dwelt upon by the Apologists were, the incredibly short time the Gospel took to accomplish its end; the extent of the conquest, being nothing less than the known world; against an opposition the most unanimous, violent and persevering that can well be imagined; and all this, achieved by means apparently insignificant and inadequate. Particular allusion is made to the means being moral, in opposition to the effects of fraud, eloquence or physical power.

Here then was just the complement which Christianity seemed to need, not indeed for its own sake, but for that of its followers. By the time this proof began to ripen, the persecuted Church required all the assistance and all the encouragement and comfort that could be vouchsafed to her: and who can say what a support it was to the exile in the mines, and to the martyr on the rack, to know that his sufferings but served to further the rapid advancement of Christ's kingdom, and to fulfil Christ's predictions?

The whole attainment was too wonderful to be human; and we may reflect, in conclusion, that if this argument availed to prove and edify in the times of the Fathers of the Church, how much more should it prove and edify now. Wherefore, this argument seems especially in place as a final chapter; its influence extending and even increasing to our own days. Fifteen centuries have rolled away, only to leave us additional assurances of the divinity of the Gospel in its peaceful and continued success, when compared with the violent extension of Mahommedanism, the fraudulent spread of Popery, and the various clamorous but temporary triumphs of fanaticism or infidelity.

JUSTIN MARTYR.* "Why should we mention an innumerable multitude of those who have been converted from a life of incontinence, and learned these [Christ's] precepts? From† Jerusalem twelve men went forth to the world; they were unlearned, not knowing how to speak; but by the power of God, they preached to every nation, that they were sent by Christ to teach the Word of God to all the world."

"We have‡ witnessed the desolation of Judæa, and have seen such men as we ourselves, men out of every nation, persuaded by the preaching of the Apostles, and renouncing their previous manner of life, so that Christians more numerous and true, have been made from the Gentiles than from the Jews or Samaritans."

"With us § information may be obtained upon these [religious] points from those who have not received even the rudiments of learning; who although unlearned and speaking a strange language, have wisdom and faith in their hearts, so as to make it evident that these things were not done by human wisdom, but by the power of God."

"By how much the more‖ we are afflicted with torments, by so much the more does the number of the faithful and true worshippers of God increase through the name of Jesus." Our author mentions this in connection with the fulfilment of prophecy concerning the Gentiles. To the same intent¶ he reminds the Jew that "there are some countries in which none of his nation ever dwelt; but there is not so much as

* *Apol.* I. c. 18. † *Ib.* c. 49. ‡ *Ib.* c. 68.
§ *Ib.* c. 78. ‖ *Dial. cum Tryph.* c. 10. ¶ *Ib.* c. 17.

one nation of men, whether Greek or barbarian, Scythian or Arabian, amongst whom prayers and thanksgivings are not offered up to the Father through the name of Jesus crucified."

THEOPHILUS* notes as a matter of astonishment that the Hebrew prophets who uttered such divine truths were illiterate and unskilled men, often being mere shepherds or husbandmen.

CLEMENS ALEXANDRINUS† ascribes the rapid success of the Gospel to the superintending providence of God. "The divine power shining upon the earth has with a celerity not to be surpassed, and the widest benevolence, filled the earth with the seeds of salvation. Without his care so great a work in so short a time could never have been accomplished. Our Lord, who was despised because of his outward condition, is now adored as the expiator, the Saviour, the gentle one, the Divine Word manifested as truly God, equalled to the Lord of all, proving whence he was, and who he was, and what he taught and did."

TERTULLIAN. "Some‡ among you are changed from what they were, and are become Christians, as soon as they learn what our religion really is. They begin to hate what they were, to profess the opinions they hated, and to swell our numbers. Our enemies exclaim that the whole state is overrun with us; they lament it as a great calamity that Christians are found in the country, in the cities, in the islands; that persons of both sexes, and of all ages, and stations, and dignities, come over to that name; but yet not even this fact is sufficient to rouse their minds to imagine there is any latent good in Christianity."

* *Ad Autol.* Lib. II. c. 35. † *Hortat.* c. 12. ‡ *Apol.* c. 1.

"Among* yourselves many have given exhortations to the patient endurance of pain and death, as Cicero in his Tusculan disputations, or as Seneca, Diogenes, Pyrrho, and Callimachus; yet none of this verbal advice ever gained so many followers as the Christians have obtained by the instructions which their actions have delivered."

He farther speaks† of Christians as forming "almost the majority in every state," and declares that "if the cruel laws against the Christians were enforced, Carthage would be desolated."

In describing‡ the diffusion of Christianity throughout the world, he enumerates the countries whither the Gospel had already extended, and includes "all the extremities of Spain, and the different nations of Gaul, and parts of Britain inaccessible to the Romans, but subject to Christ."

MINUTIUS FELIX.§ "The daily increase of vast numbers is so far from being a disparagement to our religion, that it is a testimony in its favor; for Christians are faithful adherents to their holy profession, and are continually augmented by heathen converts."

ORIGEN,|| as a preliminary to his proofs of the canonical inspiration, mentions that, "no legislator or teacher among the Greeks or barbarians ever begat in nations who followed after them, such a surprising adherence to his own laws as Moses did; and although philosophers, with some appearance of truth, published what seemed reasonable and plausible, they never could succeed in persuading a multitude of people of different nations, as the apostles had done. The fact is," he explains, "these legislators and teachers, however much they desired to disseminate their principles

* *Apol.* c. 50. † *Ad Scap.* c. 2. c. 5. ‡ *Adv. Jud.* c. 7.
§ *Octav.* c. 31. || *De Princip.* Lib. IV. s. 1.

throughout the earth, soon found it impossible, and prudently forebore. But now all Greece and all the circle of the earth contains numbers, who having forsaken the laws and customs of their ancestors, observe the Mosaic law and the discipline of Jesus Christ, and that too in spite of the hatred of idolaters, and at the greatest risk of their own lives."

Our author is led* by these reflections to notice other remarkable circumstances connected with the spread of Christianity; "that in so short a time and with so many snares laid for them, the Christians, though continually put to death and despoiled of their property, (their indigence therefore showing that success could not have arisen from any power in the teachers themselves) have propagated the Gospel throughout the world."

"What necessity† is there to produce other prophecies of Christ, whilst there is that song inscribed 'pro dilecto,' wherein his tongue is said to be 'the tongue of a ready writer, and his form more lovely than the sons of men, because grace is diffused from his lips?' For this refers to Christ having in so brief a period filled the whole earth with his doctrine, and the true worship of grace. In his days too, righteousness and abundance of peace have appeared, which shall doubtless endure to the consummation, when 'he shall rule from sea to sea, and from the river to the ends of the earth.'"

"Nor should the divinity‡ of the Scriptures be doubted on account of their simplicity, because the weakness of our understanding cannot enter always into the secret splendor of ideas, concealed in humble and abject speech; for 'our treasure is hid in earthen vessels, that the excellency of the power may be of God, and not of us.' 2 Cor. iv. 7. If the usual methods of demonstration had been adopted to convert the human race, the cause might have been misunderstood;

* *De Princip.* Lib. IV. s. 2. † *Ib.* s. 5. ‡ *Ib.* s. 6.

but now it is clear to any one using his eyes, that our influence with the multitude was not placed in persuasive words of man's wisdom, but in the exhibition of spirit and power. It is this heavenly wisdom alone that can reveal to us the mystery hid from the beginning, but now manifested in the writings of the prophets, and in the advent of the Lord."

A comparison having been instituted* between the risks and sufferings of Christians and the calamities to which Socrates, Pythagoras, and other philosophers were exposed, our author remarks that "the Athenians did not persecute for any length of time, as the Romans have done with regard to us, though after all without succeeding in their object."

To Celsus objecting† that Christ was but the head of an upstart sect, called Christians, Origen proceeds to show the unfairness of such a depreciating expression. "I answer," says he, "that a doctrine so lately introduced as ours, should meet with such wonderful success that in almost every part of the habitable world, a great number, both of Greeks and barbarians, learned and unlearned persons, should readily and triumphantly forsake the religion in which they were born and bred, and to which they were preëngaged, by many strong and almost indissoluble ties, and on a sudden discover such an extraordinary zeal for a new religion as to be willing to sacrifice their reputation, and their fortune, and even their lives for the profession of it, which can hardly be said of any other doctrine, though it have all external advantages to recommend it; I say, things being thus, we must be strangely blinded by the force of prejudice, if we do not observe a more than ordinary appearance of the providence of God in this sudden, uncommon, and most blessed change. For‡ when everything looked unfavorably on so daring an undertaking, and threatened that the Gospel should be confined to a very narrow compass; when the Roman emperors in their

* *Cont. Cels.* Lib. I. s. 4. † *Ib.* s. 26. ‡ *Ib.* s. 27.

successive reigns, the governors of provinces, and generals of armies, the magistrates of particular cities, the soldiery and the common people, — in a word, when all persons that were in authority or had any influence or interest, declared open war against the Christian religion; even then, under all these great outward disadvantages, it bore the sacred and undeniable marks of a divine original, applied itself to the conversion of the most wicked men, forced its way in spite of the united malice and vigorous efforts of earth and hell, gained ground against the stoutest opposition, and being superior to all its enemies, who were neither few nor contemptible, exerted a marvellous power over the minds of men, and turned all Greece and a great part of the barbarian states into trophies of honor, to the memory of its God-like founder. Nor did he [Jesus] act like a tyrant, who by the help of a prevailing party takes occasion to violate the known laws of the land in which he lives; nor like a robber, who comes with armed bands; nor like a wealthy man, who by the help of bribes, induces others to come over to his interests, whether by right or by wrong, and whose proceedings manifestly deserve our censure; but like one, who came to teach an ignorant and degenerate world what views they ought to entertain of God, and how they might regulate their conduct so as to maintain an humble and familiar correspondence with the majesty of Heaven. As to Themistocles and others who gained an unusual reputation, and did great services to their native country, this must be said to draw a shade over their greatest glory, that everything seemed to smile on their just and honorable attempts, and as it were to pave the way to victory. How different the path the Saviour trod to the cross; the most awful tragedy that ever was enacted!"

Having* remarked that the base origin of the apostles, often carped at by Celsus, is a proof of the power of God in

* *Cont. Cels.* Lib. I. s. 67.

using them as instruments, Origen proceeds: "We say and know that the divine power of our blessed Saviour has been happily seen and felt through all the habitable world, wherever churches are founded, consisting of persons reclaimed from the most glaring vices. And the name of Jesus at this very day composes the ruffled minds of men, dispossesses demons, and works a gentle and amiable temper in all those who make profession of Christianity from a higher end than worldly interest, and who sincerely believe what it teaches concerning God, Christ, and a future judgment."

He says farther,* "I defy Celsus and all the world to prove that a doctrine introduced by one who reclaimed so many persons from every scandalous vice, effectually engaging them to enter upon a virtuous course of life, deserves to be vilified with the title 'the plague of the world.'"

To another cavil, raised on the ground† that Christ did not immediately produce an effect upon the mass of society, our author replies: "We can prove that he did; for when he came into the world, justice seemed to regain her native seat, the neighing of war-horses, the clangor of trumpets, the flash of arms, the piercing groans of the sick and wounded, were heard no more; but a wonderful calm succeeded the late confusions." This, he considers, was arranged in the providence of God to prepare the way for the success of the Gospel, by subjecting the entire world to the Roman empire, so that the Apostles might not be hindered in carrying out their orders, "Go, teach all nations." "How," he inquires, "could this have been practicable, if the people of different countries had lived under princes of their own, without any mutual intercourse, instead of under the single jurisdiction of an Augustus, who is well known to have encouraged commerce and prevented war?"

"I cannot conceive,"‡ he continues, "how our Saviour, if he was only a man, as Celsus supposes, could have been so

* *Cont. Cels.* Lib. II. s. 29. † *Ib.* s. 30. ‡ *Ib.* s. 79.

weak as to imagine that his doctrine would obtain the desired success, and that he should surmount all difficulties and dangers, and prove in the end superior to the united force of the people, the senate, the Emperors of Rome, as well as all foreign potentates. If we do not allow that he had a divine as well as a human nature, how can we account for his making so many and such remarkable converts on a sudden, and when the disadvantages were so great under which he labored? Had they all been educated men whom he dealt with, I confess the wonder would somewhat abate; but the greater part by far were destitute of reason, and little better than brutes in a human state, and, what is worse, were slaves to their unruly passions, and on that account more difficult to reclaim; so that we must needs resolve this matter into its being the power and wisdom of God, let the unbelieving Jew and the learned Greek gnash their teeth as they please, and produce what they can to the contrary."

He again* applies this argument by contrasting the paucity of Æsculapius' followers with the abundance of those who confess Jesus. This affluence and popularity, he affirms, would never have taken place, had not some wonderful benefit been derived from this faith. Amongst the disciples of Christianity, he enumerates "many who were delivered from weary burdens, from alienation and distraction of mind, and from infirmities which Æsculapius was never able to heal."

"It is not† to be wondered at that the discourses of philosophers, so aptly and ornately composed, had some weight in the correction of a few vicious persons; but when we see that the teaching which Celsus calls spiritless and mean, was endowed with all the efficacy of enchantment, so that multitudes are recalled from vice to virtue, and exhibit such constancy that for the sake of their religion they despise death, do we not well to wonder and ascribe it to a supernatural

* *Cont. Cels.* Lib. III. s. 24.

† *Ib.* s. 68.

cause? The success of the first preachers of the Gospel was not due to any force of Attic eloquence, but to a power of persuasion given them by the Spirit of God. Hence it is they prevailed so promptly everywhere; yea, that the words of God spoken by them, changed those whom nature and custom had led captive in sin, and corrected and converted to its own will those whom neither man nor law could tame."

"Let any one* show in what other than the Christian way, not merely one here and there, but a great number, can be recalled to a better life; that so we may judge by comparison which is the doctrine that tends most to virtue."

Our author† farther observes that though, as Celsus says, "the style of the Greeks is more studied than that of the Scripture writers, yet that the latter, besides having purposely written in plain and familiar language, for the sake of the mass of the people, have their words accompanied by a certain power from God, producing effects such as the dogmas of the schools never attained. On this account it is that the disciples of Jesus, though rude and unskilled in philosophy, are to be met with in every kingdom of the earth, and that instead of single auditors, as the sophists had, Christian teachers have captivated whole nations to their doctrines and morals."

Finally,‡ he argues under this head, that "it is an evidence of divine interference that the Jewish republic, city, temple, and sacrifices should cease, just as they could no longer answer their purpose; and that when a new doctrine is issued for the benefit, not of a single nation, but of all people, the counsels of men cannot prevail against it; but the more kings and governors and people persecute its followers, the more their numbers increase and their cause strengthens."

* *Cont. Cels.* Lib. IV. s. 53. † *Ib.* Lib. VI. s. 2. ‡ *Ib.* Lib. VII. s. 26.

CYPRIAN* offers a fine illustration of the power of the Gospel over the individual man, in the train of thought that had led to his own conversion and baptism the year before. He remarks how impossible at first it seemed that he could ever leave those rooted and habitual customs, which time and circumstances had riveted to the very frame of his being. "Whenever was it known," he would ask himself, "that a man becomes a learner of frugality, who has been a liver in luxury and riot? How rarely that any one becomes content with plain apparel, who has been used to sparkle in gold, jewels and embroidery!" How then could his ambition, his intemperance, his pride and anger, his covetousness and cruelty, be restrained and laid aside? Such were his soliloquies; "for," says he, "I was deeply entangled and ensnared in the errors of my former life, which I deemed it impossible ever to disengage myself from. Thus I seconded the evil propensities of my nature, and by choice added strength to them by indulgence and despair. But when the Spirit of God had descended upon me, things appeared easy which before looked difficult and discouraging. I distinguished thenceforth that earthly principle which being born of the flesh exposed me to sin, and that new principle which I had derived from the Spirit of God, and which had entirely devoted me and bound me to his service." This new nature† he ascribes to the power of God's grace, a fountain ever flowing, whose waters of life no determinate channel restrains, being received into our hearts by faith; "Whence," he adds, "we having qualified ourselves for the reception of it by proper preparations of prayer and all holy dispositions, derive the power of expelling the deadly poison of sin, and cleansing the stains contracted through its pollution, of composing dissension, and of making the violent and intractable tame and civilized."

* *Ad Donat.* c. 3.

† *Ib.* c. 4.

ARNOBIUS* offers in proof of the divinity of Christ, that his religion has overcome all decrees, and dissolved the silly and fatal superstitions of the Gentiles. "The human race," he contends,† "is so naturally incredulous, that unless the affair is as clear as the sun itself, it will never be received extensively in the world." He adds to this that the early propagation of Christianity incurred such a gratuitous hatred and execration, as can only be endured and explained on the supposition of sincerity in its promoters. "Why is it, if as you say [he is addressing an imaginary objector,] the history of our affairs is false, that in so short a time the whole world is full of this religion? Who can unite into one, nations separated by winds and climate, so that they give themselves to God, and set no value on their own comfort and lives?" "Are you not," he exclaims again‡ in a like strain, "struck with the fact that already throughout all lands in so brief a period of time, this wonderful name has been spread, so that there is now no people, however barbarous or cruel, that has not turned in love to Christ and assumed a tranquil state of mind? Orators of the greatest genius, grammarians, counsellors and physicians, and even professors of philosophy, seek our instructions and despise their own! And although punishments are inflicted, and threatening edicts published, the people seem to be more excited by the stimulus of prohibition, and apply themselves to the study of our faith. Could there be so many conversions in the face of such opposition unless the affair was divine?"

Once more§ he calls attention to "that power which, originating in Christ and his Apostles, has spread itself throughout the whole world, subduing the passions of men, and causing nations dissimilar in their manners to run together in one mind and one faith. For it is well known what is done

* *Adv. Gent.* Lib. I. c. 15.

† *Ib.* c. [illegible].

‡ *Ib.* Lib. II. c. 3.

§ *Ib.* c. 7.

in India, in Persia, in Arabia, in Syria, in Egypt, in Asia Minor, in Greece, and in every isle and province lit by the sun; and lastly at regal Rome itself, where men, though interested in the arts and ancient superstitions of Numa, delayed not to leave the religion of their forefathers, and to unite themselves to the truth."

LACTANTIUS* suggests in proof of the truth of the Christian religion, that "it both understands the cunning nature of demons, and subdues them by its spiritual arms. With what terror it fills them, any one may know who would see how they fled, when adjured by Christ, out of the bodies in which they dwelt. How is it," he asks, "that they only flee at the name of the true God?"

EUSEBIUS.† "The things foretold by the prophets in the Hebrew tongue long since, are in our own time being witnessed in operation, and fulfilled; and if you desire any other proofs of the excellences of the truth, showing that it is not of a mortal nature, but is really the Word of God, and that the power of God in the Saviour has been revealed not by words only, but by deeds, attend now. What king,‡ philosopher, lawgiver, or prophet, ever effected so much that he should be preached throughout the whole earth; and who bade his disciples go and testify of him and suffer for his sake, and with the Word brought the deed to pass? What prince,§ what armies ever, in spite of the constant opposition of all, went and prospered everywhere? Who‖ ever before had a people after his own name, not in a corner of the world, but among all barbarians and Greeks alike; and¶ by the doctrines which he taught (being well confirmed by deeds) turned men, yea, even the Egyptians, from idolatry;** and drove out demons, so that the fountain of Castalia became

* *Div. Instit.* Lib. IV. c. 27. † *Theoph.* Lib. III. c. 3. ‡ *Ib.* c. 4. § *Ib.* c. 8. ‖ *Ib.* c. 9. ¶ *Ib.* c. 10. ** *Ib.* c. 13.

silent, with that of Colophon; the Pythian divinations ceased, the Clarian, the Nemean, and likewise those of Delphos, Miletus, and Lebadia, so much boasted of in ancient times? And where now are Amphilochus and Mopsus, Amphiaraus and Æsculapius, or the image of Ammon that was in the desert of Lybia? These* are clear and irresistible proofs, confirming the divine power of the Saviour, who is therefore living and operative." Our author brings this argument to bear upon his own time more particularly, by designating the churches rebuilt by Constantine under the very eyes of their destroyers, some of whom had themselves been converted meanwhile to the new doctrine. He continually reverts† with surprise to the wide diffusion of Christianity, and to its overcoming every opposition; "for enemies," he observes,‡ "have not ceased to contend with it from first to last. Yet,§ nevertheless, places of instruction are everywhere established, and congregations are gathered from among all, ascribing in songs of victory, honor to the life-giving Word of God. Egyptians,‖ Scythians, Italians, Moors, Persians, and Hindoos, all and at once, have become wise through the knowledge of God."

"If any one will consider¶ what numbers of Christians and churches, with vast congregations, are said to exist in the East; and how many there are of men and women desiring to come over to holiness in Persia and India, and in like manner in the western parts of the world; that throughout the whole of Spain, and Gaul, and the country of the Moors and Africans, in the islands of the ocean, and in Britain, men subscribe to Christ; — if, I say, one will consider these things, he will understand what is the power of that prophetic word which declared, 'many shall come from the east and the west, and shall sit down with Abraham, Isaac and Jacob, in the kingdom of heaven.' And** this too has

* *Theoph.* Lib. III. c. 17. † *Ib.* c. 34. ‡ *Ib.* c. 37. § *Ib.* c. 76.
‖ *Ib.* c. 79. ¶ *Ib.* Lib. IV. c. 4. ** *Ib.* c. 6.

been effected by means of poor and illiterate men; for had Christ brought it about by means of the intellectual, the wise, the rich, the illustrious, we might have supposed the matter to have been human; but he made use of no such disciples; on the contrary, they were poor and despised, men ignorant in speech, Scythians in language, and in character humble and mean. Thus by divine power, fishers became preachers."

In allusion* to the conversion of Constantine, our author says: "Now no more, as in former times, are the babblings of impious men heard in the palace, but priests and pious men worship together, and celebrate the divine Majesty. The Gospel of glad tidings connects the human race with its Almighty King, and the nations of the four quarters of the world are instructed at the same moment in his precepts."

ATHANASIUS † pities "the blindness of the heathen in not seeing that the works of Him who was lifted up on the cross have filled the whole earth, proving that he is the God and Saviour of all men. To refuse to believe in Christ, because of the scandal of his temporary humiliation, is as if any one should deny that the world is lit by the sun, because it was obscured by a cloud."

GREGORY NAZIANZEN ‡ observes, that the multitude of Christians is greatly to be wondered at.

CHRYSOSTOM § shows how much more effect Christ has produced than the philosophers, or Apollonius, and asks what impostor ever had so many churches. He proposes to prove the power of Christ, and therefore his divinity, from the establishment and extent of his Church. He contends that it is not the work of a mere man to establish in so short

* *Euseb. Orat.* c. 10.

† *Cont. Gentes*, c. 1.

‡ *Orat.* 4 *adv. Jul.* c. 73.

§ *Doctr. des Pères*, Vol. II. p. 1.

a time, and in so depraved an age, such a religion over the whole earth as can deliver men from many errors and evils. But what he conceives to be "the most inexplicable part of the affair is, that Christ has accomplished this without arms, money, or soldiers, but simply by the instrumentality of eleven poor humble peasants, who have been enabled to persuade a multitude of men to change their opinions, not only as to things present, but as to things to come. The laws of countries have been abrogated, the most ancient customs abolished, the most inveterate habits uprooted, for the purpose of introducing entirely opposite usages and institutions. Men have been led to resign their evil inclinations in favor of a life the most difficult to follow, and from which they were by nature the farthest removed. Jesus Christ withdraws us from sensual pleasures, to mortification; from the love of riches, to that of poverty; from luxury, to temperance; from envy, to charity; from the broad and easy road, to a strict and narrow way. Moreover, this success has been attained in the face of a universal opposition. Christ himself finished his life by the most ignominious of deaths, and his followers have furnished a host of martyrs." The facts of Christ's crucifixion, and the subsequent spread of the Gospel, are contrasted as matters which can neither be denied, nor explained away. "Multitudes of men, converted from being ravening wolves, to the gentleness of lambs, and who speak of immortality, of the resurrection, and of the ineffable blessedness of another life, far better than ever the Pagan philosophers did, attest the marvellous power actuating them; and this influence is by no means confined to any particular place or city, but has penetrated solitudes, deserts, villages, islands, ports, and the very vessels that traverse the sea. Nor is it attached to any particular rank; kings have submitted their diadem to the faith of the Crucified One, as well as all classes of their subjects. The event also has shown that it was no transitory authority, which was gained by the

Apostles; for even at the present day, notwithstanding the violence and tortures, prejudice and depravity of their enemies, the Gospel continues in full force; whilst the mightiest kings and princes have often lived to see their own laws abrogated."

AUGUSTINE* argues that "the resurrection of the body was once considered incredible; but now the whole world believes that Christ's body was taken up into heaven. Strange that men, ignorant of all arts, without rhetoric, logic, or grammar, plain fishermen, should be sent by Christ into the sea of this world, only with nets of faith; and still more, that they should draw such innumerable sorts of fishes, and among them many philosophers." He considers this to be as antecedently incredible as the resurrection of the body, and yet both are found predicted by Christ.

After showing† how unequal the most sublime maxims of philosophy were to persuade the people, and that it is better to have God in the heart than Plato in the mouth, our author remarks that "these and greater truths have been propagated over the earth by the Gospel of Jesus Christ: which wonderful conversion proves him to have had an authority more than human." He then speaks of the multitudes who have turned to Christ in the islands, in the deserts, in solitudes, having abandoned the wealth and honors of the world, in the cities, in the towns, in the country, so that at this day almost all men, everywhere declare, with one voice, that they have their hearts lifted up unto the Lord.

Our investigation is thus brought to a close, and leaves little more to be said but by way of recapitulation or reflection.

In the course of this Essay it has been my endeavor to suggest what were the evidences adduced by the Apologists in defence of Christianity; to explain the circumstances,

* *De Civ. Dei*, Lib. XXII. c. 5. † *De Ver. Relig.* c. 3.

sense and design, with which they were urged; and to illustrate and prove the whole by sufficient, direct citation.

The result, it must be granted, is to establish both the reputation and claims of the foregoing arguments. They are found to be the inventions of wise and good men who have long since gone their way, like Daniel escaped from the lion's den and the fiery furnace, "to stand in their lot at the end of days:" as such, they are to be revered for the sake of their authors' characters. They are found to be the identical addresses which, under God, helped to allay the most furious moral tempest that mankind was ever in; and, after the manner of the Saviour's words on the sea of Galilee, hushed the winds and the waves into a great calm: as such, they are to be studied for the influence they once exerted in the world. They are found to be methods of conviction at once scriptural and philosophical, original and thorough, even (as it may be said of them) to the satisfying of the subject, not by exhausting its materials, but by indicating and occupying its limits: as such, they are to be prized in each succeeding age, for their own intrinsic and enduring worth. Lastly, and just on these accounts, they are found, though the fruits of bygone discussions, to be as unquestionable as ever: as such, they are capable of being advantageously employed by ourselves; an advantage to us above all others, and without which, it is presumed, the present thesis would never have been appointed for our consideration; but of which I feel sure, it has proved itself possessed in an eminent degree. What other or more weighty considerations than these can be desired to establish the value of any human opinion? And hence arises the reciprocal obligation we are under with regard to them:

"Quisquis magna dedit, voluit sibi magna rependi."*

* Whoever has conferred great favors, wishes equal favors in return.
Am. Ed.

It would seem as if we can scarcely do our duty, with regard to the sacred cause which these pleas were intended to promote, and of which every professing Christian may still be called the modern apologist, in face of the array of sceptical and mythical error, of the superstition, of the folly, of the licentiousness that almost distinguish our age, without casting back an occasional glance over the whole field of controversy. True we have not to encounter the ancient opposition in precise terms. Centuries have rolled away: the immediate conflict has become a matter of history; the weapons, the mode of warfare, the foe, are in some respects changed. But it is equally true, as we have before observed, that this change is a limited one: specific, but not generical; "a man's foes are those of his own household" still; the weapon, though varied in shape, must yet be of metal; in other words, our difficulties are but new cases of old objections; our enemies but fresh classes of the ancient schools of infidelity and heresy; our appeals but the arguments revived, of these time-worn apologies. Surely then it will be both wise and prudent in us, to mark at least the *general* plan pursued by these our predecessors in the moral suasion of mankind. I can only notice some of the most prominent features of this plan.

Observe, that the earliest defenders of Christianity were willing to test the truth of their cause in *any* and *every* accredited way; by argument or abstract reasoning, more plausible than the speculations of philosophy; by testimony or external evidence, more trustworthy than the traditions of other systems; and by experience or subjective proof, more efficient, ample, and durable than that of any human influence whatsoever; in short, that they placed Christianity upon a truly rational, a truly historical, a truly moral foundation. Such a religion, they justly concluded, was unique, must be true, must be divine.

A system that could thus levy tribute upon the whole world of mind and matter, from metaphysics down to modern facts, seemed to speak with an authority which neither scribes nor philosophers had ever thought of assuming. Our authors, therefore, inflamed with Christian zeal, and as men who felt themselves debtors in many ways both to the Greeks and barbarians, to the wise and unwise, did not feel themselves authorized in withholding anything out of this variety and plenitude, that was at all likely to attract the attention of their fellow men to the momentous concerns of the soul. A star had led the magi to Bethlehem; other providential tokens might conduct, though by indirect ways, to equally blessed results.

But observe again, that as the Apologists took care to collect, so they also were mindful to combine these various arguments. They had arranged all the spokes of the wheel pointing to a common centre, they now bound them together with a tire. Union, in the case of the evidences, they conceived to be strength and symmetry, adaptation and use. No doubt they occasionally applied themselves, in the heat of their spirit, to some particular train of reasoning, called forth by the stress of the times, just as an experienced pilot inclines the bow of his ship to meet some threatening wave; but, as the same pilot, when the storm is over, returns to his true course, so are they seen, while allowing the variation, preserving the rule of combination. Indeed, to such an extent was this habit of presenting the whole forefront at once to the enemy carried out, that with a few exceptions, it would be impossible to distinguish the Apologists one from another by any peculiar mode of ratiocination; and perhaps nothing they did went further towards convincing the world of the divine character of Christianity, than their perpetual exhibition of its comprehensiveness, completeness and perfection.

Observe, moreover, with reference to the practice of our authors, the one object to which they turned these united appliances, viz., the exaltation of the risen Saviour. Like the great apostle, into whose labors they had entered, and whose spirit they had imbibed, they preached not themselves, but Christ Jesus the Lord; and were servants to others for his sake. One object, one motive made them more than content to sink their own will and renown in their Master's, and their own happiness in that of their fellow-creatures. To these ends they welcomed even the stake, the rack, the mine. What an impassable gulf does a principle like this place between the Christian and the heathen philosopher; between the self-seeking of the latter, and the self-dedication of the former! Granting that they were both moral (which, however, is not the case), here is a further difference in kind, as well as in degree. To compare them, is to bring the cold and inanimate statue into competition with the warm and active hero it represents, the true messenger of God doing more than an angel's work, "the highest style of man!" And how can so miraculous a contrast (for it is nothing less) be explained in the case of a uniform series, like that which the Apologists present, but on the supposition of the renewing of the natural mind by the Holy Spirit's power, even as the subjects of it themselves declared, one and all? Would that such an influential object were always ours, and that we who call ourselves Christians in these peaceful but ensnaring days, bore more constantly in mind the responsibilities incurred, together with the dignity assumed, by reason simply of our name and profession!

Once more, it is a point not to be overlooked in the general plan of apologetical defence, that the anti-nicene Fathers of the Church occupied true Protestant ground. They clearly show the practicability, and at the same time the propriety, of proving the truth of Christianity independently, and without the aid of any tradition or unwritten word. "The means of becoming acquainted with the will of God, according to the Fathers, are Scripture and reason: the latter subordinate to the former."* It is, probably, the obvious inference from this matter of fact, that has led some of the Romanists, as Perrone, Wiseman, Cardinal de la Luzerne, with others,† to confess that they rely in the *first* instance for proof of the authority of the Church on Scripture, considered merely as a human document, and sustained by human testimony; and *then* employ the authority of the true Church, to determine its interpretation, and to establish its inspiration; but this, while it acknowledges the dilemma they are in, only transfers the difficulty from one horn to another. It was a case of not arguing at all before: it is as clearly a case of arguing in a circle now.

These are but a few hints respecting the scheme of the Apologists; others equally important have, no doubt, suggested themselves to the reader's mind, which he can prosecute more at leisure.

The author has only farther to hope, in committing his humble attempt to the public, that with such a directory as is thus placed in their hands, some may be induced to renew their interest in the evidences for the truth of Christianity; and that all the people of God who may honor its pages with a perusal, may feel constrained by the whole survey, to unite and encourage one another in language which David himself meant to be figurative and prophetic: "Walk about Zion, go round about her; tell the towers thereof. Mark ye well her bulwarks, consider her palaces; that ye may tell it to the generation following. For this God is our God for ever and ever; He will be our guide even unto death."

* Tennemann's *Man. of Phil.* p. 212.
† Palmer *On Develop. and Consc.* c. 2, p. 33.

VALUABLE WORKS

PUBLISHED BY

GOULD AND LINCOLN,

59 WASHINGTON STREET, BOSTON.

SACRED RHETORIC: Or, Composition and Delivery of Sermons. By HENRY J. RIPLEY, Prof. in Newton Theological Institution. Including Ware's Hints on Extemporaneous Preaching. Second thousand. 12mo, 75 cts.

An admirable work, clear and succint in its positions and recommendations, soundly based on good authority, and well supported by a variety of reading and illustrations. — *N. Y. Literary World.*

We have looked over this work with a lively interest. The arrangement is easy and natural, and the selection of thoughts under each topic very happy. The work is one that will command readers. It is a comprehensive manual of great practical utility. — *Phil. Ch. Chronicle.*

The author contemplates a man *preparing to compose a discourse* to promote the great ends of preaching, and unfolds to him the process through which his mind ought to pass. We commend the work to ministers, and to those preparing for the sacred office, as a book that will efficiently aid them in studying thoroughly the subject it brings before them. — *Phil. Ch. Observer.*

It presents a rich variety of rules for the practical use of the clergyman, and evinces the good sense, the large experience, and the excellent spirit of Dr. Ripley; and the whole volume is well fitted to instruct and stimulate the writer of sermons. — *Bibliotheca Sacra;*

An excellent work is here offered to theological students and clergymen. It is not a compilation, but is an original treatise, fresh, practical, and comprehensive, and adapted to the pulpit offices of the present day. It is full of valuable suggestions, and abounds with clear illustrations. — *Zion's Herald.*

It cannot be too frequently perused by those whose duty it is to *persuade* men. — *Congregationalist.*

Prof. Ripley possesses the highest qualifications for a work of this kind. His position has given him great experience in the peculiar wants of theological students. — *Providence Journal.*

His canons on selecting texts, stating the proposition, collecting and arranging materials, style, delivery, etc., are just and well stated. Every theological student to whom this volume is *accessible* will be likely to procure it. — *Christian Mirror, Portland.*

It is manifestly the fruit of mature thought and large observation; it is pervaded by a manly tone, and abounds in judicious counsels; it is compactly written and admirably arranged, both for study and reference. It will become a text book for theological students, we have no doubt: that it deserves to be read by all ministers is to us as clear. — *N. Y. Recorder.*

THE CHRISTIAN WORLD UNMASKED. By JOHN BERRIDGE, A. M., Vicar of Everton, Bedfordshire, Chaplain to the Right Hon. The Earl of Buchan, etc. *New Edition.* With Life of the Author, by the REV. THOMAS GUTHRIE, D. D., Minister of Free St. John's, Edinburgh. 16mo, cloth.

"The book," says DR. GUTHRIE, in his Introduction, "which we introduce anew to the public, has survived the test of years, and still stands towering above things of inferior growth like a cedar of Lebanon. Its subject is all important; in doctrine it is sound to the core; it glows with fervent piety; it exhibits a most skilful and unsparing dissection of the dead professor; while its style is so remarkable, that he who could *preach* as Berridge has *written*, would hold any congregation by the ears."

THE CHRISTIAN REVIEW. Edited by JAMES D. KNOWLES, BARNAS SEARS, and S. F. SMITH. 8 vols. Commencing with vol. one. Half cl., lettered, 8,00. Single volumes, (except the first,) may be had in numbers, 1,00.

These first eight volumes of the Christian Review contain valuable contributions from the leading men of the Baptist and several other denominations, and will be found a valuable acquisition to any library.

Aa

IMPORTANT WORK.

KITTO'S POPULAR CYCLOPÆDIA OF BIBLICAL LITERATURE. Condensed from the larger work. By the Author, JOHN KITTO, D. D., Author of "Pictorial Bible," "History of Palestine," "Scripture Daily Readings," &c. Assisted by JAMES TAYLOR, D. D., of Glasgow. With *over five hundred Illustrations.* One volume octavo, 812 pp., cloth, 3,00.

THE POPULAR BIBLICAL CYCLOPÆDIA OF LITERATURE is designed to furnish a DICTIONARY OF THE BIBLE, embodying the products of the best and most recent researches in biblical literature, in which the scholars of Europe and America have been engaged. The work, the result of immense labor and research, and enriched by the contributions of writers of distinguished eminence in the various departments of sacred literature, has been, by universal consent, pronounced the best work of its class extant, and the one best suited to the advanced knowledge of the present day in all the studies connected with theological science. It is not only intended for *ministers* and *theological students*, but is also particularly adapted to *parents, Sabbath school teachers, and the great body of the religious public.* The *illustrations*, amounting to *more than three hundred*, are of the very highest order.

A condensed view of the various branches of Biblical Science comprehended in the work.

1. BIBLICAL CRITICISM, — Embracing the History of the Bible Languages; Canon of Scripture; Literary History and Peculiarities of the Sacred Books; Formation and History of Scripture Texts.
2. HISTORY, — Proper Names of Persons; Biographical Sketches of prominent Characters; Detailed Accounts of important Events recorded in Scripture; Chronology and Genealogy of Scripture.
3. GEOGRAPHY, — Names of Places; Description of Scenery; Boundaries and Mutual Relations of the Countries mentioned in Scripture, so far as necessary to illustrate the Sacred Text.
4. ARCHÆOLOGY, — Manners and Customs of the Jews and other nations mentioned in Scripture; their Sacred Institutions, Military Affairs, Political Arrangements, Literary and Scientific Pursuits.
5. PHYSICAL SCIENCE, — Scripture Cosmogony and Astronomy, Zoology, Mineralogy, Botany, Meteorology.

In addition to numerous flattering notices and reviews, personal letters from *more than fifty of the most distinguished Ministers and Laymen of different religious denominations in the country* have been received, highly commending this work as admirably adapted to ministers, Sabbath school teachers, heads of families, and *all* Bible students.

The following extract of a letter is a fair specimen of individual letters received from *each* of the gentlemen whose names are given below: —

"I have examined it with special and unalloyed satisfaction. It has the rare merit of being all that it professes to be, and very few, I am sure, who may consult it will deny that, in richness and fulness of detail, it surpasses their expectation. Many ministers will find it a valuable auxiliary; but its chief excellence is, that it furnishes just the facilities which are needed by the thousands in families and Sabbath schools, who are engaged in the important business of biblical education. It is in itself a library of reliable information."

W. B. Sprague, D. D., Pastor of Second Presbyterian Church, Albany, N. Y.
J. J. Carruthers, D. D., Pastor of Second Parish Congregational Church, Portland, Me.
Joel Hawes, D. D., Pastor of First Congregational Church, Hartford, Ct.
Daniel Sharp, D. D., late Pastor of Third Baptist Church, Boston.
N. L. Frothingham, D. D., late Pastor of First Congregational Church, (Unitarian,) Boston.
Ephraim Peabody, D. D., Pastor of Stone Chapel Congregational Church, (Unitarian,) Boston.
A. L. Stone, Pastor of Park Street Congregational Church, Boston.
John S. Stone, D. D., Rector of Christ Church, (Episcopal,) Brooklyn, N. Y.
J. B. Waterbury, D. D., Pastor of Bowdoin Street Church, (Congregational,) Boston.
Baron Stow, D. D., Pastor of Rowe Street Baptist Church, Boston.
Thomas H. Skinner, D. D., Pastor of Carmine Presbyterian Church, New York.
Samuel W. Worcester, D. D., Pastor of the Tabernacle Church, (Congregational,) Salem.
Horace Bushnell, D. D., Pastor of Third Congregational Church, Hartford, Ct.
Right Reverend J. M. Wainwright, D. D., Trinity Church, (Episcopal,) New York.
Gardner Spring, D. D., Pastor of the Brick Church Chapel Presbyterian Church, New York.
W. T. Dwight, D. D., Pastor of Third Congregational Church, Portland, Me.
E. N. Kirk, Pastor of Mount Vernon Congregational Church, Boston.
Prof. George Bush, author of "Notes on the Scriptures," New York.
Howard Malcom, D. D., author of "Bible Dictionary," and Pres. of Lewisburg University.
Henry J. Ripley, D. D., author of "Notes on the Scriptures," and Prof. in Newton Theol. Ins.
N. Porter, Prof. in Yale College, New Haven, Ct.
Jared Sparks, Edward Everett, Theodore Frelinghuysen, Robert C. Winthrop, John McLean, Simon Greenleaf, Thomas S. Williams, — and a large number of others of like character and standing of the above, whose names cannot here appear.

WORKS FOR BIBLE STUDENTS.

A TREATISE ON BIBLICAL CRITICISMS; Exhibiting a Systematic View of that Science. By SAMUEL DAVIESON, D. D., of the University of Halle, Author of "Ecclesiastical Polity of the New Testament," "Introduction to the New Testament," "Sacred Hermeneutics Developed and Applied. A new Revised and Enlarged Edition, in two elegant octavo volumes, cloth, 5,00.

These volumes contain a statement of *the sources* of criticism, such as the MSS. of the Hebrew Bible and Greek Testament, the principal versions of both, quotations from them in early writers, parallels, and also the internal evidence on which critics rely for obtaining a pure text. A history of the texts of the Old and New Testaments, with a description of the Hebrew and Greek languages in which the Scriptures are written. An examination of the most important passages whose readings are disputed.

Every thing, in short, is discussed, which properly belongs to *the criticism* of the text, comprehending all that comes under the title of *General Introduction* in Introductions to the Old and New Testaments.

HISTORY OF PALESTINE, from the Patriarchal Age to the Present Time; with Introductory Chapters on the Geography and Natural History of the Country, and on the Customs and Institutions of the Hebrews. By JOHN KITTO, D. D., Author of "Scripture Daily Readings," "Cyclopædia of Biblical Literature," &c. With upwards of *two hundred Illustrations.* 12mo, cloth, 1,25.

A very full compendium of the geography and history of Palestine, from the earliest era mentioned in Scripture to the present day; not merely a dry record of boundaries, and the succession of rulers, but an intelligible account of the agriculture, habits of life, literature, science, and art, with the religious, political, and judicial institutions of the inhabitants of the Holy Land in all ages. The descriptive portions of the work are increased in value by numerous wood cuts. A more useful and instructive book has rarely been published. — *N. Y. Commercial.*

Whoever will read this book till he has possessed himself thoroughly of its contents, will, we venture to say, read the Bible with far more intelligence and satisfaction during all the rest of his life. — *Puritan Recorder.*

Beyond all dispute, this is the best historical compendium of the Holy Land, from the days of Abraham to those of the late Pasha of Egypt, Mehemet Ali. — *Edinburgh Review.*

☞ In the numerous notices and reviews the work has been strongly recommended, as not only admirably adapted to the *family*, but also as a text book for *Sabbath and week day schools.*

CRUDEN'S CONDENSED CONCORDANCE; a New and Complete Concordance to the Holy Scriptures. By ALEXANDER CRUDEN. Revised and Re-edited by the Rev. DAVID KING, LL. D. Tenth thousand. Octavo, cloth backs, 1,25

This work is printed from English plates, and is a full and fair copy of all that is valuable as a Concordance in Cruden's larger work, in two volumes, which costs *five dollars*, while *this* edition is furnished at *one dollar and twenty-five cents!* The principal variation from the larger book consists in the exclusion of the Bible Dictionary, (which has always been an incumbrance,) the condensation of the quotations of Scripture, arranged under their most obvious heads, which, while it diminishes the bulk of the work, *greatly facilitates* the finding of any required passage.

We have, in this edition of Cruden, the *best* made better! That is, the present is better adapted to the purposes of a concordance, by the erasure of superfluous references, the omission of unnecessary explanations, and the contraction of quotations, etc. It is better as a manual, and better adapted by its price, to the means of many who need and ought to possess such a work, than the former large and expensive edition. — *Puritan Recorder.*

The present edition, in being relieved of some things which contributed to render all former ones unnecessarily cumbrous, without adding to the substantial value of the work, becomes an exceedingly cheap book. — *Albany Argus.*

All in the incomparable work of Cruden that is essential to a Concordance is presented in a volume much reduced both in size and price. — *Watchman and Reflector.*

Next to the Bible itself, every family should have a *concordance.* No person can study the Scriptures to advantage without one. Cruden's is the best. — *Baptist Record.* I

DR. WILLIAMS'S WORKS.

RELIGIOUS PROGRESS; Discourses on the Development of the Christian Character. By WILLIAM R. WILLIAMS, D. D. Third ed. 12mo, cl., 85c.

This work is from the pen of one of the brightest lights of the American pulpit. We scarcely know of any living writer who has a finer command of powerful thought and glowing, impressive language than he. The volume will advance, if possible, the author's reputation. — DR. SPRAGUE, *Alb. Atlas.*

This book is a rare phenomena in these days. It is a rich exposition of Scripture, with a fund of practical religious wisdom, conveyed in a style so strong and massive as to remind one of the English writers of two centuries ago; and yet it abounds in fresh illustrations drawn from every (even the latest opened) field of science and of literature. — *Methodist Quarterly.*

His power of apt and forcible illustration is without a parallel among modern writers. The mute pages spring into life beneath the magic of his radiant imagination. But this is never at the expense of solidity of thought or strength of argument. It is seldom, indeed, that a mind of so much poetical invention yields such a willing homage to the logical element. — *Harper's Monthly Miscellany.*

With warm and glowing language, Dr. Williams exhibits and enforces the truth; every page radiant with "thoughts that burn," leave their indelible impression upon the mind. — *N. Y. Com. Adv.*

The strength and compactness of argumentation, the correctness and beauty of style, and the importance of the animating idea of the discourses, are worthy of the high reputation of Dr. Williams, and place them among the most finished homiletic productions of the day. — *N. Y. Evangelist.*

Dr. Williams has no superior among American divines in profound and exact learning, and brilliancy of style. He seems familiar with the literature of the world, and lays his vast resources under contribution to illustrate and adorn every theme which he investigates. We wish the volume could be placed in every religious family in the country. — *Phil. Ch. Chronicle.*

LECTURES ON THE LORD'S PRAYER. Third ed. 32mo, cl., 85c.

We observe the writer's characteristic fulness and richness of language, felicity and beauty of illustration, justness of discrimination and thought. — *Watchman and Reflector.*

Dr. Williams is one of the most interesting and accomplished writers in this country. We welcome this volume as a valuable contribution to our religious literature — *Ch. Witness.*

In reading, we resolved to mark the passages which we most admired, but soon found that we should be obliged to mark nearly all of them. — *Ch. Secretary.*

It bears in every page the mark of an elegant writer and an accomplished scholar, an acute reasoner and a cogent moralist. Some passages are so decidedly eloquent that we instinctively find ourselves looking round as if upon an audience, and ready to join them with audible applause — *Ch. Inquirer.*

We are constantly reminded, in reading his eloquent pages, of the old English writers, whose vigorous thought, and gorgeous imagery, and varied learning, have made their writings an inexhaustible mine for the scholars of the present day. — *Ch. Observer.*

Their breadth of view, strength of logic, and stirring eloquence place them among the very best homiletical efforts of the age. Every page is full of suggestion as well as eloquence. — *Ch. Parlor Mag.*

MISCELLANIES. New, improved edition. *(Price reduced.)* 12mo, 1,25.

☞ This work, which has been heretofore published in octavo form at 1,75 per copy, is published by the present proprietors in one handsome 12mo volume, at the low price of 1,25.

A volume which is absolutely necessary to the completeness of a library. — *N. Y. Weekly Review.*

Dr. Williams is a profound scholar and a brilliant writer. — *N. Y. Evangelist.*

He often rises to the sphere of a glowing and impressive eloquence, because no other form of language can do justice to his thoughts and emotions. So, too, the exuberance of literary illustration, with which he clothes the driest speculative discussions, is not brought in for the sake of effect, but as the natural expression of a mind teeming with the "spoils of time" and the treasures of study in almost every department of learning. — *N. Y. Tribune.*

From the pen of one of the most able and accomplished authors of the age. — *Bap. Memorial.*

We are glad to see this volume. We wish such men abounded in every sect. — *Ch. Register.*

One of the richest volumes that has been given to the public for many years. — *N. Y. Bap. Reg.*

The author's mind is cast in no common mould. A delightful volume. — *Meth. Prot.* **Bb**

THEOLOGICAL SCIENCE.

BY THE REV. JOHN HARRIS, D. D.

THE PRE-ADAMITE EARTH: Contributions to Theological Science. New and revised edition. 12mo, cloth, 85 cts.

It opens new trains of thought; puts one in a new position to survey the wonders of God's works, and compels Natural Science to bear her testimony in support of Divine Truth.—*Phil. Ch. Observer.*

If we do not greatly mistake, this long looked for volume will create and sustain a deep impression in the more intellectual circles of the religious world.—*London Evan. Mag.*

The man who finds his element among great thoughts, and is not afraid to push into the remoter regions of abstract truth, be he philosopher or theologian, or both, will read it over and over, and will find his intellect strengthened, as if from being in contact with a new creation.—*Albany Argus.*

Dr. Harris states in a lucid, succinct, and often highly eloquent manner, all the leading facts of geology, and their beautiful harmony with the teachings of Scripture. As a work of paleontology in its relation to Scripture, it will be one of the most complete and popular extant.—*N. Y. Evangelist.*

He is a sound logician and lucid reasoner, getting nearer to the groundwork of a subject generally supposed to have uncertain data, than any other writer within our knowledge.—*N. Y. Com. Adv.*

We have never seen the natural sciences, particularly geology, made to give so decided and unimpeachable testimony to revealed truth. The wonders of God's works, which he has here grouped together, convey a most magnificent, and even overpowering idea of the Great Creator. We wish that we could devote a week, uninterruptedly, to its perusal and re-perusal.—*Ch. Mirror.*

Written in the glowing and eloquent style which has won for him a universal fame, and will secure a wide circle of readers.—*N. Y. Recorder.*

The elements of things, the laws of organic nature, and those especially that lie at the foundation of the divine relations to man, are dwelt upon in a masterly manner.—*Watchman and Reflector.*

A work of theological science, not to be passed over with a glance. It applies principles or laws to the successive stages of the Pre-Adamite Earth; to the historical development of man; the family; nation; Son of God; church; the Bible revelation, and the future prospects of humanity.—*Transcript.*

MAN PRIMEVAL; Or, the Constitution and Primitive Condition of the Human Being. A Contribution to Theological Science. With a fine Portrait of the Author. 12mo, cloth, 1,25.

*** This is the second volume of a series of works on Theological Science. The first has been received with much favor; the present is a continuation of the principles which were seen holding their way through the successive kingdoms of primeval nature, and are here resumed and exhibited in their next higher application to individual man.

His copious and beautiful illustrations of the successive laws of the Divine Manifestation, have yielded us inexpressible delight.—*London Eclectic Review.*

The distribution and arrangement of thought in this volume are such as to afford ample scope for the author's remarkable powers of analysis and illustration. In a very masterly way does our author grapple with almost every difficult and perplexing subject which comes within the range of his proposed inquiry into the constitution and condition of Man Primeval.—*London Evangelical Mag.*

Reverently recognizing the Bible as the fountain and exponent of *truth*, he is as independent and fearless as he is original and forcible; and he adds to these qualities consummate skill in argument and elegance of diction.—*N. Y. Commercial.*

Dr. Harris, though a young man, has placed himself in the very front rank of scientific writers, and his essays attract the attention of the most erudite scholars of the age.—*N. Y. Ch. Observer.*

It surpasses its predecessors in interest. To students of mental and moral science, it will be a valuable contribution, and will assuredly secure their attention.—*Phil. Ch. Chron.*

It is eminently philosophical, and at the same time glowing and eloquent. It cannot fail to have a wide circle of readers, or repay richly the hours which are given to its pages.—*N. Y. Recorder.*

The work before us manifests much learning and metaphysical acumen.—*Puritan Recorder.*

THE FAMILY: Its Constitution, Probation, and History. Being the third volume of the Series. *In Preparation.*

THE PREACHER AND THE KING;

OR, BOURDALOUE IN THE COURT OF LOUIS XIV.

Being an Account of that distinguished Era. Translated from the French of L. BUNGENER. Paris, fourteenth edition. With an Introduction, by the REV. GEORGE POTTS, D. D., New York. 12mo, cloth, 1,25.

It combines *substantial history with the highest charm of romance;* the most rigid philosophical criticism with a thorough analysis of human character and faithful representation of the spirit and manners of the age to which it relates. We regard the book as a valuable contribution to the cause not merely of general literature, but especially of pulpit eloquence. Its attractions are so various that it can hardly fail to find readers of almost every description. — *Puritan Recorder.*

A very delightful book. It is full of interest, and equally replete with sound thought and profitable sentiment. — *N. Y. Commercial.*

It is a volume at once curious, instructive, and fascinating. The interviews of Bourdaloue, and Claude, and those of Bossuet, Fenelon, and others, are remarkably attractive, and of finished taste. Other high personages of France are brought in to figure in the narrative, while rhetorical rules are exemplified in a manner altogether new. Its extensive sale in France is evidence enough of its extraordinary merit and its peculiarly attractive qualities. — *Ch. Advocate.*

It is full of life and animation, and conveys a graphic idea of the state of morals and religion in the Augustan age of French literature. — *N. Y. Recorder.*

This book will attract by its novelty, and prove particularly engaging to those interested in the pulpit eloquence of an age characterized by the flagrant wickedness of Louis XIV. The author has exhibited singular skill in weaving into his narrative sketches of the remarkable men who flourished at that period, with original and striking remarks on the subject of preaching. — *Presbyterian.*

Its historical and biographical portions are valuable; its comments excellent, and its effect pure and benignant. A work which we recommend to all, as possessing rare interest. — *Buffalo Morn. Exp.*

A book of rare interest, not only for the singular ability with which it is written, but for the graphic account which it gives of the state of pulpit eloquence during the celebrated era of which it treats. It is perhaps the best biography extant of the distinguished and eloquent preacher, who above all others most pleased the king; while it also furnishes many interesting particulars in the lives of his professional contemporaries. We content ourself with warmly commending it. — *Savannah Journal.*

The author is a minister of the Reformed Church. In the forms of narrative and conversations, he portrays the features and character of that remarkable age, and illustrates the claims and duties of the sacred office, and the important ends to be secured by the eloquence of the pulpit. — *Phil. Ch. Obs.*

A book which unfolds to us the private conversation, the interior life and habits of study of such men as Claude, Bossuet, Bourdaloue, Massillon, and Bridaine, cannot but be a precious gift to the American church and ministers. It is a book full of historical facts of great value, sparkling with gems of thought, polished scholarship, and genuine piety. — *Cin. Ch. Advocate.*

This volume presents a phase of French life with which we have never met in any other work. The author is a minister of the Reformed Church in Paris, where his work has been received with unexampled popularity, having already gone through *fourteen* editions. The writer has studied not only the divinity and general literature of the age of Louis XIV., but also the memories of that period, until he is able to reproduce a life-like picture of society at the Court of the Grand Monarch. — *Alb. Trans.*

A work which we recommend to all, as possessing rare interest. — *Buffalo Ev. Express.*

In form it is descriptive and dramatic, presenting the reader with animated conversations between some of the most famous preachers and philosophers of the Augustan age of France. The work will be read with interest by all intelligent men; but it will be of especial service to the ministry, who cannot afford to be ignorant of the facts and suggestions of this instructive volume. — *N. Y. Ch. Intel.*

The work is very fascinating, and the lesson under its spangled robe is of the gravest moment to every pulpit and every age. — *Ch. Intelligencer.*

THE PRIEST AND THE HUGUENOT; or Persecution in the Age of Louis XV. Part I., A Sermon at Court; Part II., A Sermon in the City; Part III., A Sermon in the Desert. Translated from the French of L. BUNGENER, author of "The Preacher and the King." 2 vols. 12mo, cloth. ☞ *A new Work.*

☞ This is truly a masterly production, full of interest, and may be set down as one of the greatest Protestant works of the age.

UNIVERSITY SERMONS.

SERMONS Delivered in the Chapel of Brown University. By the REV. FRANCIS WAYLAND, D. D. Third thousand. 12mo, cloth, 1,00.

☞ DR. WAYLAND has here discussed most of the prominent doctrines of the Bible in his usual clear and masterly style, viz.: Theoretical Atheism; Practical Atheism; Moral Character of Man; Love to God; Fall of Man; Justification by Works impossible; Preparation for the Advent of the Messiah; Work of the Messiah; Justification by Faith; The Fall of Peter; The Church of Christ; The Unity of the Church; The Duty of Obedience to the Civil Magistrate; also, the Recent Revolutions in Europe.

The discourses contained in this handsome volume are characterized by all that richness of thought and elegance of language for which their talented author is celebrated. The volume is worthy of the pen of the distinguished divine from whom it emanates. — DR. BAIRD'S *Christian Union.*

Few sermons contain so much carefully arranged thought as these. The thorough logician is apparent throughout the volume, and there is a classic purity in the diction, unsurpassed by any writer, and equalled by few. — *N. Y. Commercial.*

The author has long been before the public as one of our most popular writers in various departments of science and morals. His style is easy and fluent, and rich in illustration. — *Evan. Review.*

No thinking man can open to any portion of it without finding his attention strongly arrested, and feeling inclined to yield his assent to those self-evincing statements which appear on every page. As a writer, Dr. Wayland is distinguished by simplicity, strength, and comprehensiveness. He addresses himself directly to the intellect more than to the imagination, to the conscience more than to the passions. — *Watchman and Reflector.*

Just issued, a noble volume of noble sermons, from the distinguished President of Brown University. These discourses are fine specimens of his discriminating power of thought, and purity and vigor of style. — *Zion's Herald.*

DR. WAYLAND'S name and fame will cause any thing from his pen to be eagerly sought for; and those who take up this volume with the high expectations induced by his previous works, will not be disappointed. The discourses are rich in evangelical truth, profound thought, and beautiful diction; worthy at once of the theologian, the philosopher, and the rhetorician. — *Albany Argus.*

This volume adds to Dr. Wayland's fame as a writer. This is commendation enough to bestow upon any book. — *Puritan Recorder.*

DR. WAYLAND is one of the prominent Christian philosophers and literary men of our country. His style is elegant and polished, and his views evangelical. — *Watchman, Cincinnati.*

His style is peculiarly adapted to arrest the attention, and his familiar illustrations serve to make plain the most abstruse principles, as well as to enstamp them upon one's memory. It is, in fact, scarcely possible to forget a discourse which we read from Wayland, and we have ever found his works to be highly suggestive. We think no minister's library complete without it. — *Dover Star.*

We must call the attention of our readers again to this attractive volume of sermons. They come from one who has attained a national reputation, and embody the views matured by the careful study of many years upon the most important topics in theology. — *Phil. Ch. Chronicle.*

It would be spending time to little purpose to attempt a eulogy on a work emanating from such a source. — *N. Y. Baptist Register.*

THE PERSON AND WORK OF CHRIST. By ERNEST SARTORIUS, D. D., General Superintendent and Consistorial Director at Konigsberg, Prussia. Translated from the German, by the REV. OAKMAN S. STEARNS, A. M. 18mo, cloth, 42 cts.

A work of much ability, and presenting the argument in a style that will be new to most American readers. It will deservedly attract attention. — *N. Y. Observer.*

DR. SARTORIUS is one of the most eminent and evangelical theologians in Germany. The work will be found, both from the important subjects discussed and the earnestness, beauty, and vivacity of its style, to possess the qualities which recommend it to the Christian public. — *Mich. Ch. Herald.*

A little volume on a great subject, and evidently the production of a great mind. The style and train of thought prove this. — *Southern Literary Gazette.*

Whether we consider the importance of the subjects discussed, or the perspicuous exhibition of truth in the volume before us, the chaste and elegant style used, or the devout spirit of the author, we cannot but desire that the work may meet with an extensive circulation. — *Christian Index.*

A WREATH AROUND THE CROSS;

Or Scripture Truths Illustrated. By the REV. A. MORTON BROWN, D. D. With a Recommendatory Preface, by JOHN ANGELL JAMES. With beautiful Frontispiece. 16mo, cloth, 60 cts.

☞ This is a very interesting and valuable book, and should be in every house in the land. Its great excellence is, it *magnifies the cross of Christ.* It presents the following interesting subjects: "The Cross needed; The Way to the Cross; The Cross set up; The sufferings of the Cross Mediation by the Cross; Life from the Cross; Faith in the Cross; Submission to the Cross; Glorying in the Cross; The Cross and the Crown." No better book can be put into the hands of "inquirers after truth."

This is a beautiful volume, defending and illustrating the precious truths which cluster around the atonement. These truths are set forth in a lively and popular style. — *Phil. Ch. Chronicle.*

May it find its way into every Christian family, and be read by every member. — *Ch. Secretary.*

The theme is the centre of all evangelical religion, both doctrinal and experimental. It is the excellence of this work, that it keeps so constantly in view this grand instrument of salvation, that it might have been entitled a "walk," as well as a "wreath," around the Cross. — *Religious Herald.*

"Christ, and Him crucified," is presented in a new, striking, and matter-of-fact light. The style is simple, without being puerile, and the reasoning is of that truthful, persuasive kind that "comes from the heart, and reaches the heart." We wish this Christian classic a wide circulation, hoping that many, under its direction and influence, may be found "looking unto Jesus." — *N. Y. Observer.*

A highly-approved work, issued in elegant style. The author presents the most important doctrines of our holy religion, in a form not only intelligible, but in attractive lights, adapted to allure the eye of faith, and hope, and love to the glorious objects revealed in the gospel. — *Phil. Ch. Observer.*

PHILOSOPHY OF THE PLAN OF SALVATION: A Book for the

Times. By an AMERICAN CITIZEN. An Introductory Essay, by CALVIN E. STOWE, D. D. 12mo, cloth, 63 cts.

⁂ This is one of the best books in the English language. The work has been translated into several different languages in Europe. It has been republished by the London Tract Society, and also adopted as one of the volumes of "Ward's Library of Standard Divinity," edited by Drs. John Harris, J. Pye Smith, and others. A capital book to circulate among young men.

One of the most original and valuable works of recent publication. — *N. Y. Christian Intelligencer.*

A useful book, written with great spirit and point. — *Phil. Presbyterian.*

In many respects, this is a remarkable book. — *N. Y. Observer.*

We have expressed our decided opinion as to the exalted merits of this transatlantic essay on the truth of the Gospel. We think it is more likely to lodge an impression in the human conscience, in favor of the divine authority of Christianity, than any work of the modern press, as it seeks an avenue to the human heart somewhat different from the ordinary mode of approaching it. —*London Meth. Mag.*

It is logical, both in its arrangement and in its reasonings. It is the work of a clear and vigorous thinker. It proposes to solve these two questions, — *Is Christianity true?* and, *What is true Christianity?* Few volumes have issued from the American press that bear the stamp of originality and profound thought so deeply imprinted on every page. — *Puritan Rec.*

This is really an original book. Every sentence is pregnant with thought, and every idea conduces to the main demonstration. The various paragraphs are bound together as closely as the successive steps of a mathematical argument. At the same time, neither abstruseness vails the method, nor subtilty polishes away the power of the reasonings employed. Its conclusions come home with certainty to the business and bosom" of every man. The book is the work of a reclaimed sceptic. — *Edinburgh United Secession Magazine.*

Though written with great simplicity, it is evidently the production of a master mind. There is a force of argument and a power of conviction almost resistless. — *London Evangelical Magazine.*

The book before us is one of singular merit. As a piece of clear, vigorous, consecutive thinking, we scarcely know its superior. We would not hesitate to place it side by side with Butler's Analogy, merely as a specimen of close and unanswerable reasoning, while it is far superior with regard to the evangelical view which it gives of the plan of salvation. — *Edinburgh Free Church Magazine.*

"*The president of Knox College, Illinois,*" says, "I have just taken the senior class through the Philosophy of the Plan of Salvation. It is decidedly the best vindication of the Old Testament Scriptures against the assaults of infidelity, and one of the most useful class books which I have ever met."

A Welsh minister, in Michigan, brought a copy from Wales. It has been translated into Welsh, and is circulated broadcast over the hills, through the hamlets, and in the mines of his native land.

CHRISTIANS DAILY TREASURY.

A RELIGIOUS EXERCISE FOR EVERY DAY IN THE YEAR.

By E. TEMPLE, author of the "Domestic Altar." A new and improved edition. 12mo, cloth, $1,00.

☞ A work for every Christian. No one should be without it. It is indeed a "Treasury" of good things.

If any book of modern date has fallen in our own way that deserves a second and a third commendation, it is this. We wish most heartily that this volume were the daily companion of every disciple of Christ, in the land. "Temple" is calm, logical, Scriptural, devout, full of light, if not "without any darkness at all." Could not other copies be obtained, we would not part with our own for ten times the cost of it. — *Congregationalist.*

The outlines or materials for reflection and meditation. They are designed for the Christian in his daily walk with God. — *Puritan Recorder.*

It should be found on the table of every Christian and receive his daily attention.— *Ch. Times.*

It differs materially from any thing that we have met with. The author has a most happy talent at conveying much important truth in a few words. It is altogether an admirable work, worthy to be read by every Christian who deserves to be quickened and sanctified by divine truth, and worthy to be studied by every minister who aims at simplicity and perspicuity in the construction of his sermons. — DR. SPRAGUE, *Albany Atlas.*

A useful evangelical volume, designed to assist Christians in the work of daily meditation on the divine word. — *Christian Herald.*

A grand work for the centre table of every Christian, or for the most private place, where they hold communion with the Invisible. — *Albany Ch. Spectator.*

It is one of the best of the kind that we have ever examined. It is a *treasury* of evangelical truth forcibly expressed, in a manner well adapted to awaken thought. — *Phil. Ch. Observer.*

This work might appropriately be called a guide to meditation. The plan strikes us as a very happy one. Many do not know *how* to meditate. A careful use of this volume, will do very much to form habits of profitable meditation on Scripture. — *Phil. Ch. Chronicle.*

Were these "Exercises" less animated and life like, we might almost call them *skeletons;* but skeletons have not flesh and blood, as the reader finds these to have. We prefer them to any thing of the kind we have before seen. They are especially adapted for daily reading; and designed to furnish themes for profitable meditation. — *Dover Star.*

This is a precious compendium of pious reflections, upon happily-selected Scriptures. It is very superior to the numerous works of this character already published, and will afford alike pleasure and profit in the study of the minister, and in the closet of the private Christian. — *American Pulpit.*

We give it our most decided recommendation. It differs from the generality of works of a somewhat similar style, in that they consist of reflections, while this more particularly forms the outlines or materials for reflection and meditation. We feel confident these *outlines* will be found highly acceptable to the Christian in his daily walk with God. — *Baltimore Lutheran Observer.*

There is no volume on the same general plan, and having the same aim as this, can compare with it, for its suggestive properties and comprehensiveness. — *Ch. Mirror.*

It breathes the spirit of the gospel. It is eminently suggestive and practical. The Christian who shall daily appropriate its treasures, will, at the end of the year, find himself greatly enriched. It deserves a place in every Christian's library. — *N. Y. Recorder.*

This excellent treasury furnishes rich, practical, and devotional instruction. It is well to feed daily on such spiritual food. — *N. Y. Observer.*

This work is a treasure, indeed, to any one who will study its daily lessons.— *Ch. Index.*

THE IMITATION OF CHRIST. By THOMAS A KEMPIS. Introductory Essay, by T. CHALMERS, D. D. New and improved edition. Edited by the REV. HOWARD MALCOM, D. D. 18mo, cloth, 38 cts.

⁂ "This work has, for three hundred years, been esteemed one of the best practical books in existence, and has gone through a vast number of editions, not only in the original Latin, but in every language of Europe. Dr. Payson, in conversing with a young minister once said, "If you have not seen "*Thomas a Kempis,*" I beg you to procure it. For spirituality and weanedness from the world· *I know of nothing equal to it.*"

That the benefit of this admirable work may be enjoyed by all, the translation of Payne, which best agrees with the *original*, has been revised and adapted to general use, by Dr. Malcom. **Mm**

MIALL'S WORKS.

FOOTSTEPS OF OUR FOREFATHERS; what they Suffered and what they Sought. Describing Localities and portraying Personages and Events conspicuous in the Struggles for Religious Liberty. By JAMES G. MIALL, author of "Memorials of Early Christianity," etc. Containing thirty-six fine Illustrations. 12mo, 1,00.

An exceedingly entertaining work. It is full of strong points. The reader soon catches the fire and zeal of those sterling men whom we have so long admired, and ere he is aware becomes so deeply enlisted in their cause that he finds it difficult to lay aside the book till finished. — *Ch. Parlor Mag.*

A book to stir one's spirit to activity and self-sacrifice in the work of God. It portrays the character, the deeds, the sufferings, and the success of those heroic non-conformists who stood up for the truth against tyranny. It is a book worthy of a large sale. — *Zion's Herald.*

A work absorbingly interesting, and very instructive. —*Western Lit. Magazine.*

The title of this book attracted our attention; its contents have held us fast to its pages to the very close. Its story is of principles and sufferings with which every American who prizes his birthright, and would know how it has been secured, should be familiar. It embraces graphic sketches of localities and scenes, of personages and events, illustrative of the grand struggle for religious liberty. It is fascinating in style, and reliable for substance. It is full of antiquarian lore, and abounds in charming local descriptions. Most earnestly do we recommend it. — *Watchman and Reflector.*

The events narrated and scenes described by the author give us interesting and impressive views of the great sacrifices made by the noble sufferers for the priceless boon of spiritual freedom, which American citizens claim as their birthright. — *Ch. Observer.*

This volume is devoted to biographical notices of those noble minds who made the grand discoveries of civil and religious liberty in England, and who counted not their lives dear, so that the Bible and the freedom of conscience should descend upon their children's children. The anecdotes of these men and their times are full of interest, and are drawn from the most authentic sources. — *Nat. Intel.*

This is a most captivating book, and one that the reader is compelled to finish if he once begins it. We really wish that every family in our land could have a copy. It has kept us perfectly enchained from beginning to end. — *Newport Observer.*

MEMORIALS OF EARLY CHRISTIANITY; Presenting, in a graphic, compact, and popular Form, Memorable Events of Early Ecclesiastical History, etc. By JAMES G MIALL, author of "Footsteps of our Forefathers," etc. With numerous elegant Illustrations. 12mo, cloth, 1,00.

☞ This, like the "Footsteps of our Forefathers," will be found a work of uncommon interest.

We thank Mr. Miall for this volume, which our publishers have reprinted in quite handsome style. There are plain truths plainly told in this volume about ancient Christianity and the practices of the Christians of ante-Nicene times which we could wish *churchmen* would lay to heart and profit by. — *Episcopal Register.*

It is well written, *more* interesting than a *romance*, and yet full of instruction and warning for the present generation. — *Hartford Times.*

A work of no ordinary value as a faithful exponent of early church history, and we can most cheerfully commend it to all. Every Sabbath school should be supplied with copies of it. — *Ch. Secretary.*

Mr. Miall is a Congregational minister in England, and a popular writer of unusual power. He has the power of graphic delineation, and has given us pictures of early Christianity which have the charm of life and reality. We regard the volume as one of unusual interest and value, and our readers are assured that its glowing pages will excite their admiration. — *N. Y. Recorder.*

This is an extremely interesting work, embodying classic and ecclesiastic lore, and calculated to do much good by bringing the church of *to-day* into closer acquaintanceship and sympathy with the church of the early past. — *Congregationalist.*

A very successful attempt to *popularize* the history of the church during the first three centuries. The *results* of extended research are offered to the general reader in a style of *uncommon interest.* The mass of readers know far too little on church history. — *Watchman and Reflector.*

We have in this volume, embodied in a lucid and attractive form, some of the most important facts of early ecclesiastical history, in illustration of the original purity and power of Christian faith. It is a work of labor, and labor very successfully applied. — *Puritan Recorder.*

A volume of thrilling interest. It takes the reader through a very important period of secular and ecclesiastical history. We are glad to see this work. It cannot fail of doing good. — *Western Lit. Messenger.*

www.ingramcontent.com/pod-product-compliance
Lightning Source LLC
LaVergne TN
LVHW020230110826
845151LV00003B/880

* 9 7 8 1 4 2 5 5 3 1 0 8 9 *